BREAKDOWN

BREAKDOWN

N. S. SUTHERLAND

STEIN AND DAY/*Publishers*/New York

First published in the United States of America, 1977
Copyright © 1976 by Stuart Sutherland
All rights reserved
Printed in the United States of America
Stein and Day/*Publishers*/Scarborough House,
Briarcliff Manor, N.Y. 10510

Library of Congress Cataloging in Publication Data

Sutherland, Norman Stuart.
    Breakdown.

    1. Sutherland, Norman Stuart. 2. Mental illness—
Personal narratives. 3. Psychotherapy. I. Title.
RC464.S93A33   616.8'9'00924 [B]   75-37980
ISBN 0-8128-1941-1

To Gay and Julia

'Post-therapeutic confessionals, written under intense abreactive pressure and unneutralized exhibitionism, often betray their underlying motives of subtle revenge towards the disappointing treatment.'

J. Kavka (Member of the Chicago Institute for Psychoanalysis), from *Contemporary Psychology*, 1975.

Contents

	Preface	ix
1	Onset	1
2	Background	8
3	Psychoanalysis	16
4	The Hospital	26
5	Treatment	44
6	Recovery	56
7	Aftermath	63
8	The Nature of Mental Illness	77
9	The Origins of Mental Illness	88
10	Freudian Theory and Practice	95
11	Evaluation of Freud	103
12	Popularity of Freud	109
13	Varieties of Analysis	120
14	Analysts and Their Patients Today	133
15	Other Forms of Individual Psychotherapy	140
16	Group Therapy	152
17	The Wilder Shores of Therapy	161
18	Behaviour Therapy	166
19	Manipulating the Brain	184
20	Psychotropic Drugs	195
21	Ethics and Mental Illness	210
22	Improving Methods of Treatment	231
23	The Choice of Treatment	244
	Glossary	249
	Notes	251
	Author index	267
	Subject index	271

Preface

A few years ago I suffered a precipitate mental breakdown. Although at the time my experiences were agonizing, in retrospect I became fascinated with their unexpected nature. Concern for my own plight and that of others in similar distress led me as a professional psychologist to concentrate my thinking over a two-year period on the care and treatment of the mentally unwell.

In the first part of this book, I record as honestly as I can my own experiences of mental illness. In the second, I review present methods of treatment and set out conclusions based on my own experiences, my professional knowledge and the reading I have undertaken since my breakdown. Mental illness is so common that everybody reading these words will at some time or another be confronted with the problem – either in themselves or in someone close to them. Everyone needs to be well-informed about the subject. Faced with a breakdown, it is not enough to make for the nearest professional helper: the experts differ so much amongst themselves that it is necessary for the individual to exercise choice in the sort of treatment he will seek.

This book attempts to provide information that will help the individual in making a choice that is right for him or her; it is written for the general reader and no previous knowledge of the subject is assumed. There are of course many popular books on mental health, but the majority present only one point of view and do not attempt a systematic comparison between the different methods of treatment available. The book covers a wide area some of which goes well beyond my professional expertise. I have tried to be accurate, but mistakes may have crept in, particularly in the realm of psychiatry: since it is rare to find two psychiatrists – or for the matter of that two psychotherapists – who agree with one another, it can safely be assumed that none will agree with me.

The topic of mental illness is beset by many contentious issues. To expound the evidence and discuss each issue in detail would require many volumes. For the sake of lucidity, but at the risk of dogmatism, I have not burdened the text with detailed qualifications or with references to learned work. The interested reader can obtain pointers to the sources of my information from the notes at the back of the book. I have also provided a brief glossary to assist anyone in doubt about the nomenclature for the different approaches to mental illness.

I have been greatly assisted in the preparation of this book by many friends, both lay and professional. I would like to thank in particular R. H. Cawley, R. A. Farrand, F. W. Finger, P. N. Johnson-Laird, N. J. Mackintosh, Sonia Melchett, M. W. Richey, M. B. Shapiro and J. P. Thorne. Although they have all helped in different ways, none of them would agree with all the opinions expressed. I would also like to record my thanks to Ann Doidge for the patience and skill she exercised in typing successive drafts of the manuscript.

Finally, I wish to thank the many professional helpers – doctors, analysts, psychiatrists, clinical psychologists, occupational therapists, nurses and social workers – who cared for or treated me during the various phases of my illness. I have protected their anonymity, but where I judged it important to record an event I have spared neither their feelings nor my own. In more than one sense, it can truly be said that without them this book could not have been written. Regardless of how far each succeeded in helping me, I am sincerely grateful to all who tried.

N. S. Sutherland
March 1976

BREAKDOWN

I

Onset

About three years ago, in my mid-forties, I had a sudden and severe mental breakdown. There was nothing unusual about the breakdown itself, nor about the events in my own life that led up to it. The only exceptional feature was that I am a psychologist and should therefore be able to view the events of my illness from two standpoints – subjectively as the patient and more objectively as the detached professional observer.

Until I broke down I had always regarded myself as reasonably well-balanced: although I had sometimes worried about physical illness, the thought that I might be subjected to the torture and humiliation of a severe mental illness had never entered my head. For many years I had been outgoing, efficient, continually active and reasonably cheerful: I thought of myself as well-meaning, though possibly somewhat insensitive both to my own and others' feelings. It never occurred to me that one day my existence would disintegrate within the space of a few hours. For half a year I lived in mental anguish, a prey to obsessive and agonizing thoughts. I had neither interest in nor ability to cope with the outside world which formerly I had found so fascinating. I hated myself and I hated others, and so unremitting and painful were my thoughts that I was virtually unable to read: I could not even concentrate sufficiently to peruse the daily paper. In five months all I read were a dozen case histories of neurotic breakdowns which were sufficiently similar to my own to seize my interest. For someone accustomed to spending most of the day reading and writing, the complete inability to do either was a singularly refined torture.

There were two aspects of the breakdown that were particularly painful, and took me by surprise since I had never experienced anything similar. The onset of my neurosis was marked by levels of physical anxiety that I would not have believed possible. If one is almost involved in a road accident, there is a delay of a second or two and then the pit of the stomach seems to fall out and one's legs go like jelly. It was this feeling multiplied a hundredfold that seized me at all hours of the day and night. My dreams were often pleasant, but as soon as I woke panic set in and it would take a few moments to work out what it was about. The realization brought anguish: an irrevocable and cataclysmic event had occurred from which I could imagine no recovery. Sleep was difficult to come by even with the help of sleeping pills, to which I soon resorted. I would awake in terror twenty or thirty times a night. I would sometimes doze off in the daytime, and dream pleasant dreams for what seemed an eternity only to wake panic-stricken to discover that I had been asleep for no more than a few minutes.

The second unexpected consequence of the breakdown was the most extreme boredom. I could concentrate on nothing except my own pain. At first I would try to go to the theatre, or the cinema, but invariably I had to leave after a few minutes. In my previous existence, there had always been something to look forward to: now there was nothing, except the fitful mercy of sleep. I spent the day longing for the night to come.

I am conscious that, without being a poet, it is difficult to capture in words the quality of the pain and boredom that I suffered. Indeed it is difficult even to recall in my present mood the bitterness of my experience: perhaps nature is merciful in making it so difficult to remember pain, and it is said that no woman would ever bear a second child if she could remember the agony of her first birth. A friend recently pointed out that I have a tendency to dramatize. He said: 'If you have a breakdown, it has to be the biggest and best of all time, just as if you have seen a donkey and a girl in Port Said, you come back saying it was the only show of its kind to be done on rollerskates.' My breakdown was not the biggest and the best, but it was severe enough, and I believe my experiences were characteristic of those of other sufferers.

The reader may wonder what dire misfortune could have occurred to reduce to such misery someone who had counted himself as having a happy marriage and many friends, who was pursuing an interesting and not unsuccessful career, and who enjoyed many other diversions. The breakdown was in fact triggered by a banal, if somewhat old-fashioned, emotion – sexual jealousy. For some years I had known that my wife – Josie – had been having a sporadic affair with another man. I had been upset when I first heard about it from her, but had tolerated it since I had always regarded sexual jealousy as a particularly despicable and selfish emotion. Moreover, I had myself had a number of casual affairs, although I had always taken care to avoid any kind of involvement: I therefore had no right to recriminate. She had confided many of the details of her affair to me, and I had even admired some of the extravagant gifts with which it was punctuated. She had, however, told me that the man involved was someone I did not know. When eventually I discovered the truth, my reactions were very different.

About three years after Josie's affair began, I returned from a trip abroad to find her unusually cold. In the deepest part of the night, she revealed the name of the man: despite the lapse of a further three years I still cannot bring myself to write the word 'lover'. It turned out to be a fairly close friend of mine whom I had known for many years. I found this news desperately upsetting, possibly because my attitude towards him had always been ambivalent. In retrospect it seems as though he had always behaved towards me in a spirit of petty rivalry and I had tolerated this behaviour, ascribing it to gaucheness rather than to animosity. He was in many ways the opposite of how I pictured myself: he appeared to be emotionally closed up, mean and humourless, but along with such less desirable traits he possessed one that I admired – he was completely self-reliant and needed sympathy from nobody. The self-reliance was accompanied by a boastful smugness that I and some of our mutual acquaintances found hard to bear: some referred to him as 'the lout', and I had from time to time found myself defending his behaviour as arising from awkwardness rather than from malice. In the light of what took place, I cannot of course pretend to be presenting a fair or sympathetic portrait of him: the description is intended primarily to reveal my own feelings. It is given to few to be completely objective about such matters.

Whilst the affair had been going on, Josie and I had together been seeing this friend and his wife fairly regularly. I was sometimes given to shocking people by my candour, and I actually discussed my wife's affair on more than one occasion when the four of us were together. I sometimes supplied details from my own imagination, and I remember on one occasion, having described how devoted he was to her, adding, 'Apparently he only has one fault: he's far too quick and has no sense of rhythm.' He was driving a car at the time and nearly collided with a bus, though it was only later that I realized the cause of this lapse.

When I discovered the truth, I was at first merely badly shaken by the duplicity involved and by the fact that he was somebody about whom I already had mixed feelings and with whom I probably had a strong but unacknowledged sense of rivalry. Over the years my wife had confided many sexual details of the affair and now proceeded to supply many more in a spirit, so it seemed at the time, of trust, though in retrospect it appears to have been more a way of punishing me for my own misdeeds. I was also annoyed with and ashamed of myself; I should have been able to infer what was going on – the signs were patent. I recalled visions of my wife giving him tidbits from her plate in restaurants, and many other such indications.

The reader may well ascribe some of what I have written to rationalization. However this may be, in recording my feelings I am in no way trying to justify either my breakdown or my jealousy. Indeed, perhaps above all, I was ashamed of giving way to the loathsome emotion of jealousy. Nevertheless, I managed to hold myself together after a fashion for a further two months. My natural inclination was to wreak physical injury on the lout, but my reason told me that such behaviour was uncivilized. So foolishly determined was I to be civilized that I eventually arranged to have a drink with him when I was passing through London. He proceeded to exculpate himself by saying that my wife had thrown herself at him, a statement that was neither chivalrous nor true. My breakdown dated from that moment. I drove sixty miles home in a frenzy: I was fortunate not to kill myself. I had of course felt sexual jealousy before, but it is one thing to have twinges that can be suppressed by other interests; to be overwhelmed by this emotion to the exclusion of all other thoughts is different in kind.

My mind worked on two levels. I tried to comfort myself with the thought that there were elements of innocence in the affair. He was flattered beyond measure to find an attractive woman who liked him, whilst she not unnaturally enjoyed his attentions and such extravagant tokens of regard as being told: 'I had always known that there was something better in life.' Although such remarks are characteristic of the successful womanizer, I think in his case they came from the heart and the pair of them were swept away on a high tide of romance. I believed even then that he was sincere, and since the affair appeared to be good for

Josie I felt I should have been able to rejoice on her behalf and accept it. Once again, I beg the reader to remember that I am describing the affair as I saw it in my attempts to comfort myself. My description may not have captured its real flavour: it is intended only to reveal how I felt.

Although, even at my worst times, such ideas ran through the back of my mind, they did nothing to alleviate the more dominant cast of thought marked by the black passions of jealousy, hatred and panic. My anxieties were compounded by my own inability to forgive myself for being unable to behave rationally.

How I passed these early days of the breakdown, I find difficult to remember. I could not bear to be separated from my wife, and most of the time was spent in her company. I followed her around the house and on shopping expeditions: if I lost sight of her in the supermarket I would panic and think I would never see her again. I played tennis with her until the sight of her bare legs acted as such a spur to my jealousy that I had to give it up. It was as though only a single track in my brain was operating – whatever I tried to do led back to the same agonizing groove of jealousy. I was obsessed with visions of Josie's affair, and for hours on end my mind would be crowded with a succession of hideously detailed visual images of the sexual activities that she had so vividly related.

At times I did fight to regain some measure of control. I would drag myself into my office for two or three hours at a time thinking I was being very courageous. When I went to work, I could do none: instead I bored my colleagues with my troubles and telephoned home every half-hour. I was supposed to be examining a doctoral thesis, and for a fortnight I struggled with it morning and afternoon sitting in my garden. I tried to make notes on the contents, but I never succeeded in understanding a paragraph: my notes, penned with a shaking hand, turned out to be gibberish. From the outset of my breakdown, I tried from time to time to resume my normal activities. There was one book on psychology that I pathetically carried around with me and which several times a day I would attempt to read. In the ensuing five months I must have opened it several hundred times, but I never succeeded in getting past the first page.

There were three activities that gave me some slight respite. Two were pursuits that in my normal state I would have condemned as a waste of time: they were driving a car and doing *The Times* crossword. Perhaps I could concentrate on these tasks because neither requires one to carry forward anything in memory from one moment to the next. I could not

read because I could never remember the sense of what I had just read;
to solve a crossword, however, one does not need to remember the answer
to one clue in order to tackle the next, and I could find just sufficient
gaps in my obsessive thought-processes to enable me laboriously to
complete a puzzle clue by clue.

The third source of relief was talking. When they would listen, and at
first many were prepared to listen, I bored my friends with the story of
my woes. Provided this was the sole subject of conversation I could concentrate on what was being said and make intelligible replies. The relief
was admittedly short-lived, since as soon as the conversation ceased I was
as bored as ever. Moreover, repeating my troubles brought diminishing
returns, and I eventually became almost as bored with them as did my
friends. Breakdowns take many forms, and it is popularly thought that
anyone who can talk about their problems cannot be in too bad a condition; in my own case 'getting it off my chest' did not provide any long-
term help.

The early days of my breakdown were marked by a further curious
feature. I was seized by a compulsion to tell my wife not merely of every
disloyal act that I had ever committed but of every disreputable thought
that had ever crossed my mind. I knew I should not do this, but un-
prompted, some incident would come to mind and I would shake with
anxiety as I struggled not to reveal it. I would even force myself to go out
and walk alone, hoping that the compulsion would die away, but it never
did: whilst I kept it to myself, my anxiety level would go on rising until
eventually it forced me to vomit forth whatever I had on my mind.

My bizarre behaviour naturally upset my wife, and she alternated
between tender concern and violent hatred. From moment to moment I
never knew in which mood I would find her. She preserved her sanity
and retained her customary charm and equanimity in her dealings with
others, but her behaviour to me was almost as out of control as mine
towards her.

The following incident illustrates the depth to which we were reduced.
It is not typical of either of us – in normal circumstances Josie is a woman
without rancour or malice – but I tell it here because it *is* typical of what
can happen when things go wrong between two people with a deep
involvement in one another. In a moment of anger, Josie insisted that I
write letters to three girls with whom I had had affairs. When I wrote the
letters, I thought them unkind, though in retrospect they seem quite
mild, but at the time, despite or perhaps because of my breakdown, I was
in an idealistic mood: even in the extremes of my agony, I was hoping

that the marriage would survive and indeed be strengthened by the revelations we had made to one another not merely about our infidelities but about our innermost thoughts and longings. It seemed to me wrong to build our own happiness on writing unkind letters to others. Nevertheless I had no choice but to write the letters with Josie standing over me. When they were completed, she seized them from me. I was in a desperate state and swallowed half a bottle of whisky. With the cunning of the trapped, I went into another room and addressed and stamped three pairs of identical envelopes. I pocketed one of each pair and gave the other to Josie. She sealed up the letters and ran out of the house. I pursued her and, when we reached the pillarbox, I seized them from her and put them in my pocket saying: 'You can't post those.' Her anger flared, I put my hand in my other pocket, produced the empty envelopes and handed them to her. She posted them. I later tore up the letters and flushed them down the lavatory and out to sea. Over the next twelve hours, my anxiety about having deceived Josie built up to intolerable levels. Without telling her, I wrote out letters that were as nearly as I could remember identical to the originals and posted them. When I returned to the house, I told her exactly what I had done.

During this initial phase of my illness, the phrase '*folie à deux*' came to have a new meaning for me. I could not help thinking even then that the extreme swings in Josie's attitude to me were reminiscent of some of the brainwashing techniques used to break down prisoners, and were likely to perpetuate my state of dependence, panic and misery.

After about ten days in this condition, I sought the help of a general practitioner, and he referred me to a psychoanalyst.

2

Background

Before describing the bizarre events of my skirmish with psycho-analysis, it is necessary to give some background information both about myself and about this book. I write it with several aims.

First, it recounts my personal experience of a mental breakdown. In Britain, one in six women and one in nine men spend some part of their lives in hospital as psychiatric patients; in America over half the population consult psychiatric services at least once before the age of sixty. Despite its prevalence, there is still a formidable degree of ignorance and prejudice surrounding mental illness and its treatment. By retailing my own painful experiences, I hope both to give some idea of what it is like to those who have never suffered, and perhaps to give some comfort to those who either now or in the future find themselves in my situation. They are not alone in their suffering. Of more importance, breakdowns are not irreversible, no matter how much they seem so at the time. Until I collapsed myself, I found it difficult to sympathize properly with friends who were to a greater or lesser degree neurotic. For forty-five years I had never known what it was like to be depressed or anxious, and although, being slightly hypochondriacal myself, I could sympathize with friends who were physically ill, I was unable to understand at an emotional level the feelings of someone suffering purely mental torment – and this despite the fact that I am myself a psychologist, and had therefore read a great deal on the subject of mental illness.

My second aim is to convey information about the pitfalls and the benefits of the many different methods of treatment. Most people who become mentally unwell stumble into a particular kind of therapy almost by accident: despite my own knowledge of the subject, this happened to me, but I was just sufficiently in possession of my professional faculties to escape from a method of treatment that was wholly unsuitable for my case and was making me worse rather than better. Many laymen do not realize what the alternatives are. Even if someone is too ill to choose a sensible treatment for himself, it is important that his friends and relatives should know enough to steer him away from forms of treatment that are at best useless and at worst harmful. There is much that is unknown and uncertain in the field of mental health, but at least I hope to be able to clarify some of the contentious issues that surround the problem.

Finally, many of the things that happened in the course of my illness were so bizarre and unexpected that they demand to be recorded. Although I was unable to laugh at the time, some of the incidents that occurred in the course of my treatment seem in retrospect extremely funny: others point a moral.

Shortly after the most severe stage of my breakdown, I published two brief articles on it in the *Sunday Times*: their reception encouraged me to write a fuller description. I received numerous letters about the articles from psychoanalysts, psychiatrists, quack therapists and patients, and I shall subsequently quote extracts from this correspondence.

To return to my own story, it may be wondered how it was that the rather commonplace events described in the previous chapter brought about a severe breakdown in someone who to all outward appearances had been most fortunate in his lot in life. I can only say that the events in question, which I saw as a double betrayal of my rather simple-minded trust, still seem in retrospect to have been precisely shaped to unlock my inner uncertainties. I have always been afraid of terminal illness and death, but I assumed that short of such a prospect nothing could disturb my sanity. The world seemed so full of fascinating things to do and to observe that the idea that a trauma in one's personal relations could drain the interest from everything else would have seemed laughable. I could understand that death, illness, starvation or physical pain, whether my own or of someone close to me, could cause me misery, but I never expected to be rendered wretched and useless by events that involved none of these banes. Sydney Smith spoke only for the sane when he wrote: 'If with a pleasant wife, a good house, many books and many friends who wish me well, I cannot be happy, I am a very foolish silly fellow and what becomes of me is of very little consequence.'

It is likely that we all have our breaking points, though what destroys one man may barely pierce the skin of another. We all have wishes, conflicts and uncertainties of which we are unconscious, but of what makes one crack under this misfortune, another under that, we know very little. Inherited factors may to some extent predispose to neurosis, but my own ancestors and relatives seem a singularly unneurotic, not to say phlegmatic, lot. As in all individual cases, one can only speculate about what it was about my background that rendered me liable to a breakdown in middle age.

I was born at a time when middle-class parents were prone to follow current medical fashion about upbringing. The dogma was that babies should not be picked up when they cried and should be fed at set times. When I was two years old and my brother was born, the nurse told my mother not to see me for a fortnight. My mother obeyed the nurse rather than her own instincts and, so I am told for I have no memories of that period, I sat outside her locked bedroom door and howled for fourteen days. Such an experience may be harmful or it may not.

My parents lived a narrow suburban existence and were very much in love with each other. They were upright but not overstrict, and were dutiful and in many ways self-sacrificing in the way they brought up their sons. They were distinctly Calvinistic in their attitudes towards drink, gambling, sexual licence and all other such indulgences that are today taken for granted. My father was kind, sensible, placid and without ambition: he made a virtue of necessity and would have been genuinely contented with any lot in life. He was intelligent and well-read and inspired both his sons with an interest in literature and things of the mind. My mother was perhaps more ambitious. She encouraged us to work hard and took considerable pride in our achievements. Neither of my parents were given to self-questioning or moral doubts: they believed in the virtues of hard work and strict honesty and were perhaps a little surprised that not everyone adopted, let alone lived up to, the same standards. My relations with my younger brother were close, and untinged, as far as I can recall, with 'sibling-rivalry': the dark passions that Freud assumed to lurk within the family were unknown to me, though I may merely have succeeded in repressing them. You might say that for that day and age, I had a singularly normal and conventional upbringing.

Until I reached adolescence, I was cheerful, outgoing, gregarious and successful. Over the next few years, I became considerably less sure of myself and more introverted: by my late teens I was a clever but rather shy schoolboy. Once on the field, I enormously enjoyed playing rugby football, but I dreaded the train journeys to play against other schools: I could neither enjoy the coarse sexual and scatological banter of my team mates, nor approve of the sport of wrecking trains. I was a prig. I was particularly shy with girls – until I was nineteen, I doubt if I had ever been in the sole company of a girl of my own age. My awkwardness and lack of close contact with girls was to prey on my mind for some years to come.

Over the next few years, my character underwent a further change. I adopted, half consciously, a technique whereby I forced myself to behave in a confident and outgoing way regardless of what I felt underneath. In the matter of banter, which I continued to hate, I taught myself to give better than I got. I learned to hide my sensitivities, and soon few either dared to or could touch them. As so often happens, the mask became the man, and I came eventually to feel as confident and extroverted as I behaved. At about this time I completely gave up listening to music or reading poetry, since I found both too upsetting emotionally.

I took up my first academic appointment at the age of twenty-six, and married shortly afterwards. I taught and undertook research at the University of Oxford over the next twelve years, with the exception of two years spent working in the United States. I never fitted in to life at High Table, and my experiences there may have fostered some of my more intolerant attitudes. I came to abhor pretentiousness, snobbery and hypocrisy – by which marks, along with cattiness, much High Table conversation was distinguished. As a junior fellow of a college, it would have required more courage and more disregard for my own career than I could muster openly to rebel against the system. I therefore sat in silence whilst one or other of the senior fellows would expatiate on how and where the badge on his Rolls-Royce had been stolen or would describe the dinner he had attended the previous evening where he was the only guest without at least an earldom. I was, however, never able to conceal my boredom. Subsequently I gave more open vent to my dislike of snobbery and pretentiousness, and even welcomed the opportunity of meeting people who displayed these qualities, since I came to enjoy puncturing them. I saw my rudeness as a form of knight errantry.

When I was thirty-seven, I became a professor of psychology at the

University of Sussex. I had always worked hard, but I now plunged into a whirlpool of ceaseless activity that became a veritable vortex in the years before my breakdown: it may have been this vortex that finally sucked me under.

The popular stereotype of the leisured existence of university teachers has always mildly annoyed me. All professional people are busy and professors are no exception. In the pitifully exiguous hours of the day, I strove to find time to teach; examine; organize courses; attend university and government committees; travel to conferences; prepare reports; advise publishers; edit learned journals; interview students and potential students; appoint lecturers, secretaries and technicians; write references for students and staff past and present; and find sources of finance for the department I directed. In the interstices between these and other activities, I tried to pursue what I regarded as my real vocation – my scientific research and writing. I enjoyed almost everything I did, and of course many of the activities were voluntary, even though I told myself I had a duty to undertake them. I mention this hectic way of life only because it may have contributed to my ultimate breakdown. The pace of my existence had three further relevant effects.

First, I never allowed time to think about myself. Most people, I take it, occasionally ponder in the bath or whilst shaving. I bathed rarely and hastily; I shaved only in my car and, if I was lucky with the traffic lights several days running, would acquire a thick stubble. A former secretary recently told me, without rancour, that I used to dictate letters whilst seated on the lavatory: although I have no recollection of so doing, it sounds plausible. I therefore charged through life looking neither to left nor right, least of all inside. One or two of the numerous analysts and psychiatrists who subsequently treated me said: 'Don't you think that with all that activity, you were running away from something – perhaps from yourself?' This may be true, but it did not feel like that. I felt I was running towards something that was both useful and enjoyable.

Second, although I enjoyed organizing and administrating, I rather despised myself for spending so much time on it. Taking decisions came easily to me, and on the whole I think I showed good judgement in the staff I selected and in the direction in which I pushed my department. In the space of a few years, I built up a laboratory of psychology that was one of the foremost in Europe. Nevertheless, it all seemed too easy, and I could not help vaguely despising the skills involved. I continued to think of myself as primarily a research scientist making an original contribution to the subject; the ability to produce good original research was what I admired most in others. Amidst the welter of other activities, I found less and less time for my own research and became less productive. It occurred to me, even at the time, that I was taking on all the extraneous commitments only in order to disguise from myself the fact that I was no longer capable of producing really satisfying research: I could always tell myself that my research was becoming poorer not because my creative powers were drying up but because I was too busy with other things. Great scientists are not necessarily any cleverer than the rest of us – they are obsessed with the problem they are working on and cannot stop thinking about it. The great scientist – even the good scientist – must force himself to carry his thinking through to the ultimate point of which he is capable: this requires both lengthy periods of intense concentration and sufficient leisure to let the ideas revolve half-consciously in the mind for weeks at a time. The few whom I have known did not have to force themselves to think about their work – they could think about little else, so involved were they with it. I was so immersed in other activities that even in my few moments of leisure I rarely thought about my own research, and in consequence it suffered. The decline in my productivity was niggling at the back of my mind long before my breakdown. If one aspect of life is going really well that may be enough to help one to endure misfortunes in the remainder: in my case a marital crisis occurred just when I was becoming increasingly worried about my work.

The third consequence of all my activity was precisely its effects on the marriage. I devoted too little time and thought to the needs of my family. Indeed I worked throughout most weekends and usually spent some time in my office or laboratory even on Christmas Day. For some reason I have always loathed celebrating to order and found it difficult to make the moves appropriate to such occasions as birthdays, anniversaries and official feastdays. My habit of working at such times saved me from having to assume a mood I did not feel in order to simulate the expected jollity: it was purely selfish. I used to think that everyone would benefit if people were more direct about their own wishes. How many wearisome dinner parties are going on at this moment because the hosts think it would be rude to say that they want to go to bed and the guests are afraid to give offence by leaving too early? I have always found pubs more congenial than homes. Dr Johnson summed it up:

'There is no private house in which people can enjoy themselves so much as at a capital tavern. In a man's house let there be ever so great a plenty of good things . . . ever so much desire that everybody should be easy, in the nature of things it cannot be; there must always be some degree of care and anxiety, the master of the house is anxious to entertain his guests; the guests are anxious to be agreeable to him; and no man but a very impudent dog can freely command what is in another man's house as if it were his own. Whereas in a tavern, there is general freedom from anxiety.' ✓ ✓

My predilection for pubs, my low tolerance of boredom and my restless urges made me a less than ideal husband and father. I admire people who can sit around a house and talk about nothing in particular, but to this day I cannot emulate them, and it is difficult to describe the strangled feeling of being in a cage that made me contract every muscle of my body whenever I submitted myself to such situations. I tried to laugh off as eccentric my behaviour in leaving dinner parties (including my own) to visit the nearest pub, but my restlessness must often have given offence. Although my behaviour was selfish, I still do not understand how it could have been other than it was. I was incapable of looking interested when I was bored.

Not only did I not give enough time to the conventional activities that make up most marriages, I did not devote enough thought to understanding my wife's needs. Although I would always have acknowledged, I think, my dependence on her and my love for her, I took her too much for granted and never considered whether I was satisfying her deeper needs or even what these needs were. Despite our underlying involvement, much of our life together was superficial.

It may be that I was at a time of life which makes it difficult to bear serious emotional upheavals. Many psychiatrists believe that middle-aged men are vulnerable and that they undergo in a milder form the equivalent of the female menopause. The experience is sometimes referred to as the mid-life crisis. According to Elliott Jacques, such a crisis is particularly common in creative workers, and if they survive their work is often improved. He claims that the death-rate amongst creative artists is particularly high in the late thirties, and instances Baudelaire, Chopin, Mozart, Purcell, Raphael, Rimbaud and Watteau. Statistical evidence, however, does not support this suggestion: there is no peak in first admissions to psychiatric hospitals between the ages of thirty-five and forty-five.

When my own breakdown came it was sudden and complete, although there may have been intimations in the form of irritability, sleeplessness, heavy smoking and anxieties about physical health. My health had been worse than usual in the preceding two years. I had caught a viral pneumonia which left me mildly depressed for a few months and I suffered several other minor but persistent ailments during this time. It is possible that at some level I knew more about my wife's affair than I acknowledged to myself. It is well known that people who are subjected to strong emotions, whether to great happiness or to great sadness, are particularly prone to catch contagious diseases.

In summary, then, as in all breakdowns, so in my own case there was probably no one single cause. Josie's infidelity and the ensuing marital crisis were not on their own enough to account for the magnitude of my reaction and it is not possible to say how far the breakdown was induced by childhood traumas, my half-conscious decision to shut off many of my own feelings, the pace at which I worked or the fears of waning creativity, death, and the decline of sexual powers that accompany middle age.

3

Psychoanalysis

When, a week or so after my breakdown, I sought help from my doctor, I insisted on taking my wife with me: I felt I could say nothing behind her back. The doctor seemed rather startled at my agitated condition. I pleaded for reassurance that I would recover, but he could give none. He advised us both to see a psychoanalyst who specialized in treating discordant married couples. I asked with touching naivety whether the doctor thought Josie and I would be able to continue to live together or whether the passions let loose would force us apart. That was how it felt then, and was to feel for many months to come: I wanted only to live in peace and happiness with my wife, but there seemed to be strange forces within ineluctably driving us apart. He answered sensibly enough: 'Nobody can guarantee that you will be able to live together. Whatever happens will be for the best.' I interpreted this innocent remark as the pronouncement of a sentence worse than death.

In accepting the doctor's advice to see a psychoanalyst, I had considerable misgivings. My own experience as a psychologist* had made me

* Psychoanalysts believe that neurosis is caused by conflict between unconscious wishes formed in childhood, and that it can be cured only by helping the patient to become conscious of such wishes and to accept them at an emotional level. In Britain the majority of analysts do not have a medical degree. Psychologists study normal as well as abnormal behaviour and in general have a more eclectic and empirically-based approach. These distinctions are discussed in more detail later in the book. If in doubt about the meaning of a term, the reader should consult the glossary on page 249.

sceptical about the value of analysis, but in my despair anything seemed worth trying, and I agreed to go. I continued to see the analyst once or twice a week for the next six weeks. He lived about forty miles away, and I used to drive to see him with hope in my heart – despite my intellectual doubts about analysis, at an emotional level I felt perhaps someone could help and I pinned my faith on him.

He lived in a quiet suburban house. He was a tall, thin, slightly shy and gentle man in his forties. He warned me that he charged seven guineas a session, which was really a London price, but he always had more patients than he could cope with. He allowed me to ramble on rather incoherently about my problems and my background and occasionally he made a few interpretations. I had the feeling that he was slightly bored with the whole proceedings: he seemed to spend most of his time either examining his wristwatch or gazing into the sunlit garden from which came the noise of children playing. The very normality of such sights as children at play came as a poignant reminder of times when I too had been normal.

For several sessions he saw me together with my wife in an effort, as he put it, 'to take the steam out of things'. He did his best to alleviate my distress by pointing out the benefits to be derived from a breakdown ('better understanding of yourself and others') and by uttering the magic word 'collusion' whenever I blamed myself for having treated others badly. 'Collusion' is a Catch-22 of much modern psychotherapy – if you let someone else be nasty to you, you are colluding with them and just as guilty. In general he tried to find something good to say about our situation. 'You seem to communicate well together', he said, and he pointed out the benefit of the flurry of compulsive sexual activity in which we were indulging. He produced some mild alleviation in guilt, but my boredom and anxiety persisted in as extreme a form as ever.

He was a genuinely kind and considerate man, and although he used some Freudian interpretations he also used his common sense. I told him that I was thinking of going up to London and beating hell out of 'the lout', whom I felt like murdering. To my surprise, he said: 'That would be a much more sensible thing to do than what you are doing at the moment – you would be better to take it out of him than to go on taking it out of yourself.' I said: 'I never expected an analyst to advise me to indulge in physical violence' and he replied: 'You would of course have to make the violence commensurate with the crime and be careful not to inflict any long-term injury.'

Some of his dicta were more bizarre. It emerged that, despite the mental pain I was in, I had not shed tears since the onset of the illness. He implied that this was regrettable: 'That means there is some underlying emotional disturbance of which you are not conscious; we must try to bring it to the surface.' I went home and then and for the next week or so I used regularly to practise crying, but the tears would not come. However, I made sufficient noise for others in the house to overhear, and my children would explain to their guests: 'Don't worry – that's only Daddy practising his crying.' When I told the analyst a week later of my attempts at tears, he remarked: 'I was afraid that would happen.' I contemplated more serious deeds than crying, and would open the bedroom window and climb out, half-wanting to dash myself to death on the concrete two stories below, but I usually did this when other people were around. My suicidal gestures were more a cry for help than in earnest, though some of them were sufficiently realistic to have imperilled my life had I slipped.

Another recurrent theme brought up by the analyst was that: 'There is something puzzling about your case – you don't seem to want to get better. We must get to the bottom of that.' Needless to say, we never did. Of course one side of me wanted desperately to recover, but on the other hand I was so preoccupied with my obsessions that I could not imagine them going away. The tendency to promise insights that were never vouchsafed was something common to all the therapists I encountered and I found it irritating. One's hopes would be raised in the course of a session by the therapist implying that next time we would try to get to the root of a particular problem, only to be dashed when further probing petered out with no new insights and no relief. I am, it is true, particularly impatient, but other patients whom I subsequently met also felt that they were sometimes given false hopes. I should have realized better than most that there is no magic a therapist can offer to effect a sudden recovery. The analyst himself made some play with my impatience. He thought the suffering induced by my breakdown might help me to adopt a more stoical attitude.

My doubts about analysis and my knowledge of psychology probably made me a particularly difficult patient. I was prone to argue with any attempt at interpretation and to try to catch the analyst out in inconsistencies. The sessions often turned into arguments about the value of psychoanalysis and other forms of treatment.

After four or five consultations he announced that my problems were too complex to be treated in joint therapy with my wife, and suggested that I should undergo an individual analysis. He had accepted me as an acute case hoping to be able to produce some alleviation in a few sessions, but this had not proved possible: he had commitments to many other clients whom he saw two or three times a week for several years, and was not sure whether he could fit me in as a long-term patient. He agreed to see me on my own for a few more times, but then he went on holiday. At that point he referred me to another analyst in London. I put up only a feeble resistance to continuing in analysis. I asked whether it would not be better to seek some form of drug treatment, but he scoffed at this: 'All that would do is to change your mood.' To anyone who has never felt real depression or anxiety, a change of mood may sound rather a trivial thing: but for many who are mentally unwell, it can be a matter of life or death.

The analyst whom he originally suggested could not take me, since he also was too busy: he suggested another who, he said, was 'perhaps a bit young for you, but he is extremely good and I think you will respect his intelligence'.

My new analyst lived in London. To reach him necessitated an hour's train journey along the stretch of railway line which had been used by my wife to reach the station hotel in London where she had made assignations with her lover. The train journey and the sight of the hotel at the other end reduced me to complete panic, and I would arrive at the second analyst shaking with terror. He occupied a small flat permeated by the smell of cooking. On my first visit he was late, and his wife showed me into a squalid consulting room where I lay down on a greasy couch and gave way to real tears for the first time in thirty or forty years. I think he was rather gratified by my tears – transference had already begun before I had set eyes on him. He said: 'Did you think I had deserted you then?' He turned out to be a young man dressed in student dropout gear. I found his youth disconcerting, since it was hard to believe that anyone so young could understand the emotions that had attacked me in middle age.

Although in all questions of mental health it is difficult to assign cause and effect, I believe that the seven or eight sessions I had with him increased my distress by making me more anxious than ever. When I told my own doctor, who was himself a devotee of psychoanalysis, that analysis was making me worse, he said predictably: 'Maybe you had to be made worse before getting better' – another Catch-22 of the trade.

I am sure the young analyst was genuinely anxious to be helpful, but he sometimes set about it in a heavy-footed way. He may have felt threatened by me, since I was a well-established psychologist and I had little faith in psychoanalysis. My doctor had been to great lengths telling me that I must be completely honest with the analyst. I accordingly gave him my views on the value of analysis, on the fact that he must have only recently completed his own training analysis, and judging by the poverty in which he seemed to live was not a great success. He countered this attack by telling me that he owned a large house elsewhere in London and had more would-be patients than he could take.

Although he tried to lift some of the load of guilt I was carrying, he made a number of remarks that I found very threatening. He said: 'It seems you have missed out on all the best things in life.' At one stage he diagnosed me as a repressed homosexual, and in the course of my telling him some incident from my childhood he leant forward and said something deeply shocking. I apologize to the reader, but to understand the nature of my reactions it is necessary to quote his actual words. They were: 'Did you not feel then as though you wanted your father to fuck you until the shit ran out?' If I had ever entertained any such feeling, I had long since forgotten it, but I found the suggestion most upsetting.

Indeed around this time I read, in a lucid moment, a clinical case about someone who exactly fitted my picture of myself. He suffered from tormenting obsessions similar to my own, had like myself a deaf mother, and had been a compulsive womanizer. He had been under analysis for twenty years without showing any signs of improvement. He was diagnosed as a repressed passive homosexual, the womanizing being of course his way of disguising his homosexuality to himself. There seemed no hope for me. I should have realized, had my judgement not been impaired by the illness, that according to Freudian doctrine the only men who are not repressed passive homosexuals are unrepressed passive homosexuals. I recounted this clinical case history to one of my colleagues who happened to have a medical degree, and told him that I was apparently beyond all hope. He said: 'When I was a medical student, I used to think I had every disease under the sun. It is very easy to think you have all the aspects of a syndrome, but I don't suppose you really have. For example, were you ever a compulsive womanizer?' I said that I thought I had been at one time, and he said: 'How many women did you sleep with?' I said, in jest: 'I can't remember – a few hundred.' He replied, wholly in earnest: 'Good God, you don't call that compulsive womanizing do you?'

It is characteristic of analysts and of many other psychotherapists to turn everything upside down. Going along with other people's wishes ceases to be an easy-going virtue, it becomes collusion; chasing girls is a sign of homosexuality. When I tried to bolster the little that was left of my self-esteem by describing occasions on which I had not done things I wished to do for fear of hurting others, the young analyst said: 'You could interpret that as weakness rather than decency.'

I should not give the impression that he made no attempts to comfort me: he did, but sometimes in a rather bizarre way. He said, for instance: 'You know, I really admire you for breaking down.' When I asked him to explain this cryptic remark, he pointed out that many people charge through life without ever reflecting on their own behaviour and with no remorse for their misdeeds. Out of evil good might come: my break-down had opened the possibility of changing myself. I was far from feeling this at the time, since the breakdown seemed to have occurred for entirely selfish reasons and was in itself demeaning. It is one thing to feel depressed and anxious because the world is full of people who are dying in agony, or starving or eking out a barren, lonely existence, but it is altogether shaming to break down through an insult to one's own *amour propre*.

In addition to making efforts to comfort me, the analyst also gave some sensible advice. I had told him about my behaviour at home, much of which was like that of a small baby. I would sit around moaning and holding my head, and although I seemed unable to stop myself I was aware that this was upsetting for my wife and children. He said: 'Your wife will be able to tolerate just so much of that kind of thing, but if you continue she will be tempted to leave you. Could you not just sit in a chair and feel like a little baby without giving outward expression to your emotions?'

I went home and tried to follow his advice, but it proved to be impossible. I continued to moan and groan out loud. Such behaviour was accompanied by very mixed feelings on my part. I felt that there was an element of faking about the outward expressions of my misery: they seemed partly simulated in order to gain sympathy and attention. Yet, although I thought some of my behaviour was sham, I could not stop myself from behaving in this way. I merely added to my other worries the thought that even my breakdown was a fake. Was there nothing genuine about me?

He asked me to bring my wife to a joint session, and afterwards suggested that she was jealous of my being analysed and that the best way to cure this jealousy was for her also to become a patient of his. Being a sensible woman, she would have none of this. She pointed out that despite his own training analysis he fidgeted in his chair throughout the session and did not know what to do with his hands. Thereafter she rather unkindly referred to him as 'Pipsqueak'.

A theme that constantly recurred in my sessions with both analysts was the danger of leaving analysis prematurely: from the outset they both warned me that I would be tempted to break off treatment too soon. It would take many months or possibly years before my deep-rooted problems could be properly alleviated by analysis. It was indeed only these statements, which at the time seemed plausible enough, that kept me in a method of treatment that I now believe was wholly unsuitable to my condition. After seven or eight sessions, I was so upset by the punishment the second analyst appeared to be handing out that I began seriously to think about consulting a psychiatrist and having myself admitted to hospital to undergo physical methods of treatment. When I mentioned this to the analyst, he was horrified; he said: 'Whatever else you do, you must never let yourself be admitted to one of those places.' He seemed indeed as prejudiced against mental hospitals as are some members of the general public.

My condition continued to deteriorate, but the decision about terminating analysis was for the time being taken out of my hands, since my second analyst announced that he was going on holiday. I never saw him again, although I had not yet quite escaped the lure of psychoanalysis.

I was so annoyed with him for what I regarded as very unhelpful treatment that I did not pay his bill. When many months later I received a peremptory letter from his solicitors, I took legal advice myself and wrote to him saying that I had no intention of paying. I contested his claim on the grounds that his treatment had been incompetent. In the state of desperate anxiety in which I then was, his threatening remarks had only increased my problems: to accept such observations as that at some level of the unconscious mind one has homosexual proclivities, that one's virtues stem from weaknesses, or that one has missed out on the best things of life, it is necessary to be in a much more robust state of mental health than I then was. I also alleged that he himself felt threatened by my own knowledge of the subject and my doubts about the efficacy of psychoanalysis, and consciously or unconsciously he had been attempting to punish me. Finally, I wrote that he had claimed to be able to make me feel much better within six months of commencing therapy, that this claim was fraudulent and I had entered therapy only through false pretences on his part. Such was my fury that I think I would have been prepared to contest a legal action, but it never arose. He telephoned me a few days after I had written, and was most solicitous and pleased about the recovery I had made. It is small wonder that many analysts insist on being paid their fee, often in cash, at the end of each session.

Since the two analysts and my doctor were now simultaneously on vacation, I was left in a therapeutic limbo. My wife was anxious to take the children to Naples for a holiday. I used to carry out research on vision in the octopus there every summer, and my children had fond memories of the place and longed to go back: they had been taking important examinations at school and my own illness had been a great trial to them. They deserved a treat. Moreover, my wife and I thought that if I got away from my normal environment it might help to break up the anguished pattern of my thoughts.

By this time I was desperately worried about money: we had lodgers in our house, and so terrible was my condition that I could hardly collect the rent, and when I did collect it I forgot to record it or to bank it. The roof was leaking and the problem of finding someone to repair it seemed insuperable. I forgot who was owing me money, and when with shaking hand I wrote a cheque, there was invariably a mistake on it. I sold a car for two pounds – admittedly it was not a very good one, but it functioned. I could not face advertising it in the paper, took the first offer from a dealer, and felt relieved that I would no longer have to bear the expense of running it. The children cried when they saw it go. I was convinced that I would lose my job and my family would be destitute. Naples was to be our last extravagance before declining into hopeless poverty.

As a university teacher, I was entitled to cheap student fares on foreign railways. I therefore booked tickets to Naples through a student travel agency for a twelve-day trip. The journey was feasible only because we had some very good friends in Naples who agreed to put up our children and to find a room in a private house for me and Josie. I consulted a different doctor about whether I was in a condition to make the trip, and he thought I was. He had rather more faith in drugs than the other one and prescribed an antidepressant, sleeping pills and sedatives. I was convinced I was dying of lung cancer, and asked him whether I had club fingers: he examined them and replied, I thought very guardedly: 'They are within the normal limits.' I found this less than reassuring.

I dreaded the journey – thirty-six hours on trains and boats with no possibility of alleviating the tedium by reading since that was totally beyond my powers of concentration. All I would have to occupy me were my obsessive thoughts.

I contemplated throwing myself off the cross-Channel ferry, but the train journey was much better than I expected. By good fortune, we obtained an otherwise unoccupied compartment for the night, and I took a massive dose of sleeping tablets and slept for twelve solid hours. We arrived at Naples through the ironworks on the outskirts with their chimneys belching flame, and were met at the Ferrovia Centrale by my friends. They had not seen me since the breakdown, and were upset by my condition whilst feeling powerless to help. The husband was himself in a medical profession, and reinforced my judgement that I must have done with analysis and seek psychiatric help.

I remember, on the first evening, all of us going to a brightly-lit open-air cafe for a drink, the nostalgic sound of Neapolitan songs and the sight of the animation of Naples street life. I was now under such heavy sedation that I could drink practically nothing. The cafe was in a park along the front, and whilst the others sat at table I rolled around moaning in the dust. Such behaviour is disconcerting to others at first, but they quickly realize it is best ignored since there is little they can do to help. To my other worries was now added almost total impotence – induced partly by my mood, which was becoming more and more depressed, and partly by the drugs I was under. With their aid, I obtained the blessed relief of nine or ten hours sleep each night, but waking still brought back the pain.

I revisited many of the places I had once loved: the Museo Nazionale with its magnificent mosaics pillaged from Pompeii, Pompeii itself and Capri. None of them evoked a spark of interest – I stared listlessly and uncomprehendingly at the pictures in the museum with harrowing thoughts still racing in my mind. I could not guide the children round Pompeii, since I could not concentrate sufficiently to follow the plan. Capri had lost its beauty and charm. I could not even giggle at the vulgarity of the interior of Axel Munthe's villa, though the beauty of the formal garden and the magnificent view of the island and the sea from the belvedere evoked a slight response. The phrase 'See Naples and die' echoed through my mind: I was convinced I would never return alive to England, let alone ever revisit Naples.

I was poor company. My friends lived in an apartment on the fourteenth floor of a modern block of flats. Whilst they were eating dinner,

I would go out on the balcony and contemplate the drop. I even con-cealed myself in a corner of the balcony for half an hour in the hope that they would think I had thrown myself over – a shameful trick, though when they came looking I had enough sense to reveal myself fairly quickly.

On my return from Naples, I went back to my own doctor to tell him that I wanted to seek psychiatric advice and to attack my depression and anxiety with drugs. He was himself under analysis and was very much against this line of action. He said: 'You are going through a great emotional crisis, and drugs are not the solution. You owe it to yourself to have a prolonged analysis: if necessary you must mortgage everything you have to pay for the treatment.' So committed was he to analysis that when I suggested that giving up cigarettes and taking more exercise might help my mental state, he said: 'There is no evidence that exercise ever helped the mind' – a remark which, when I later reminded him of it, he regretted making.

In the end, I weakly agreed to have one more session with the first analyst for 'reassessment'. The reassessment took the form of advice to continue analysis in the hope of learning a new set of emotional responses: I had become preoccupied with the idea that I could never love anyone properly, and I asked him pathetically whether he could make me capable of love if I became his patient yet again. He said it would take time but he was sure this could be achieved. I asked whether I would be able to love my wife and he said: 'That I cannot guarantee: but I am sure you will be able to love someone.' Since I only wanted to love my wife, I became more upset than ever. I pointed out that new learning becomes more difficult with advancing years and doubted my own capacity for it. The analyst retorted that he had recently been seeing a woman patient of fifty-five who after a year's analysis had 'seen a flower for what it was for the first time and had burst into tears'. I think it was the sheer idiocy of this story that finally decided me to abandon analysis and seek some other form of treatment.

4

The Hospital

Having decided to seek help from a psychiatrist,* I was naturally anxious to find a good one. I had professional contacts with several psychiatrists and telephoned some of them for advice. I naturally did not want to be treated by a friend, and there was a consensus that one psychiatrist unknown to me was an excellent man. When I telephoned, he agreed to see me without an official referral from a doctor though when I told my general practitioner that I had made this arrangement he agreed to write a letter to the psychiatrist outlining my medical history.

My first interview with the psychiatrist took a very different form from the inchoate ramblings in which I had indulged with the two analysts. He spent three hours taking notes on my life, broken into systematic topics – career, early family relations, marriage and relations with friends. He then said: 'You are suffering from an agitated depression. This is not uncommon in men of your age who have achieved professional success as a result of a great deal of hard work. Your depression is an illness and must be treated as such.' He recommended

* A psychiatrist has a medical degree and specializes in the treatment of mental illness. In Britain very few psychiatrists practise analysis: they use other forms of psychotherapy and also use physical methods of treatment. The distinction between the different approaches to mental health is spelled out in more detail later in the book and is summarized in the glossary on page 249.

me to become a voluntary patient in a psychiatric hospital, if only to break up the bad pattern of interaction into which I had fallen with those around me. He also prescribed a much heavier dose of an anti-depressant drug and warned me that it would have no effect for at least three weeks other than unwanted side-effects. He told me I would remain in hell for the next month or so but that ultimately I would definitely recover – an assurance that neither the doctor nor the analysts had been prepared to give.

My wife had accompanied me to the hospital, and he spent twenty minutes talking with her. He told her that I was in a condition where I was seeing everything in a distorted way as though I were looking at the world through darkened and buckled glass. He assured her that I would recover.

The psychiatrist saw me on a Friday, and I was to be admitted to hospital on Monday. Although I had more or less agreed to admission, I agonized about it over the weekend. I am not by nature a brave person. I was still in a mood of extreme dependence on my wife, and although I could see it was not doing either of us any good I felt desperately that I needed her by my side. I thought at the time and I still think that entering hospital was the most courageous decision I have ever made.

My wife drove me there. Like all incoming National Health patients I was given a room of my own – cell-like but comfortable. The door had no lock and contained a window with a curtain outside so that nurses could observe the inmate at will. The young male nurse who admitted me was kind and considerate. He made sure that I was not carrying any drugs or alcohol, and for reasons I never fathomed he removed my electric razor, which was returned to me the day after. The reasons for retaining ordinary razors are obvious: they were issued before breakfast each morning and then recovered. Little attempt was made to explain the routine of the ward except for telling me the times of meals. It took me nearly three weeks before I discovered where and when to obtain clean sheets, though this was my own fault for not inquiring earlier.

While Josie waited on the ward, I was given a rapid physical exam-ination by a consultant whom I never saw again. A few tests were made for signs of neurological disease, and my chest, blood pressure and rectum were checked. The drugs had made me so constipated that my stools were bloody, and the consultant assured me that I had neither bowel cancer nor piles. I rejoined my wife on the ward. After lunch I sadly watched her drive away into the sunlight and was left sitting in my little cell feeling sad, lonely and very anxious.

The ward was made up of two long wings with a common room and a dining room in the middle. One wing contained male and the other female patients: there were about sixty on the ward, of whom slightly over half were women. Each wing contained a corridor with private rooms opening off it and a dormitory at the end with about a dozen beds. As patients began to recover they moved from the private rooms to the dormitory. All the inmates were there on a voluntary basis and were expected to be 'short-stay' – less than eighteen months.

The mental hospital was one of the best-equipped in England. It was set in extensive and beautifully maintained grounds and had facilities for almost every conceivable sport, including a gymnasium and swimming pool. It was free from much of the regimentation that pervades most hospitals for physical illness. Patients were up and around fully dressed in the daytime. Visitors were allowed at almost any hour. Patients were encouraged to attend occupational therapy, known as 'O.T.' – dressmaking, typing, carpentry, yoga and so on, but no compulsion was brought to bear. Breakfast was at eight and supper at five thirty.

Of more interest to most patients were 'tablet times'. The cry 'tablets' would echo through the ward at nine, one and six o'clock, and a fourth dose was obtainable from the night nurse before going to bed. Most of us who were taking drugs looked forward to tablet times and queued with alacrity. We swallowed them eagerly to the accompaniment of a draught of water from a plastic glass that each patient was responsible for rinsing and drying in readiness for the next. This was the only chore patients were expected to perform, apart from making their own beds.

Whilst taking our pills, we were closely watched by a nurse. Although it is well known that unless medicine is taken under supervision about thirty per cent of it never finds its way to the patients' stomachs, it is a remarkable fact that many hospitals still trust patients to swallow their own medicine.

Almost all the patients who were seriously unwell found the six empty hours between supper and bedtime very hard to bear. The nurses did their best to help. They organized bingo, and they tried to lure any patient who looked particularly miserable into playing one or other of the twenty or so games with which the ward was equipped, such as table tennis, snooker, Scrabble, Monopoly, or draughts. They also did their best to soothe anyone who was beside himself with anxiety. Despite these attempts to make the time pass, many patients found these hours very difficult and retired into their own miseries. There was a general feeling that not enough was being done to help us.

The ward contained three separate groups of patients, each under a different psychiatric consultant. There were alcoholics in the process of drying out, a group of patients with phobias, and the group to which I belonged, who were mainly suffering from depression.

The consultants were rarely in evidence. As in so many walks of life, as soon as they have proved themselves good at their own profession, extraneous calls on their time mount up: they practise psychiatry less and less and devote themselves instead to administering, teaching, and sitting on innumerable committees. Under each consultant was a senior registrar who in my group was a Sinhalese with a permanent and cheerful smile. There was also a junior registrar allocated to each group, in whose direct charge the patients were. Also associated with each group were one or more clinical psychologists.* All the doctors and psychologists had patients on other wards, and most also spent time working in other hospitals.

In the course of a week, patients spent on average about two separate periods of an hour or an hour and a half alone with a doctor or psychologist. The time between such sessions could feel terribly empty, and many patients saw themselves as existing in a vacuum with little being done to help. Any patient who had an appointment with a doctor or psychologist was treated by the others as being of great importance. On emerging from a session, he or she would be eagerly questioned about what went on; indeed, a patient's standing with the other patients came to be directly related to the number of occasions on which he was seen privately by the staff. The excitement generated by tablet times was also doubtless caused by the feeling that here was something that was actually being done to help.

Some of the doctors were careless about keeping appointments: they would say they would see a patient the next day and then fail to do so. This was bad for patients' morale, and some of the younger doctors were clearly unaware of the extent to which patients felt dependent upon them. To the plea that little was being done to help, the standard response of the medical staff was that everything that happened in the hospital was therapy – O.T., existence in a novel milieu, and the interactions with nurses and other patients were all therapeutic.

* Clinical psychologists have a university degree in psychology and postgraduate training in clinical work. See glossary.

As patients, we were quick to resent lack of attention from doctors, but we were equally prone to suspect that the nurses were spying on us if they paid us too much attention. Part of their duties was to make reports on the patients' mental state. They sometimes seemed a little tactless in their attempts to draw patients out on, for example, how they fared during a weekend at home. Although the nurses were trying to be kind and sympathetic, many patients felt that such inquiries were being made with the aim of having something to report in the day-book. Reports were also sent back from O.T. workers and doctors, and we had the feeling that our movements were known and recorded almost all the time. Whenever I was in my room, whether by day or night, the curtain would be removed from the window every two hours or so and a nurse would observe, replace the curtain and go away. No matter how much I told myself that such surveillance was for my own good, it was difficult not to feel that there was something sinister about it.

There was a further feature of life in hospital to which many inmates found it difficult to adjust. The younger doctors and nurses tended to treat patients as though they were insane, and this could be both infuriating and upsetting. Since all the patients were to some extent mentally ill, it may seem odd to be upset by being treated as such. The point is that none of the patients was totally out of touch with reality, and their illness only affected part of their lives. Many, for example, knew better than the nurses what pills they were supposed to be taking. However, the doctors sometimes wrote up the drug sheets in such a hurry that nurses could easily make mistakes. It could seem very important to be given the right drugs, but when the wrong ones were handed out any attempt to argue with the nurse would be treated as part of the patient's illness and recorded as such in the day-book. Because doctors and nurses could always shelter behind the belief that the patients were mad, they were in an impregnable position, and it was easy for patients to feel completely in the power of the hospital authorities. One of the alcoholics had spent several years in prison in Dartmoor; he summed up his feelings: 'I'd rather spend a year in Dartmoor than a week here.' When I asked why, he said: 'At least you can get at the screws there: here there's no one to get at.'

I should stress that in describing the common grievances of the patients I am not imputing blame to the hospital staff: I am merely trying to give an impression of what it feels like to be in a mental hospital. The point of substance is that even in a psychiatric hospital which is one of the country's showpieces and which is run in a most enlightened way at great cost to the taxpayer, patients could readily become apathetic and their feelings were easily bruised. The situation is much worse in most mental hospitals, which are run with fewer and less experienced staff. For long-stay patients, it becomes debatable how much of their incapacity to cope with life is due to their original illness and how much to being institutionalized.

I do not remember how I passed the first afternoon in the hospital. I think I talked to some of the other patients and I ate my dinner at five thirty. The food was plain but, for institutional cooking, good and plentiful. On the evening of my first day there, my anxiety began to build up. Over half the nurses were coloured: I remember wondering how nurses with home backgrounds in Jamaica, India, Pakistan, Ceylon and many different African countries could have such sympathy with the absurd neuroses of the British middle and working classes. On my first night on the ward, an attractive and vivacious little African nurse was exceptionally kind to me. She chatted about my problems and inveigled me into playing table tennis and snooker with her, and this distraction from my anxieties was extremely helpful. Many of the patients spent the evenings watching television, but throughout my stay in hospital I was far too agitated to concentrate on any programme, and although I once or twice entered the television room I was never able to sit there for more than five minutes.

The same nurse later upset me quite badly by crude but well-meant attempts to analyse my condition. I once explained that I could not join some of the other patients in a game of tennis because my motor coordination was badly impaired by my drugs. My statement was true: indeed so shaky was I that I had to concentrate very hard on crossing a road. She said: 'Oh you're always blaming your troubles on something else: if you're not blaming other people, you're blaming the drugs.' At the time this seemed very upsetting, and I was hurt for several hours: people in the state I was in are sensitive to the slightest suggestion of criticism.

At ten thirty, the patients were allowed to make themselves Horlicks, and sweet biscuits were provided. I found the nightly glass of Horlicks, with its memories of protected childhood, a great comfort. The only other drink served on the ward was heavily stewed tea, though many patients kept in the kitchen their own supplies of coffee or cocoa. Although I much preferred coffee, I never got round to investing in a jar: I was determined to spend as little money as possible, partly because I believed I would never again be able to earn and partly because I had decided to do without any self-indulgence.

At eleven o'clock on my first evening, I went to the night nurse for my final dose of drugs before going to bed. I was horrified to find that the registrar who, under the consultant, was in charge of my case had not prescribed a sleeping tablet: I had been using sleeping tablets regularly for the last six weeks, and I was convinced that without them I would not sleep. I was by now in a desperate state of anxiety, and the prospect of going without sleep – the only thing to which I still looked forward – appalled me. The night nurse was sympathetic but could not find a doctor on duty and was naturally loath to rouse one from his bed. Although he could not give me a sleeping tablet, my prescription for sedatives was written in such a way that he was able to increase the dose without going against what was written on the drug sheet – no nurse could alter in any way the drugs that were prescribed.

This particular nurse was an old-timer who had retired but still did occasional night duty as a part-time occupation. He was stocky, and possessed of demonic willpower. I talked to him from about midnight to one or two in the morning, and he told me how his only child had contracted poliomyelitis. The doctors had given up all hope of the boy ever walking again, and wished him to stay permanently in an institution. The father told me that he determined 'to lick the doctors': he insisted on his boy living at home and by the sheer exercise of his own will he gave him the strength to live and to recover. I was talking of discharging myself the day after, since in my depressed and nervous state I had by now lost faith in the hospital and its staff. He told me that he had seen 'Many like yourself when they first come in. Those that run away too soon always come back.' He said I could lick my illness but I needed help: he claimed that he himself could lick the problem of sleep for me, and he savagely willed me to sleep, seizing my arm in a grip like a vice. His faith and his will somehow enabled me to sleep, and when I woke again at four in the morning and stumbled into his office for comfort, he managed to will me back to sleep again. He was a most remarkable man and I was sorry that I never saw him again.

The following day my anxiety gradually built up throughout the morning. After lunch there was a group meeting of the whole ward: these meetings occurred weekly and were attended by nurses, occupational therapists, psychologists and doctors, as well as by patients. I was unable to sit through the meeting – I began to wring my hands and moan and eventually I rolled on the floor. The male nurse who had admitted me took me outside and we walked round and round the grounds together. He allowed me to pour out the tale of my sufferings in an attempt to talk me down. For the rest of the afternoon nurses took it in turns to walk with me through the beautiful park in which the hospital was situated.

I would not have believed it possible to feel such extreme anxiety. My heart pounded, my body shook, my stomach felt as though all the blood had drained away, and my legs felt too weak to carry me. My mind was occupied solely with my jealous thoughts: cruelly detailed and painful visual images succeeded one another in never-ending succession.

The Sinhalese senior registrar had been summoned to see me, and I spent half an hour with him late in the afternoon. He tried to reassure me, telling me that I would feel very differently in a fortnight's time, and he prescribed a stronger tranquillizer – chlorpromazine. He described very exactly what the drug would do: 'It will act within half an hour of taking it. You will find that it will remove the bodily feelings of anxiety so that your body feels calm. It will not stop your obsessive thoughts but it will blunt their edge and make them less painful so that you can bear them more easily.' It worked exactly as he had predicted.

Although the new drug made life just bearable, I remained in mental agony: I was fortunate in one thing – I was now on such a dose of different drugs that I almost invariably slept well, and sleep was always something to look forward to and to sustain me through the fears and boredom of the day.

Over the next week I began to adapt to the drug, and obtained decreasing relief. The registrar reacted by tripling the dose, but I steadily adapted to the larger dose throughout the rest of my stay. The side-effects of the drugs I was taking were most unpleasant. Apart from having very poor motor coordination, I was now totally impotent. In addition I had severe constipation and it was agony to defecate: my stools were smeared with fresh blood spilt in the effort to pass them. I suffered from these pains unnecessarily, since it was only after I had been in hospital for a fortnight or so that I discovered from another patient that the nurses would issue Senocot tablets on demand at night. Even this did not solve the problem, since in my distracted state I usually forgot to ask. The reader may wonder why I did not mention the constipation to a doctor, but during the first fortnight in hospital I think I only saw a doctor once or twice, and there seemed to be more important things to discuss than constipation. The worst side-effect of the drugs, however, was dryness of the mouth: no matter how much water I drank, the feeling of a parched tongue and throat could not be shaken off.

Like most of the other patients, I went home for long weekends, leaving the hospital on Friday evening and returning on Monday morning. The idea of spending the weekend in hospital appalled me. The boredom during the week was bad enough, despite the fact that there were always other patients and nurses to talk to, occupational therapy classes to attend and a variety of games that one could play. There was also a chance that a doctor or a psychologist would summon one for an interview, something to which I, in common with my fellow-patients, always looked forward: not only did it break the monotony, I also felt it might actually be helpful. I developed a terror that the doctors would take my weekend leave away from me, and no amount of reassurance would convince me that they had no intention of so doing. When I left the hospital on Friday afternoons I often felt for a few moments free and exhilarated. But I carried my misery with me, and the weekends were as full of terror and boredom as the weeks. I tried not to admit this to myself and caught the train back on Monday mornings with sadness.

On my return to hospital, a nurse would always come across to chat with me. I was anxious not to reveal that at weekends the pattern of interaction with my wife was a bad as ever, since I thought that if the doctors knew how I behaved at home, they might stop my weekend leave. I therefore gave very guarded replies to the nurses' inquiries, and I remember saying once rather ungraciously: 'At least it's not as bad as this place.' In fact, most of the patients were actively encouraged to go home at weekends: the few who stayed did so either because they had no home to go to or because they could not face the prospect of meeting their family or friends, and preferred the tedium of a weekend in hospital.

Many patients had good reason to fear the prejudice of 'normal' people about mental illness. As they improved, efforts were made to obtain some sort of part-time work for them in the surrounding community. This usually proved difficult, since as soon as it was known that someone had been a patient at a mental hospital, potential employers lost interest. There is still much prejudice against the mentally ill, and I realized that one of the ways in which I was luckier than the majority of patients was that I could go home at weekends and talk to friends who would (usually) be sympathetic and understanding and who would not think that being an in-patient in a mental hospital was a great stigma. It was very different for many of the others: their friends would either try to be nice whilst concealing their embarrassment or they would be downright hostile or shun them altogether.

One of the patients – a middle-aged woman who lived in well-to-do suburbia – attended one Sunday a religious ceremony connected with healing at her local church. She returned to her home with a woman who lived opposite her. The neighbour said: 'I suppose you will be moving away from here when you come out of that place.' When the patient expressed puzzlement, she said: 'Well, it would be much better for everyone in the street if you did – it would be very embarrassing to have you still around.' This was the attitude of a regular churchgoer, but to judge from the experiences of other patients it is common in the community at large.

Patients often felt they were a great affliction to their friends and family and should not trouble them with their worries. Some were so closed up that they found it difficult to talk to anyone. Many, particularly when they first came into hospital, found it a relief to be amongst fellow-sufferers in whom they could confide in return for listening to the confidences of others: they found it easier to open their hearts to complete strangers, whom after discharge they would probably never see again, than to those close to them. They also obtained some relief, at least at first, from telling the tale of their woes to doctors, psychologists and nurses, though the novelty of this usually wore off rather quickly, and patients began to find it a bore to go over their stories every time there was a change of doctors.

Although I was lucky in my friends, they too could be tactless. I remember being very hurt when, full of self-reproach, I asked a colleague of mine with whom I was on close terms what he had ever seen to admire in me: after a moment's thought he replied: 'I sometimes wonder.' After I had been discharged from hospital, whilst arguing with him in front of several other people over some intellectual issue I said: 'That argument doesn't make sense: you're mad,' and he replied: 'At least I've never been a patient in a mental hospital.' I was desperately hurt, and this provides yet another example of how prone anyone in a neurotic condition can be to take offence. I later learned that his foolish behaviour was the result of attendance at encounter groups where he had been persuaded that he must always give vent to his 'true feelings'.

Visitors to the hospital could have a somewhat similar effect. They would often be bright and smiling and comment with surprise on what a nice place the hospital seemed to be, adding that they would not mind a few weeks' rest there themselves. Perhaps they had expected to see patients shrieking and in chains. After meeting other patients, they would say: 'I can't see what's wrong with him [or her], he seems quite normal,' thus expressing the prejudice that someone who is deranged should behave in a mad fashion all the time. They did not realize that the girl who claimed that the hospital was trying to starve her, and who would constantly beg food items, was in fact suffering from anorexia nervosa and was in the habit of hoarding food in her room whilst eating so little that she was in danger of starving herself to death. Unless you have been acutely anxious or depressed yourself, it is difficult to realize that someone who is outwardly healthy and well fed, who is living in comfortable surroundings with what appear to be many pleasant recreations, and who is able to talk quite sensibly for much of the time, may be in mental anguish.

It is hard to know how to treat someone with a breakdown. The feeling that friends and family have that they can do nothing to help must be very frustrating. In my own case, I am sure that sympathy helped – at least temporarily. Being told, as I was by one friend, that my breakdown was a form of nemesis or, as some friends said, that it would do me good and help me to change myself, was distinctly unhelpful. The analysts also had a habit of saying that the breakdown was a chance to change myself, and I became very worried about how I was ever to change. I shall always be grateful to the three friends who said: 'Don't attempt to change yourself – you were all right the way you were.' If I were to sum up my own feelings on how friends and family should treat anyone mentally ill, I would say: 'Sympathize without condescension and never pass moral judgements. Try to find something to talk about to distract the sufferer.' The visitors who helped me most were those who could find something to discuss in the outside world that would take my attention away from myself.

In contrast to some visitors, patients were almost invariably kind to one another. They would go to great lengths to comfort or console one of their number who was in particular difficulties, and the phrase, 'after all, we're all in the same boat' was frequently to be heard.

For almost the whole of my stay in hospital my anxiety would from time to time rise to quite uncontrollable levels. If I was on the ward at night, I would pace from one end to the other, pausing from time to time to screw up my body or to attempt to climb a wall or even to bang my head against one. This behaviour produced a mixture of consternation and amusement in the other occupants of the ward. I went out one evening with three other patients including Jimmy, a Glaswegian alcoholic, who worked on a building site and who, although suffering from terrible anxiety himself, had adopted a protective attitude towards me and was forever greeting me with: 'Och, ye'll be all rricht, Stuart, ye'll be all rricht.' On this particular occasion, I was far from all right: I was climbing lamp-posts and threatening to dash my head through shop windows in an effort to get rid of the tortured tenseness which permeated my whole body. Somehow they managed to get me on a bus and back to the hospital.

One of the thoughts that dogged me throughout my illness was envy of normal people going about their everyday business. When I went out of the hospital to buy a newspaper or some apples, I used to feel how lucky were the newsagent and the greengrocer to live a placid life not tormented by obsessional thoughts. I was particularly envious of the hospital staff when I saw them driving away to a normal life outside the hospital.

Given that the doctors and psychologists in the hospital could only spend at most two to five hours a week seeing patients individually, one of the greatest problems facing the hospital authorities was how to occupy the patients' time. It was generally agreed that nothing could be worse than letting patients sit around and brood. The main distractions were games and occupational therapy, and nurses would constantly try to encourage patients to get off the ward during the daytime and occupy themselves by playing tennis or badminton, by swimming or by attending occupational therapy, which went on between nine thirty and twelve thirty and between two and four o'clock in the afternoon.

The head of the occupational therapy unit was a woman of great energy and faith. She tried to get to know patients and to discover their interests and talents. She constantly attempted to cajole them into taking part in play readings, poetry readings, giving or listening to lectures and musical recitals, and attending classes in dressmaking, pottery, woodwork, cookery and typing. She also organized expeditions to the local repertory theatre and to nearby exhibitions of art. Hers was a thankless task. Patients would volunteer to give talks to the others and then funk it at the last moment; they often simply forgot to come to a play reading, or the man playing the lead in a carefully rehearsed drama would be unable to appear on the opening night because he had just been given ECT. She cheerfully survived such misfortunes and continued to infect patients with her own love of the arts.

When it was her turn to take yoga or relaxation classes, she often varied the routine by introducing exercises in touching and trusting.

One patient would lie down and relax and then others would gently roll him or her from one end of the room to the other on mattresses. I could always relax sufficiently to offer no resistance to those rolling me, and I found the sensation quite pleasant. Another exercise was to pair the patients off in couples: one member of each pair was then blind-folded and was led round the room by the other. No verbal instructions were allowed: guidance was entirely by means of pressure applied by the hands and arms. Again I found this a pleasant enough diversion until I became bored with it, but lack of trust has never predominated amongst my vices.

Since I could not do anything I was used to doing, being in hospital seemed a good chance to learn something new, and I attended pottery classes for two hours almost every morning. I progressed from a dish made in a mould to a mug shaped round a beer bottle, and then to a bowl built up by adding successive strips of clay. I was baffled by the complexity of the processes that went into making such simple objects – at how difficult it was to roll clay to an even thickness or to get rid of bubbles in it, to impose with the various implements provided any pattern upon it that was other than an untidy mess, or to press a layer of clay smoothly into a mould. To obtain an even glaze required a degree of skill that was completely beyond me. It was unfortunate that having made a pot it often took a week before it could be fired and another week before the glaze could be baked: a more immediate sight of the end-product of our labours would have been more encouraging.

Misshapen though my products were, I took some pride in having made them myself: no machine process could have produced objects of such total irregularity. The pottery instructress was possessed of un-believable patience both with her pupils and with their pots: however crude one's efforts, she tried to find something to praise, and she was unsparing in the time she gave to repairing one's errors. I doubt if doing pottery taught me patience, and it certainly did not prevent my continuing obsessions, since it was possible to smooth away at the soft wet clay whilst thinking the most tortured thoughts. Despite hours of trying, I never learned to use a wheel: the trick of centring the clay cannot be imparted by words.

Patients were encouraged, though never forced, to put their former skills to use to help the hospital. A professional gardener on our ward transformed the appearance of the shrubbery beds by which it was sur-rounded. Since my own skills lay largely in writing and teaching, and I was in no condition to do either, I was hard pushed to find any useful task. Eventually I was given the job of preparing a card-index for a collection of several hundred scientific papers owned by one of the psychologists who worked in the hospital. Since the papers were heaped at random in cardboard boxes, and since the psychologist who owned them was in any case about to retire, I knew that the task was useless and this disappointed me. Nevertheless, I was determined to prove to myself that I could do something that involved a little concentration, and I spent an hour or two a day on my own in a borrowed office writing index cards with a shaking hand. Some of the articles appertained to cases like my own, and these I would occasionally manage to read or half-read in the process of cataloguing them.

During the daytime then, I tried to fill my hours with occupational therapy, progressive relaxation classes and the rather pointless indexing task. I also completed a great many more crosswords and wandered round the grounds with other patients. Many seemed to me to be in a much worse state than myself. They flitted through the ward like pathetic ghosts on the shores of Hell: some could do no more than mumble, and several were withdrawn completely from the real world and lived entirely with their inner miseries. Only the nurses and doctors and a few of the alcoholics who had already dried out seemed made of flesh. At occupational therapy, I met long-stay patients from other wards. Some had been in hospital for several years: others had been in and out for most of their lives. They were often sad, shambling creatures with slurred speech, and their condition made me feel ashamed to be in hospital at all.

In subsequent chapters I shall describe in more detail how some of the other patients behaved and felt. At the time I was often touched by the pathos of their situation, and despite my own anxieties I sometimes felt an impostor in their midst. Their troubles often seemed to have arisen from nothing and to be quite outside their own control, but I felt that I was directly responsible for my own breakdown and blamed myself for collapsing and for allowing myself to succumb to my own loathsome jealousy. At the same time, I experienced an almost directly contradictory feeling. Many patients had worries that were totally unreal: they were petrified by spiders or had paranoiac obsessions about the world plotting against them. In contrast, my own obsessions were about something that had really happened. If only some of the other patients could be persuaded to see the world as it really was, their problems would disappear: since my own obsessions were about a painfully real event, I thought there was no hope of ever overcoming them.

Early in my stay, I used to play chess with a young patient: like crosswords, chess involves little memory, and between my painful thoughts I could find just sufficient time to concentrate to make the next move. He was discharged soon after I entered, and this method of passing the evenings was taken away from me. Since I spent only four nights a week in hospital, my dread of these evenings and my despair about how to make the time pass may seem unreasonable, but then so was the rest of my behaviour. I solved the problem by persuading my wife to visit me two evenings a week and by having friends to see me as often as possible on the other two. I would usually meet them in the local town rather than on the ward. I would sadly sit in a pub with my wife in the evenings, sipping ginger beer, since the least drop of alcohol interacted with my drugs and made me feel sick and dizzy. The interchange between us was still often bad. Yet no matter how much she had abused me early in the evening, by the time we came to part she was usually contrite and loving. We would make our way to the local station from which her train left, leaving ourselves time to consume watery hot chocolate in the squalid and crowded station buffet. That buffet came to seem like a Paradise from which I was cast out every evening to make my lonely way back to the terrors of the hospital.

I have now sketched the routine of the hospital, some of my own experiences there and the feelings that most patients had in common. We all felt disappointed that we did not receive more psychotherapy and more contact hours with doctors and psychologists. All incoming patients were disappointed not to see more of the consultant who had admitted them: they had often entered hospital only because of their faith in one particular experienced man, and on admission it was a shock to discover that he was so busy that he could in fact only see patients once every three or four weeks and then not individually but in a case conference. The tedium of the evenings oppressed almost everyone, and the boredom at weekends afflicted those who did not take their weekend leave. We all felt we were very much in the power of the hospital authorities. Although we were free to discharge ourselves at any time, few were in a condition to do so, and so long as one stayed in hospital one had to agree to the conditions imposed: one woman was forbidden to communicate with her husband even by letter or telephone. This may have been good therapy for her – I never discovered why this condition was imposed – but it made the rest of us uneasy lest we suffer a similar fate. None of us liked the constant surveillance, and many of us felt oppressed because we could not deal on equal terms with nurses or doctors: we were mad, they did not need to take us seriously.

These remarks should not be taken as a criticism of the hospital authorities or staff. Like the patients, they also are human, and the sensitivity needed to avoid offending the feelings of patients in our condition is beyond most human beings. Moreover, they were extremely busy – too busy sometimes to grasp how dependent patients became upon them. Finally, there are limits to what can be done to help mental patients. Our ignorance of how best to treat them is profound. It may even be that in some cases hurt feelings are in the long run of therapeutic value, though I would like firm evidence before advocating it as a method of treatment.

Given that the patients had much in common, our behaviour was very different. The alcoholics tended after an initial period of drying out to be cheerful and sociable, though some remained desperately unhappy and reverted to secret drinking. The grounds of the hospital were full of buried bottles, purchased in the evening and available for consumption in the daytime. Some patients were quiet and uncommunicative, occupying themselves with knitting or reading. One girl who was a medical student had been in hospital for over a year and claimed to have read several hundred books but to have no memory of any of them. Some patients ran wildly round the grounds, or sat in a corner and sobbed. Others appeared superficially to be completely normal, though they were unable to function outside the hospital. I often admired the fortitude of some, particularly the women, who would sit patiently knitting or staring into space giving little outward sign of the boredom and agitation that dominated my own existence.

Only occasionally was there a scene – usually caused by one of the alcoholics returning to the ward totally drunk and shouting abuse at patients, nurses and doctors. Such offenders were often discharged at once, even when this happened late at night. They could be discharged from the hospital completely, given the option of moving to another ward, or if their condition was bad enough, detained in another ward under a compulsory commitment order. The doors of the ward were usually kept open. When they were found locked, a frisson went round the ward: either a patient had been expelled and they were locked against his unwelcome return, or a patient on the ward was thought to be in too bad a state to be allowed out.

I saw no physical violence of any kind during my stay, despite the fact that several of the patients had in their ordinary life committed violent crimes. The most traumatic episodes were suicide attempts, usually made by swallowing fifty or a hundred aspirins – a desperately painful way to die. None of these attempts succeeded whilst I was there, but one girl twice had to have her stomach pumped out; much to the annoyance of the duty doctor she always chose the small hours of the morning and he was called from his bed to perform this unpleasant task. She would disappear for a day or two to a ward in a general hospital, and having recovered sufficiently would return to the ward quieter than before.

One final misery that all, except the few on the road to recovery, had in common is that we lived without hope: few of us believed we would ever get better and there was nothing in life to look forward to.

I am conscious that, perhaps because of an inability to sympathize now with my condition then, I have not conveyed the pathos of the situation in which I and many other patients found ourselves. Our plight was better expressed in a letter written by a patient who had seen my *Sunday Times* articles, though she had clearly been in a less enlightened hospital.

'Desperate and at home I found my own doctor on holiday and his assistant, looking at his watch, had not the slightest idea how to deal with me . . . I begged a nurse just to speak to me. "GET BACK TO BED WE DO NOT HAVE TO SPEAK TO YOU ONLY TO SEE YOU ARE IN BED" were her words and to these words I have a witness. Hurt!!! I lay and cried for one hour – two hours – until the lights went on and it was day. "May I go and phone my husband?" "NO – WAIT FOR THE DAY STAFF" . . . Dr Brown said she would see me at 4 o'clock, so I sat in Ward 4 lounge and fell asleep. Can you imagine how I felt when a nurse said that I was not there and was never there at all, in fact called me a liar? . . . The day dragged by and I kept asking to see the doctor who was in charge of my case . . . I have attended meetings in hospital which are farcical and I told the doctor to stop looking at his watch and if he was too busy why bother . . . One night I woke at two in the morning and called and called for my husband. They would not call him. So I begged for a pill to sleep but no it was against the rules. So the nurse called the man in charge who also refused to make the call. I wrote my husband's name over and over again, on twenty-two pages. So I waited and at 7 a.m. when the day staff appeared again asked if I could make the telephone call. "No. No calling." "Just a call." "No. No call." So at 8 o'clock I begged someone to come with me to make the call knowing I must not leave the hospital: no – rules. So with all my strength spent I again lost confidence and had to go and phone alone, not knowing like an alcoholic I had taken the first drink – no more could I endure the silly rules and regulations made to break the will or laugh away the stupidity of it all.'

5

Treatment

Most of the psychotherapy I received in hospital was given by a clinical psychologist. Indeed I selected my consultant partly because he worked closely with this particular psychologist: although I had never met him before, I had corresponded with him professionally and he had a high reputation both as a therapist and for his research. He was about ten years older than myself, and the therapeutic techniques he practised had largely arisen out of discoveries made in my own speciality, experimental psychology. For all these reasons I was predisposed to trust and like him. He was tall, gentle, vaguely handsome, with a shock of grey hair, and his body tapered to unexpectedly tiny feet. He smiled readily and had a remarkable capacity for sympathizing with his patients' sillier fears and wishes as well as with their agonies. He treated all his patients with the gravest respect and was universally liked. It was a severe blow to many of his patients to be transferred to a different therapist.

I saw him for the first time a few days after I was admitted to the hospital. I was already talking wildly of discharging myself, and he observed that although I was free to do so I should give the hospital a fair trial. Staying there for a time might help to distance myself from my problems and hence to see them more in perspective. I should regard the hospital as a refuge from the cares of the outside world. I asked rather pathetically whether if I left they would relinquish all responsibility for me, and he said that I should not play ducks and drakes with them – another remark which though harmless enough I found most upsetting.

During the first few weeks of my stay, I had a constant fight with myself over remaining in hospital. Although my weekends at home were desperately unhappy, I told myself that they were not as bad as being in the hospital. I even thought of returning to psychoanalysis: despite my intellectual doubts, at an emotional level I still had some hankering after it and felt that I might have run away from it too soon. My wife's common-sense scorn for analysts did much to increase my resolve. Four things prevented me from discharging myself prematurely: the advice of the night nurse; the kindness of the clinical psychologist; the thought that by being kept out of the way of my family and friends I was avoiding distressing them unnecessarily; and, perhaps above all, the feeling that I must see something through.

The clinical psychologist explained that his methods of therapy were more pragmatic and empirically based than those of psychoanalysis, but he added that no method had received full objective validation, taking it for granted that as a psychologist I already knew this. Professionally I did know it, but emotionally I had been hoping for some magic that would lift my cares, and his honesty on this point came as a shock. He also explained that although some of my problems might stem from my previous history, he did not want to probe deeply into that. Despite the tenets of psychoanalysis, there is no reason to suppose that knowing the etiology of a problem is of direct help in solving it. He intended to investigate my current problems, and as they came to light to suggest methods whereby I might learn to change my behaviour: he believed that if people could be taught to behave in more appropriate ways, their feelings would undergo a corresponding change. This direct approach to patients' problems is characteristic of the method of treating the mentally ill known as 'behaviour therapy'. He added that any treatment he suggested could be undertaken only with my full agreement both as to its object and to the specific techniques to be used.

Much of his treatment was in fact based on common sense, though the common sense had been acquired only after years of experience. He said: 'It is going to be impossible for us to get to the bottom of your major problems overnight, but at least we can try to do something to help you in small ways.' He encouraged me to improve my physical health by losing weight, reducing smoking and taking more exercise. With the latter end in view, I attended yoga classes and went for walks: my motor coordination was too poor to allow me to play ball games. Of more direct help was his suggestion that I start doing the Canadian Air Force exercises: these are a graded series involving the daily performance of so many press-ups, sit-ups, and so on, finishing with jogging on the spot for a fixed number of steps. The exercises take only eleven minutes, and although I found them most unpleasant, I started doing them and have continued ever since.

One of my main symptoms was the inability to concentrate. The clinical psychologist attempted to treat this problem by a simple and direct application of behaviour therapy. He directed me to take any book whose contents I wanted to master and systematically to go through the following routine at the same hour and place each day. First, I was to read for a period over which I thought I could sustain concentration – for example, for one minute; then spend the same length of time making notes on what I had read; and finally spend the same period checking that the notes agreed with the text just read. Having found a period short enough for concentration to be maintained, the length of each of the three periods in the cycle was to be raised by one minute at a time. In this way he hoped gradually to build up my ability to concentrate.

The method is based on a technique invented with animals and known as 'shaping'. Animals can be trained to perform very complex acts by rewarding them initially for making a response that is only vaguely similar to that desired; as they come to perform the initial response more and more frequently, the experimenter narrows the range of behaviour that will be rewarded, and so the animal's performance gradually comes to approximate to the desired behaviour. Pigeons have been taught to play pingpong by this method, and it is the basic technique involved in much animal training. In more common-sense terms, if someone is unable to concentrate it will be frustrating to attempt lengthy concentration and fail: if they can concentrate successfully for short times, they are being rewarded (by success) for making the effort, and this will encourage them to practise concentration further.

The method appears to be successful with some patients. Moreover, as the psychologist pointed out, it sometimes produces a halo effect: when the patient's concentration returns, his other symptoms such as depression and obsessive thoughts are also reduced. In my own case, the technique failed: early in my stay in hospital I was too depressed and had too little faith in the advice I was given to settle down to practise concentration regularly; I tried from time to time but without success.

The psychologist tried to discover whether I had strong conflicting desires, in order to help me reconcile them; he also attempted to help me see events in a different light from that in which I was seeing them, and he laid particular stress on what was good about my situation in life. He proved as good at dialectic as the analysts, though he tried to use it to bring comfort. For example, when I expressed guilt over having had a number of casual affairs, he said: 'There are always several ways of viewing things. Some people might say that anyone who does not have the odd affair is acting falsely and denying the animal side of his nature.' He also tried to convince me that it was not unnatural in my situation to feel jealousy and even homicidal impulses, but he always counselled me against the use of violence.

He administered a personality inventory based on a self-rating scale that reveals not what one is, but how one sees oneself. I scored very high ratings on three traits – independence of thought, aggression, and 'need for succourance', in more everyday language a desire to be liked and accepted. He pointed out that if I was seeing myself as I really was, my need to be liked was in direct conflict with my aggression and refusal to be influenced by people and, other people being what they are, I could not for the most part expect both to be liked and to behave in too aggressive and independent fashion. This dilemma – if it was a real one – was never resolved.

My most distressing symptom was of course my obsessional jealousy. In dealing with this, he repeated a pattern that I had experienced with both analysts. He promised an approach to it that was in fact not implemented for many months to come. He told me that it might be possible to treat the obsessions by behaviour therapy, using a method known as 'desensitization', and for well over a year I longed for the desensitization to begin. At first the feeling that there was a powerful weapon left in the therapeutic armoury was of some comfort, but as time went by and the weapon was never used I became more and more disappointed. I do not know why it took so long before he started desensitization – perhaps he was afraid it would not work, and wanted to keep it before my eyes to give me hope whilst the illness ran its natural course. It may be that in my impatience to recover I was being unreasonable: the psychotherapist has a tricky course to steer between giving the patient some hope that he can be helped and giving him expectations that, from the nature of psychotherapy, cannot be fulfilled.

In desensitization of obsessive fears or thought-processes, the patient rehearses the thoughts in question whilst in a state of relaxation. The clinical psychologist recommended me to attend relaxation classes in the hospital with a view to using this technique. He also pointed out that learning deep relaxation was useful in its own right: once the skill was acquired, I could use it myself to reduce tension and anxiety in moments of stress.

I zealously attended classes on progressive relaxation together with anything between two and a dozen other patients. Every morning after breakfast, I would walk from the ward to the occupational therapy building where the classes were held. We lay on mattresses in a row on the floor in a darkened room, and the instructress made us systematically tense and relax all our muscles whilst breathing as deeply and regularly as possible. The instruction was given in a hypnotic tone of voice: 'When I say "Now" I want you to clench your left fist, as tightly as you can. Now. Make your fist tighter and tighter, feel the nails digging into the palm of your hand. It's a very unpleasant feeling; make it tighter and tighter until it hurts. Next, I want you to relax all the muscles of your fist – let your fingers spread out slowly. Feel the tension ebbing away through your fingers, leaving a pleasant relaxed feeling. Waggle your fingers very gently, and feel your hand growing warmer and warmer; feel it tingling and feel it becoming heavier and heavier as it grows more and more relaxed.' By the time I had systematically tensed and relaxed all the muscles of the body – hands, arms, feet, legs, thighs, stomach, torso, neck and face – I often felt as limp as a stuffed sack, and one or two members of the class would fall sound asleep.

In addition to these classes, I attended once or twice a week special sessions of individual relaxation training given by trainee psychologists. I certainly learned how to relax my body, but no matter how relaxed it became it did not ease the torment in my mind even for a moment.

Although – so it seemed to me – none of the specific methods of treatment deployed by the clinical psychologist actually improved my condition, I continued to have faith in him. I believe that his grave acceptance of my tormented fears did relieve my unhappiness temporarily, but however much I looked forward to seeing him they would come back in full force within a few hours. He never remonstrated or recriminated, even when I failed to carry out a line of action that we had mutually agreed upon. It was at his suggestion that I embarked on the task of preparing a catalogue of a collection of papers, and I think I kept at it as much through a fear of letting him down as through fear of letting myself down. This is yet another instance of the dependence that neurotic patients develop on their therapists and doctors.

I found it very hard to bear when a week or so after my admission to hospital he went on a fortnight's holiday. I felt abandoned, and fretted that the intermission in my treatment would indefinitely postpone recovery. Although I did not acknowledge that the treatment I had so far received was of any help, I clung desperately to the belief that he would eventually be able to perform some miracle and make me whole again: I longed for the day when he would be ready to begin desensitization.

As well as seeing the psychologist twice a week, I had occasional sessions with doctors. Each Tuesday morning the consultant would appear to attend a case meeting with all the staff involved with his patients, including his senior registrar, his registrar, the clinical psychologist and the senior nurses and occupational therapists. At these meetings, the cases of patients in the group to which I belonged were reviewed, and in the light of reports from the different workers it was determined how best to proceed. Every week, four or five patients would be summoned to attend the meeting. The consultant would listen to anything they had to say, ask a few polite questions, breathe a few words of encouragement, and possibly suggest some changes in treatment. How pathetically we looked forward to the summons to attend that performance, and how we envied those of our number actually privileged on a given occasion to enter. I remember week after week hanging round in the offing, hoping for a summons that usually did not come. Since the meetings were held in one of the common rooms, they were plainly visible through the glass with which it was surrounded. The doctors and nurses looked so composed as they sat around at ease crossing and uncrossing their legs while they discussed our fate.

As a new patient, I attended the meeting for a few minutes about a week after I entered hospital. I voiced my anxieties and told the consultant about my urges to discharge myself. He gently tried to dissuade me, but added that if I did decide to leave, the hospital would stand by me and give me all possible help as an out-patient. He repeated what he had said at our first meeting: the antidepressant drugs would in time take effect and bring about a change in my mood. He said: 'You have no faith in the hospital, in me or in yourself,' but urged me to give things a chance. He also tried to reassure me about my fears that my weekend leave would be stopped. I complained about my boredom and the difficulty of passing the evenings, and he said solicitously that they must try to find something for me to do. I thought I might be able to write, and obtained his permission to take into my room a huge electric type-writer. I duly fetched it from home the following weekend, intending to record some of my experiences. It lay there unused for the remainder of my stay, a pathetic emblem of my inability to recapture my previous existence. He also pointed out that the hospital afforded many oppor-tunities for recreation, and I rather ungraciously told him that even if I were well, the activities of a Butlin's holiday camp would have no appeal for me. It was not for a further four or five weeks that I again attended the weekly case conference. Although I would not acknowledge it, I was by that time in a slightly better state, and he cautiously said that I might soon be able to go home.

I also had sporadic individual sessions with the registrar in charge of my case. When I entered hospital, the registrar was a most amiable young man with a slightly bemused expression, who took careful notes on everything I said, offered some solace and left it at that. I remember feeling very upset when he said: 'Would you say then that you have always been a rather difficult person?' How could he have got hold of such a preposterous notion? When I asked about my future treatment, he observed: 'At the moment we are using implosive therapy: later it will be explosive.' I never discovered the meaning of this cryptic remark. I complained periodically that the antidepressants were having no effect, and he always gave the same reply: 'Different antidepressants suit different people. If this one doesn't work, we'll try another one, and we'll keep trying until we find one that does. In the meantime, we must just wait to discover whether the one you are on at the moment does any good.' In retrospect, I think he saw me not to offer therapy but merely to keep abreast of my case in order to monitor my drugs.

I also saw the cheerful little Sinhalese senior registrar from time to time. I liked him and used to try to waylay him on his way in or out of the ward. At one stage I was simultaneously taking two tranquillizers (chlorpromazine and Valium), an antidepressant (amitriptyline), and sleeping tablets. I asked him whether this was not too many drugs at once: I feared I could never be weaned from them. He said: 'We are well aware how dependent you become on people and things' (another threatening remark) 'but don't worry, none of them are addictive and we'll withdraw them from you gradually when you are ready for it.' Towards the end of my stay, I did in fact stop taking Valium, and since I felt none the worse for it, this was a considerable fillip to my confidence.

On another occasion, I was pacing up and down trying to restrain myself from telephoning my wife. I am not sure why I was so anxious to avoid telephoning: I think I felt I should not bother her too much. He told me to write out all my feelings about her and to show the result to the clinical psychologist who was treating me. I duly did so, but although many psychotherapists believe that writing things down is cathartic, it brought no relief to me nor has it ever. Some of the other patients did find it helpful.

In addition to individual therapy, there were twice-weekly group therapy sessions attended by my group as a whole. They were conducted by the registrar and were also attended by a senior nurse – a brisk but pleasant man from India, who was always neatly turned out. He had a ready smile, which was perhaps sometimes lacking in warmth, but he had considerable patience and rarely became ruffled, though he could be peremptory with recalcitrant patients. Each group session lasted for an hour: about half the time passed in complete silence, and we spent the remainder in sporadic discussion of what we ought to be talking about. Neither the registrar nor any of the nurses present offered guidance on this point.

The group meetings were boring and came to seem pointless. Since no compulsion was placed on attendance, only half a dozen or so of the patients out of the fifteen in my group would normally attend, and the same patient rarely came to two consecutive sessions. In addition, the composition of the group was constantly changing as old patients left and new ones arrived. In consequence, the group members never came to know one another at all well. Most were in fact reluctant to reveal their personal problems, and the group was rather fractionated. There were three women who formed a clique that I never succeeded in penetrating: they usually sat together both at meals and in the common room, but would fall silent when anyone approached them. Since we all had depressive illnesses, many of the group were withdrawn and did not relish meeting one another, though I did not fall into that category. One of our number was a rather extrovert girl who said she found talking to the depressives 'too depressing'; her social life revolved round the alcoholics, many of whom were much more cheerful than us: for this reason she rarely attended the group meetings.

I am not sure to this day what were the avowed aims of the group therapy, or even whether it had any, other than as a way of passing the time. It is usually held that to be successful it should involve sessions lasting about two hours, with the composition of the group remaining unchanged: neither of these conditions was fulfilled. The alcoholic patients had two-hour group sessions on almost every weekday, usually attended by the consultant as well as the registrar, and many of them thought them very helpful. Through these meetings the alcoholics certainly came to know one another much better than we did, and they found support in discussing methods of coping with a problem they all had in common.

When I had been in hospital for about three weeks, the registrar announced at a group session that he was leaving and was being succeeded by a 'lady doctor'. The last group meeting before her arrival was devoted to a discussion of how we felt about being treated by a new doctor who was a woman. Most patients were upset at the feeling of discontinuity induced by the change – just as they felt one doctor had got to know their problems, he was leaving, and they now had to start anew with a stranger. In addition almost all the women present felt it difficult to trust a woman doctor.

When the new doctor arrived, the patients became very upset. Although this is a characteristic reaction, some of her behaviour appeared to exacerbate the problem. She was dark-haired and small, and she moved and spoke in a busy, efficient way. Although slightly masculine, she was not unattractive. Her dealings with patients often seemed authoritarian and provocative: she may well have believed that such a stance was of therapeutic value. When I raised a query about my drugs she silenced me: 'I prescribe the drugs here; I'm the doctor and I am wholly responsible for your drugs.' Again when I quoted to her something the clinical psychologist had said concerning the possibility of discharging me she said: 'I'm in charge of your case and I take all decisions about your discharge.'

She suggested I was behaving like a child of seven, and produced from my case notes instances of childish behaviour, asking whether I did not think they were 'unbecoming for someone of your status'. However correct her observations were, they seemed very threatening at the time. She also upset many of the other patients: she announced to one that she was not going to handle her case with kid gloves, and was critical of the neurotic behaviour of others. Several of the women patients emerged in tears from their first interview with her. One claimed that the doctor had slammed the door in her face: when this was brought up at a group meeting the registrar replied that she had done no such thing, the door was difficult to close because it had just been painted.

Although I usually found sessions with her upsetting, I still longed to be summoned to her office and would be disappointed when I asked a nurse: 'Is Dr Bloggs seeing me today?' only to be told that she was too busy. I remember being touched by one act of kindness on her part. As I was walking out of the hospital to go home for the weekend, she drove in through the gates and stopped her car to ask me how I was feeling and wished me a pleasant weekend.

Her arrival transformed the atmosphere in group meetings. The doctor attacked the patients and the patients attacked one another. In every session one or more women would burst into tears and flee from the room. The first time this happened, nobody paid much attention, and the doctor rounded on the patients and said: 'Why do none of you go after Sue when she is in so much distress?' Sue's two closest friends explained that she often walked out of group meetings, and that in her present mood she would be unapproachable. A new patient who had done almost all the talking at the meeting said she would go after Sue, whereupon Sue's friends urged her not to follow, saying it would only upset her more than ever. The new patient left the room and came back crying ten minutes later, having been severely rebuffed by Sue. Bad feelings were provoked between Sue's friends and the new patient, who appeared to them to have interfered unwarrantably in something she knew nothing about; things were not made any better by the doctor putting her arms round the new patient and saying: 'I'm very proud of you: you're a brave girl.'

This incident was typical of the way in which emotions boiled up over trivial incidents in the ensuing group sessions. A further instance was a long discussion about a patient in another group who was alleged to be a gossip and to have other undesirable but unspecified habits. The registrar wanted the patient who had criticized the other woman to arraign her in front of a full meeting of the whole ward, but the patient who was complaining was not unnaturally reluctant to do so.

Although I and other patients were upset by this doctor's behaviour, she may well have thought that some patients would be helped by being provoked, and indeed it is quite possible that some of us, including myself, were in fact helped.

In addition to the group therapy given to three separate groups of patients, the ward met as a whole once a week in a session also attended by doctors, nurses, O.T. workers and clinical psychologists. Again, everyone was puzzled about the function of this meeting, since once the quality of the food had been discussed, and some comments made on what games had gone missing and why the swimming pool was not open on Friday afternoon, there appeared to be nothing else to talk about and much of the meeting would pass in complete silence. Some of the nurses would use this meeting as an opportunity to castigate patients who had misbehaved. For example one girl who was not herself an alcoholic had on several occasions come back to the ward in the evening very drunk. This behaviour was most upsetting for the alcoholics. The charge nurse on the ward was a buxom African woman with beautiful white teeth and a skin of purest ebony. Although she often smiled, we were all scared of her tongue. She gave the offending girl a public dressing-down at a ward meeting, and the girl promised in floods of tears to behave better in future. A patient who had unsuccessfully tried to commit suicide was berated for her antisocial behaviour, which had put the medical staff to a good deal of trouble in the middle of the night and had upset other patients.

Although a few patients would usually give verbal support to anyone subject to public vilification in this way, it seems unlikely that the experience would be helpful to them. Most of the patients and particularly those with suicidal tendencies already held themselves in very poor esteem; to be publicly shamed could only lower their self-regard further, and might delay recovery. I was myself in danger at one stage of being arraigned before the ward meeting. A woman patient approached me and said she wanted to raise a rather delicate problem. I am unfortunately sometimes given to belching: usually I do so quite unconsciously, though in formal society I suppose I sometimes use this method of expressing distaste for snobbery, pomposity and hypocrisy. My eructations had not gone unmarked by some of the women patients on the ward, and this particular woman gently warned me that some of them intended to raise the subject at the next group meeting. I thanked her for her courtesy in forewarning me, and promised to try to bring my wind under better control. I think I succeeded: in the event no more was heard of the matter.

I am afraid that the picture I have drawn of the treatment administered in the hospital is somewhat gloomy. Later in the book I will discuss in more detail the general issue of the aims and effectiveness of psychotherapy. My professional knowledge and scepticism about the value of most methods of treatment may have made me a particularly difficult patient. Moreover, during almost my whole stay in hospital I was in such a state of panic that it is doubtful if any psychotherapy could have had much curative value. Indeed the treatment I received was probably intended less to cure than to provide some comfort until such time as the storm of my anxiety would abate either spontaneously or through the action of the antidepressants: one of the doctors said as much to me. The nurses usually behaved with great kindness and patience; the clinical psychologist provided comfort and suggested ways within my very limited power by means of which I could begin to help myself. If I saw less of the doctors than I would have liked, that was because they were all overworked. Some of the younger doctors may have been lacking in sensitivity to the feelings and needs of their patients, but it may require more experience than they had to develop such sensitivity when confronted with patients as readily upset as were most of us. The group therapy was perhaps the weakest point of treatment: I had a feeling that it had been introduced because it was fashionable rather than because anyone had much faith in it, and I doubt if any of the staff involved had had any training in this method of treatment.

I was in fact extremely lucky in being able to use my own professional knowledge to select the hospital to which I was admitted. It was one of the National Health Service's showpieces, run at great expense to the taxpayer. Most mental patients both in Britain and America find themselves in incomparably worse surroundings; they are frequently housed in ugly ramshackle buildings and herded together in overcrowded dormitories. The number of nurses and doctors is often wholly inadequate for the number of patients. In such circumstances it is more difficult to control patients without strict regulations, and their freedom is correspondingly curtailed. Had it not been for the gloom of the patients themselves, the atmosphere in which I found myself was more like that of a holiday camp than a hospital. Moreover the renown of my hospital ensured that it could attract nurses and doctors who were amongst the best trained in the country. The staff certainly felt that something could be done to help the patients, and their optimism communicated itself to us. How much more terrible is the plight of those incarcerated in long-stay wards with inadequate facilities where the doctors and nurses have no more hope of improving the patients' lot than do the patients themselves.

6

Recovery

When I first entered hospital it was midsummer. It was an unusal English summer with prolonged fine weather, and many of my memories of the hospital are anomalously tinged with the glow of that continuous sunshine. Even on that second afternoon when, in the extreme of my anxiety, I was walked round the grounds by one nurse after another, I remember noticing the beauty of the hospital's park: the majestic trees, the flowering shrubs, the scented lawns were all enveloped in the same summer calm, in complete contrast to my own mood of torment. I remember being surprised to come suddenly on a freshly-mown cricket pitch and wondering who if anyone ever played there. In the last fortnight of my stay, summer was turning to autumn, and the early stages of my recovery were associated with a paler sun and with the crisp air and heavy dew through which I walked each morning to my ritual relaxation exercises.

On his return from holiday, the clinical psychologist devoted a whole session to a discussion of how to help me give up smoking. Amongst my other fears whilst in hospital was that of killing myself through cigarettes: I had been a heavy smoker for twenty years, and in hospital my consumption was around fifty cigarettes a day. I was so intensely miserable that I thought that to stop smoking could hardly make me worse: it therefore seemed a good time to try. I had made many previous unsuccessful attempts to give up, and had studied the literature on the problem with some care. I knew that there was no objective proof that any method worked, but I was sufficiently desperate to wish to use something as a crutch. If I succeeded, I thought it might restore some modicum of self-respect.

We discussed and rejected many methods. The psychologist suggested that I should put aside the money saved by not smoking and use it to reward myself with some self-indulgence like occasional expensive meals. Unfortunately, I was so depressed that I could think of no treat I would enjoy. He rejected the possibility of punishing me for smoking with electric shocks as both unethical and inefficacious: smokers so treated soon cease smoking in the situation where they are going to receive a shock, but smoke just as much at other times. The use of substitute drugs to mimic the effect of nicotine in the bloodstream has been found not to help. Committing a large sum of money repayable only after a period in which one has not smoked may help in the short term: I had so little faith in my ability to stop that I was not prepared to put up the money. Arousing anxiety by showing smokers films of lung cancer operations or wards of patients suffering from emphysema or chronic bronchitis is also known to be ineffective. As one smoker said at a time when the newspapers were full of reports about the harmful effects of smoking: 'It has made me so scared I have had to stop reading the papers.' I was also not prepared to be locked in my room without cigarettes for a fortnight: this might extinguish the smoking habit in my room, but as soon as I emerged and found myself in other surroundings, I thought I would go straight back to it. Nor was there any point in taking tranquillizers to help me through the first stages of nicotine withdrawal: I was already taking massive doses of such drugs.

Eventually we decided that on a prearranged date I would simply stop smoking. The clinical psychologist would give me as much support as he could. Such is the human desire for praise that verbal support – praise for success in stopping for a period and sympathy for any failures, together with an exhortation not to be dismayed by a single lapse but to keep on trying to give up – could well act as the most potent form of reward. Moreover, it could help one to persevere rather than abandoning the attempt at the first failure. The clinical psychologist added something I thought very helpful: he said that smoking was a physiological addiction, and it was only possible to give up if I was prepared to be miserable for a period of up to a year. On stopping, I simply had to regard myself as suffering from an illness and over the period of convalescence I must accept that it might be impossible to work or function efficiently, or indeed to be happy. Any work well executed or any happiness experienced after giving up could be welcomed as an unexpected bonus, but to give up successfully one should be prepared to accept the worst. He also suggested circulating my friends and relatives with a letter asking them to treat me gently whilst undergoing the pangs of withdrawal, but this was never carried out.

It was agreed that when I went home on the next weekend, I would have a chest X-ray to establish that my lungs were currently all right. I had an extremely sympathetic chest physician in my home town who arranged for the X-ray: the few minutes waiting for the results were, as always, agonizingly anxious, but I returned to the hospital with the knowledge that there was nothing showing on an X-ray.

On the following day, I saw the clinical psychologist and agreed to give up there and then. Over the next few days, I fought constantly to prevent myself cadging cigarettes from other patients, and on about five occasions my resolve broke down: I also smoked outside the hospital one evening when I went out for a meal with a visiting friend who was a heavy smoker. Nonetheless, I persisted in the attempt. Instead of smoking, I consumed vast quantities of apples – about thirty a day. When I went home the following weekend, I knew I could not smoke since there was no possibility of doing so without my wife seeing me, and she was determined that I should cease. By the time I returned to hospital I was convinced that I would never smoke again.

Although I had managed to stop smoking, I still felt as depressed as ever, though during that week I did manage to read a complete novel and even derived a little enjoyment from it – I think it was Peter de Vries's *The Cat's Pyjamas*. However, I would not admit either to myself or to anyone else that I was any better, though both my friends and the clinical psychologist told me I was behaving more normally. He said that in his experience there were usually three stages in the recovery from depression. First, outward behaviour improved and this could be observed by other people; second, the patient himself came to see that his behaviour had improved; the final symptom to disappear was usually the patient's own agonizing feelings – another example of a change of feelings being dependent on a change in behaviour.

My actual recovery – if it was a recovery – was as sudden and dramatic as the breakdown itself. After spending a week without cigarettes, I returned home for the weekend. The Friday evening, all day Saturday and most of Sunday were passed as usual in a state of anxiety and depression. In the morning I lay in bed trying to sleep for as long as I possibly could since it was only in sleep that I could obtain forgetfulness. I mooched around the house by day, doing the odd crossword puzzle, and I accompanied my wife shopping. In the evenings I would meet friends in a pub, though I could only risk a single pint of shandy myself.

At six thirty on the Sunday evening my mood changed dramatically. I was upstairs finishing off the *Sunday Times* crossword puzzle, when I heard a record being played in the sitting room beneath me. The tune was at that time 'top of the pops', and I had heard it over and over again whilst in hospital. It was called 'Eye Level', and was an orchestrated piece with a good thump to it and a dying fall. Banal though it was, it seemed to combine joy and sadness. I suddenly found myself enjoying it, rushed downstairs and turned it up full volume. I can now appreciate that it is not in fact a great piece of music, but at the time I thought it the most inspiring music I had ever heard. It filled me with happiness and hope. That evening I not only read the Sunday papers with some interest, but for the first time in five months I did something that looked towards the future: I made a note of several books reviewed that I wanted to read.

The following day, instead of taking a train to hospital, I persuaded my wife to drive me. I was convinced that I was better and that the woman registrar would see this and agree to my discharge: I would load my things in the car, drive off home and be happy ever after. I had an appointment that day with the clinical psychologist, and told him that I was much better, thanking him profusely for all his help. He said that if I wished to discharge myself there was no point in my staying, but since the woman registrar (under the consultant) was in charge of my case, I must also see her. I told all the nurses excitedly that I was better, though I behaved in a less exuberant fashion in front of the other patients, since I did not want to compare my own good fortune with their sad lot.

I attended a group therapy session after lunch, in which I fell into an argument with the woman registrar over how far one should exercise tact in apprising people of their faults: I think she was on the side of honesty, I of tact. I grabbed her after the session to explain that I was better and wanted to discharge myself. She promised to see me later that afternoon, and I hung about the ward waiting for her. After supper, I discovered from the nurses that she had gone home. I was crestfallen. Discharging myself from the hospital had itself become an obsession.

I was of course free to pack my belongings and drive off, but it had been impressed on me, as on all patients, that we must take our drugs exactly as prescribed, and by spending the night at home I would miss my night and morning doses: the nurses were not allowed to issue drugs to take home except on the instructions of a doctor.

I discovered from the nurses that there was another registrar still on the ward: he had only just taken up his post at the hospital and was in charge of a different group of patients. I went up to him as he came out of his office, explained that I was better, and that through no fault of my own I had not been seen by my own registrar: he was a benevolent-looking young man, and much to my surprise agreed to prescribe drugs to tide me over the night. I returned joyfully home with my wife and came back to the hospital the following day. I gathered from the nurses that the senior registrar, the woman registrar and the clinical psychologist were having a case meeting, and since the clinical psychologist had said he would discuss me with the woman registrar I assumed that one of the topics for consideration would be my discharge. By lunchtime, I had still not seen the woman registrar, but I caught her coming out of her office with the clinical psychologist. I approached her and said: 'Is it all right? Can I go home?' She said: 'I cannot agree to your discharge.' When asked whether she would prescribe drugs, she was evasive.

My hopes were once again dashed, and I had a miserable lunch: I felt it probable that my change of mood had been in part due to the anti-depressant drug, and I did not feel I could take the risk of returning home and abruptly withdrawing from all the drugs I was taking.

When I was called to her office after lunch she said: 'You have always been too impulsive – now you want to spoil your chances by acting impulsively yet again and discharging yourself prematurely.' I tried to explain that I felt better and there seemed no point in staying in hospital: I also pointed out that the clinical psychologist had agreed with me. She said: 'You are not to play him off against me. It is my decision whether to prescribe drugs.' She picked up a note that was lying on her desk, read it and then said: 'I have decided not to withhold your drugs if you do not follow my advice. I advise you to stay in hospital, but if you discharge yourself I will prescribe your drugs. I want you to promise to attend the next case meeting with the consultant: he is ultimately in charge of your case. You should also continue to attend the hospital in the daytime and to come to group therapy.' I readily agreed to these conditions, and that afternoon I packed my belongings in the car, including the huge electric typewriter that had sat unused for five weeks in my room.

I attended the case meeting two days later: the consultant was most affable. He agreed that I should live at home, implied that I should soon start tapering off my drugs and wished me success in my marriage and a speedy return to work. He recommended me to continue to attend the hospital once or twice a week to see the clinical psychologist and the registrar: he thought I should go to group therapy only if I found it helpful. In practice, I gave up the group therapy almost immediately.

At my next meeting with the woman registrar, I asked her when I should begin to reduce my drug dosage. She said that it would be a good idea to begin soon, and, wrongly, I formed the impression that she wanted me to reduce them of my own accord. I cut down the tranquillizing drugs that I was taking. Although I was now cheerful, I was still given to bouts of anxiety and was hyperactive and sleeping less than usual, and it seemed to me to require considerable self-control to reduce my drug intake. When next I saw her, I told her with pride that I had succeeded in reducing the dosage of tranquillizers, and instead of bestowing the praise that I had expected, she said: 'You have no business to go in for self-medication: you must take the drugs I prescribe in the exact doses I specify.'

My sessions with her had now turned into a series of heated arguments often unconnected with my own condition: for example, we spent half an hour in a fierce dispute about the character and habits of American citizens. The interaction between us was painful to me and exasperating for her. She said: 'You treat me not as a doctor but as a woman'; when I discussed her with one of the nurses he said: 'Ah, I expect you are in love with Dr Bloggs.' The breaking point in our relationship came when I smuggled a tape-recorder into her office and recorded a complete session. In my exuberance, I regarded it at the time as a piece of harmless mischief, but my judgement was sadly lacking. When I told her what I had done she offered to let the consultant hear the tape, but I thought it best to destroy it. It was decided that further treatment should come not from her but from the consultant. I continued to see both him and the clinical psychologist every few weeks for the next year.

Two questions can be asked about my recovery. First, what was it that brought it about? As usual in such cases, it is impossible to give any certain answer. Was it the antidepressant? The support of the clinical psychologist? Giving up cigarettes? The realization that many others were much worse off? Was it being needled by the woman registrar that restored some fight and spirit? Or was it merely that most depressions are self-limiting, and restorative processes usually occur even without medical intervention? This illustrates the difficulty of testing methods of treatment: all cases are different, and in the individual case one can never be sure of the factors that bring about recovery.

Whatever the cause, my mood had altered drastically, and within twenty-four hours I had moved from a state of hopeless gloom in which I could see no future for myself to a mood of optimism and fascination with the world around me. My external situation had also completely changed: I was back with my family and I also returned to work immediately. A clinical psychologist once told me that one of the most certain ways of overcoming a breakdown was for the patient to receive an unexpected piece of good news. He instanced someone who had been hospitalized for two years with obsessive compulsions that completely disabled him. This patient was left a legacy of £30,000 and overnight his compulsions disappeared: he became cheerful and immediately discharged himself from hospital. Whether my own mood change was in part facilitated and prolonged by the change in my own circumstances I do not know. At the time I reflected on the words of my first psychoanalyst, who had said: 'All that having drug treatment and going into hospital will do for you is to change your mood.' The difference between abject misery and happiness was not such a trivial matter.

The second question that may be asked is whether I had really recovered. Although I did not realize it at the time, I had not. I had bounced from a mood of deep depression to one of high elation, and although this was fun for me it was as upsetting for those around me as was my depression.

7

Aftermath

Shortly after discharging myself from hospital, I telephoned one of my psychiatrist friends to tell him that I had made a complete recovery and that I was grateful for his advice to seek proper psychiatric care and for his suggesting the name of an excellent consultant. I was full of praise for the medical treatment I had received and I happily informed him that the breakdown had been one of the best things that had ever happened to me, that I now had a new lease of life and was working with great energy and effectiveness. He thanked me for telephoning and said that it was rare for someone who had taken such advice to express their thanks. He also asked whether I was continuing to see the consultant, adding: 'Depressions are funny things, and they rarely disappear suddenly without after-effects.' I thought at the time that his concern about whether I was still receiving treatment was a little sinister, but I was so elated that I put it to the back of my mind.

In practice I acted for the next three months or so in a way that was almost as mad as my behaviour during the depression. My mood was characterized by a complete lack of shame or reserve, wild optimism about the future combined with reckless spending of money in the present, a fascination with the external world of people, things and books, an inability to stop talking and a tendency to indulge in pranks.

A typical instance of one of these japes was the following. I purchased in a sex shop on the Tottenham Court Road an object known in the trade as a 'tickler', and invented, I believe, by the Arabs: it consists of a ring of goatskin with the hairs still attached. The salesman's promise that it would give my wife 'ecstasy' was not borne out by the event. Next time I was in London, I made a point of passing the shop with Josie and pulled her in before she realized the nature of the establishment. I accosted the salesman, pulling the tickler out of my pocket, and said: 'Look here, I bought this from you last week and it's virtually useless.'

He replied politely: 'What seems to be the problem sir?'

'You said it would really turn my wife on, and it's done nothing for her. Has it darling?'

She confirmed my opinion, and I continued: 'Not only that but it's far too small: it's practically chopped my penis in half.'

'I'm sorry about that sir, we could find you one in a bigger size.'

'Even if you have a large enough one in stock, that's not going to help my wife, is it?'

'We like to give satisfaction to our customers, sir: if you care to look around, maybe we can exchange it for something else.'

I accepted his offer and selected for fun some other device that looked as though it would be no more helpful than the original tickler. On being shown it, he said: 'I'm afraid that costs four pounds, sir, whereas the tickler was only two: perhaps you wouldn't mind paying the two pounds difference.'

I slapped him on the shoulder and said boisterously: 'I'm one of your best customers – you're surely not going to haggle over a mere two pounds.'

He said helplessly: 'Take it away.'

By this time I had accumulated a considerable audience. Sex shops are for the most part frequented by furtive-looking men in raincoats, who keep their hands in their pockets and by examining the objects on display out of the corners of their eyes are able to keep up the pretence that they are not really interested in the wares. I now turned to the salesman and said in a voice of thunder, thinking to discover how far his shop catered for all tastes: 'By the way, do you happen to have any canes or whips?'

At this point my wife sought refuge in the street. The salesman replied: 'I'm sorry, sir, we used to stock them, but we no longer do. If you like to come with me to the bookshop next door, they occasionally keep them under the counter.'

I followed him into a sex bookshop. Up to this point he had been talking rather after the fashion of an assistant in a Savile Row tailor's, but when he accosted his friend behind the counter of the bookshop he reverted to his native cockney.

'Got any kines in at the moment, George?' he asked.

'Sorry, Fred, we're outa stock: 'ad a big consignment in only last week, but they sold like 'ot cakes and we're fresh out of kines.'

I expostulated: 'I really don't know what this country is coming to: one week there's no sugar to be had, the next everywhere is out of lavatory paper, and now it's virtually impossible to buy a cane in the whole of London.'

I do not normally engage in pranks of this kind, and the story illustrates the extent to which hypomania can abolish all reserve. Apart from thinking that my own jokes were funnier than they were, my judgement was sapped in ways that could have been more dangerous. Having whisked my wife into a sex shop, I later bought her a fur coat more suitable for a tycoon's mistress than for the spouse of a comparatively penurious professor. I also ordered a car that was large enough and expensive enough to have bankrupted me, but fortunately the model was in short supply, and by the time it was available I had sufficiently come to my senses to cancel the order, albeit with some financial loss.

I was convinced that I would make a fortune by writing a highly successful introductory textbook on psychology: a successful text of this sort can net its author several hundred thousand dollars in royalties if it is widely adopted in American universities. It seemed to me that I was just the person to write such a book, though I overlooked petty details such as when I would find the time to do it and how I would actually manage to gear it to the interests of teachers in some of the less well-known American universities of which I had no experience. I fired off letters to six American publishers pointing out my pre-eminent qualifications for writing a work of this kind and asking for a $25,000 advance; I did not scruple to inform them that in addition to being widely adopted for the teaching of introductory courses to undergraduates in psychology, the book would undoubtedly be 'the best and most popular account of modern psychology for the general reader.'

Even in my elated condition, I was a little disappointed at the publishers' response. One of them politely declined my offer on the grounds that his publishing house was too small to be able to afford me, but wished me every success in my dealings with other publishers. Others used phrases such as 'the economics of book publishing have become rather restricted' and 'the heightened competition plus increased splintering of the market, make it more difficult to achieve sales figures of the sort you have in mind.' One of them went so far as to ask to see a synopsis and a specimen chapter with a view to negotiating a contract, but I was so restless and excited that I could not sit long enough at my desk to work out such tedious matters of detail: I was convinced that once a contract was signed and an advance safely in the bank, the book would somehow write itself with the minimum effort on my part.

In my elated state, I was receptive to new ideas provided they could be understood without lengthy concentration. I established a friendly relationship with an assistant in a men's clothing shop who had a distinctly 'gay' manner and was prepared to put up with my volubility. In my previous existence, I had been, to put it mildly, careless about my appearance, but I was now anxious to acquire smarter apparel as behoved a potential millionaire. He selected new clothes for me, including such things as a velvet jacket that I could ill afford, though this did not deter me at the time. He also taught me how to tie my ties with a Windsor knot and my shoe-laces with a 'tennis' knot: in the past I had done up both ties and shoe-laces rather casually, and they were as often untied as tied. It is odd how one can remain ignorant for so many years of useful tricks such as these. He also suggested changes in my hair style, including the growing of sideburns, and referred me to a good hairdresser – 'Don't forget to ask for Lennie: I wouldn't let anyone else touch my own hair,' he said, giving it a pat.

I was without reticence, shyness or reserve. I found I could lead community singing in pubs and could buttonhole strangers and tell them the story of my life, whether or not they wished to hear it. Every book I read, every film I watched, every play I attended and every painting I saw were the greatest works of their kind there had ever been, and in my attempts to communicate my enthusiasms to others I was often puzzled at how rarely they came to share them.

I also discovered a hitherto unsuspected ability in myself to 'camp things up' and from time to time made mock passes at homo- and heterosexual men alike, much to the alarm of both. My behaviour in this respect would doubtless have delighted my analysts, and I felt I was a credit to them, though whether I was giving vent to suppressed homosexual urges or acting out of mere bonhomie neither I nor anyone else can ever know. As a Peter de Vries character put it: 'My unconscious was now doing a magnificent double-take. I was defending myself against defending myself against latent homosexuality by pretending to be one.'

In my previous existence, I had always had a taste for the bizarre and was gratified when, as I sometimes did, I found myself in curious situations. In the state of supremely elevated confidence in which I now found myself, however, I discovered a facility for making the bizarre occur to order. One illustration must suffice. It is drawn from the period when I went through a second high phase about a year after the first, by which time I had resumed smoking. I was returning home from London on a late-night train, when I found I was out of cigarettes. I went down the corridor looking for someone smoking, and the first smokers I encountered were ensconced comfortably in a non-smoking first-class compartment. They were two girls and a man. I entered and said: 'Give me a cigarette or I'll call the guard.' They kindly offered me cigarettes and I stood and chatted.

It turned out that one of the girls worked in a massage parlour in my home town. The massage was strictly for men, and was of the variety that in the terms of the trade offers 'relief'. She received £2 for each half-hour session, and the owner of the parlour also pocketed £2. If she volunteered services beyond the expected massage and manual masturbation, she could make her own terms for additional payments. She had for many years made a good living at this profession, and was able to provide her small daughter with two ponies and to maintain her and her own parents in some comfort in the country. She told me how fond some of her clients, many of whom were lonely and old, became of her and of the gifts they brought her. She varied her activities by working the trains back from London in the evening, where she found many businessmen were glad to avail themselves of her services in the train lavatories at £10 a time. She approached only first-class passengers and always picked on shy-looking men, since in her experience they were the most likely clients.

When we were about twenty miles from our destination, she suddenly got up, slapped me on the shoulder and said: 'I've taken a fancy to you: come into the lavatory and I'll wank you off for nothing.' I put in a polite plea of *nolle prosequi* on the grounds that my wife was fast asleep in the next coach, and should she wake I might have difficulty in explaining any joint occupation of the train's toilet facilities.

Whilst one is entitled to divulge personal details of one's own life, it can rarely be done without causing pain to others, and I distressed my family by my lack of reticence. Having failed to secure a contract for an introductory book on psychology, I was seized by the idea of publishing a detailed account of my breakdown in a Sunday paper: I had read that one paper had recently paid someone a vast sum for publishing extracts from an extremely frank book on his mother's life. I now told everyone that I was going to make my fortune by divulging sensational facts not about the dead but about the living.

Several of the living did not share my enthusiasm for the project. Indeed I received a stern letter from a doctor who had been a friend of mine and who was in the same firm as the doctor who had persuaded me to embark on analysis. It began by saying that although I might not like it, it was written primarily out of concern for myself, and went on to point out correctly that I was in a hypomanic condition. He warned me not to publish an account of my medical treatment whilst in that state and concluded by threatening to resort to the Medical Defence Union if I in any way impugned the professional skills of his colleagues or himself. This doctor was also a devotee of psychoanalysis, and his statement that the letter was written primarily out of concern for me suggests that the insight psychoanalysis gives into one's own motives is not necessarily very deep.

Several of my friends were also concerned lest I publish an account of my breakdown. They were afraid I would do myself harm by it – such is the taboo against admitting that one has been through a period of mental instability. When I asked a friend what harm it could do, he thought for a minute and replied: 'Suppose you ever want to join the Athenaeum: they would never admit you after publishing something like that.' Despite my elation, I had sufficient insight into my condition to realize that I was not my normal self, and I had already decided that whatever I wrote would need careful vetting to make sure that I was not writing anything too damaging either to myself or to others.

The elation could be interpreted as a way of covering up a continuance of my original anxiety state and depression. I slept little, waking very early in the morning: when I woke it was as though a searchlight illumined my mind, and I began going over exciting plans for the future which precluded any return to sleep. Moreover, although I was now reading and writing a great deal, I was not able to concentrate in the way I could when normal. My mind wandered when I attended talks on psychology, and although I wrote at great speed I found it difficult to undertake the more tedious and painstaking process of revising and systematizing what I had written. In addition, I was given to sudden bouts of anxiety which would come on for no apparent reason and leave my heart pounding and my body weak. Finally, several times a day I was still attacked by obsessive and harrowing thoughts which I could overcome only by burying myself in activity.

It is of course a standard psychoanalytic tenet that elation is a defence put up to conceal from oneself unresolved conflicts and anxieties. Despite the underlying fears, most of my elation was enjoyable to myself if not to others. I had completely lost the fear of death that had previously assailed me from time to time in moments of inactivity. I can remember when I first discovered that everyone had to die: I was about eight years old at the time and was being driven up a hill in an old Rover car by a friend of my father's, and I can still visualize the dashboard of the car and the appearance of the road. He imparted the dreadful news that everything ends in death: at first I was incredulous, but then I realized he must be right. Whilst elated, I could accept the fact that we all must die, but it had ceased to worry me: the phrase 'Fate cannot harm me' echoed through my brain.

I was comparatively lucky with my hypomania: I did not take any irrevocable rash decisions, although I emerged from my elated state much more impecunious than when it began. Since hypomanics usually have little or no insight into their condition, some behave in recklessly extravagant ways that can lead to bankruptcy or the alienation of all their friends and relatives. We know as little of the causes of elation as of the causes of depression. My psychiatrist told me that my own elation was 'a rebound effect of the depression' and had not been caused by the drugs I had taken. Indeed I managed to give up all drugs within a month of leaving the hospital. States of abnormal elation sometimes occur with no preceding depression, and the sufferer may be reluctant to seek psychiatric help unless pushed to it by relatives or friends.

My hypomania lasted for three or four months, and then I gradually descended into a further prolonged depression. It was very unpleasant, although it did not have the quality of agony that accompanied my previous collapse, in which I was totally unable to concentrate. I now tried to escape from reality by lying in bed dozing fitfully until noon or one o'clock; I was once again unable to take much interest in the external world. I was told by both the clinical psychologist and the psychiatrist that I must force myself to get up in the morning and to fill my day with normal activities. With a great effort I managed to teach, read and write, though my writing was unsatisfying and lacking in verve. I again became a prey to anxiety and obsessive and painful chains of thought. After seven months without cigarettes, I found myself entering a cigarette shop and buying a packet, and I added the shame of having reverted to smoking to my other worries.

Over this period, I managed to complete a revision of my articles on the breakdown. I eliminated the more highly personal material, and wherever I was in the slightest doubt of the veracity of what I had written, I deleted it. After much further delay, the pieces were published: nine months had elapsed since my renewed depression, and I had been in a mentally abnormal state for over a year and a half.

I had been most worried about how the articles would be received. I had written them from a <u>mixture of</u> motives: I felt I could give an account of what it was like to undergo a breakdown that would be of some interest to the general reader; I also thought that the public should be better informed about mental health and the different types of treatment, and that an account of my own experiences might bring some comfort to those who were either undergoing what I had been through myself or had close friends and relatives suffering from mental illness; I wished to point out the dangers of some methods of treatment and to make some attempt in a small way to remove the stigma that still attaches to mental illness. I was also fascinated, in retrospect, by my own bizarre experiences and by the subject of mental health in general, and I wanted to communicate some of this fascination. I also needed the money that the articles would bring and the satisfaction of writing something that would, I hoped, be read with interest by many people. Despite all this, I was anxious about how readers would respond. Perhaps my more cautious friends were right and I should not expose myself publicly in this way. I was open to the charge of washing dirty linen in public in return for money or notoriety; although I felt no animus towards anyone who had been involved in my treatment, I had in all honesty to write that I did not think all the treatment had been helpful, and I could be accused of taking a petty revenge on people of whom I had run foul – the attitude of some psychoanalysts to patients who write about their psychotherapy is summed up by the quotation on the fly leaf. Worst of all, perhaps the articles were badly written and would evoke only boredom in the reader.

I have spelled out my feelings at the time the articles were published in some detail, since I think it was the reception of the articles, at least in some quarters, that brought me back to a more normal frame of mind. Many people whom I scarcely knew came up to me in public places and thanked me for having written them: they would often reveal that they too had been through similar experiences and that it was some comfort to see it all set out in print. Others wrote to me to say that their own experiences, particularly in the hands of analysts and in psychiatric hospitals, had been so similar to mine that they could hardly believe I was writing about myself not about them. I was surprised at how many of my acquaintances told me they too had had breakdowns: it is an experience to which most people do not readily admit except to fellow-sufferers. I was gratified at the number of people I encountered who had actually read the articles with some interest. In short, I was immensely relieved by the way they were received, and a little flattered.

Not everyone approved: the doctor who had first referred me to an analyst thought it very sad that I had published them and said I had not done myself justice – a remark that an analyst might have interpreted as projection. My psychiatrist colleagues had divided opinions: some thought that what I had written needed saying, others did not like the implicit criticism of some members of their profession and thought it dangerous to inform the general public of the difficulties and dangers inherent in some methods of treatment.

I am conscious that both in the present book and in the articles I may have failed to convey the full agony of my own experiences. I consider I was lucky to recover and it is hard to recapture the mood of torment. I quote below some further extracts from the letters written to me: they both express the feeling of pain better than I can and also demonstrate that my own experiences were by no means atypical:

'... These terrible nervous feelings and the awful sense of isolation, of being boringly, frighteningly alone – a spiritual isolation.'

'The words' [quoted from my articles] "an event tailor-made to cause me the maximum possible hurt" carried SUCH meaning for me. The degree of pain not only went right off the scale of previous experience but far exceeded anything I could describe or imagine. I know the torment of disintegration, and the "irrevocable and cataclysmic" – words which often fall on uncomprehending ears – the self recrimination, and the incredible loss of the previous personality, leading to self-unbelievable behaviour and tortured impairment of function.'

'Bed was my sanctuary where I could shut the world out for a few short hours.'

'Where I am going or what will happen I do not know, I need help desperately, but seem to fall victim to all the wrong things, I guess it's me. I do not want to see my children because I cannot bear the reproach in their eyes.'

'The articles read, in parts, like a carbon copy of my own experiences during the seven years in the "living hell" of depressive anxiety.'

'Your account gives rise to such a variety of thoughts and feelings, so parallel, it seems, to your own.'

'I was very much reminded of my own similar experiences. So many of the points the professor made struck me as being very pertinent and typical of one's feelings at being an in-patient of a psycho-therapy unit.'

I should perhaps trace out the forms of therapy I have received since I left the hospital just over two years ago. During my first period of elation and the subsequent depression, I visited the clinical psychologist almost once a week. Over part of this time he saw me together with my wife and attempted to encourage us to improve our behaviour to one another. We still often harped back on past wrongs, and although we could both see this was childish and pointless we did not have sufficient self-control to avoid painful and boringly repetitive recrimination. Her jealousy vented itself in anger, mine usually in sadness. We would repeatedly vow to the psychologist to behave better to one another, only to reappear next week admitting that we had not kept our promises. He eventually said ruefully that if anyone were to ask him whether he had been able to help Josie and Stuart he would have to admit that he had not: he was an honest man. Towards the end of my second depression he again began seeing me alone and introduced the long-awaited desensitization treatment for my jealous obsessions but my depression turned once more to elation, and the jealousy abated of its own accord.

About this time the consultant in charge of my case decided to refer Josie and me to another psychiatrist who specialized in 'marital therapy'. We saw him together with a girl social worker: the presence of therapists of each sex avoids the problem that a single therapist may be in sympathy with only one of the couple in distress. The psychiatrist was pleasant and anxious to be helpful, and I am grateful to him for the time he spent with us. He had the restrained manner of one who has been to one of the better English private schools, and I thought he found it difficult to empathize with my own tempestuous emotions.

For entirely different reasons Josie and I were difficult patients. She has more pride than I, and found it difficult to reveal herself to comparative strangers. On one occasion she mentioned some intimate thoughts to me and I said: 'You ought to tell that to the psychiatrist,' to which she made the magnificent rejoinder: 'That's far too personal a matter to discuss with a psychiatrist.' She was also given to claiming that she was too ill to see a doctor. She found it difficult to accept the artificiality of some of the exercises we were asked to perform, through a fear of looking ridiculous. The psychiatrist, for example, suggested that to encourage mutual trust she should place her hands in mine and let me support her. We were also asked to perform another standard therapeutic trick, namely to take it in turns to let our bodies go plastic whilst the other arranged the body into a pose characteristic of the way he or she saw the partner. Such games were not for Josie.

Although rather more willing to give things a try, possibly because I was more desperate, I shared much of her cynicism about the possible benefits of marital therapy. Moreover, my own knowledge often led me to ask for a justification of any step the psychiatrist proposed, and it cannot be much fun for any therapist to be called on by the patient to account for every move he makes. I tried to play this down, but I was at first very anxious that no misunderstandings should occur, and I had an annoying tendency to correct what I regarded as any errors of interpretation or verbal slips made by the psychiatrist. Although I was genuinely anxious to keep the record straight, such insistence on precision could well have appeared to be gratuitous hostility on my part.

Moreover, it is difficult for therapists seeing a couple once a fortnight or so to come to know and understand them: the occasional remark would reveal how deep such misunderstandings could go. For example, at one point the social worker suggested that my wife, not having a career, might be jealous of her. This rendered Josie speechless with embarrassment, since although she might relish the thought of being a successful couturier, actress or dealer in fine art, the idea of being a social worker lacked sufficient glamour for her to feel anything but mild good will towards anyone undertaking such work.

Perhaps to avoid misunderstandings, the psychiatrist at one point suggested that we should sit down and say exactly how we felt about one another. I went over some of the material reproduced above, and added that I thought that underneath he probably felt real concern, but that his approach was rather intellectual and that, perhaps because of his upbringing, he might have difficulty in revealing his feelings. I suspect such frankness is rarely helpful in personal relationships, and no matter how much a therapist may try to put down hostility from patients to projective or other mechanisms, they are themselves just as vulnerable as the rest of us.

Some of the psychiatrist's sayings and advice were not a little bizarre. At one point, and for no clear reason, he took an inventory of our family trees. The identity of my wife's grandfather was lost in mystery, and on learning this he remarked: 'Ah, then your grandfather is just a face-less penis to you.' For some time, one of the worst aspects of my own jealousy was that it was provoked most strongly in sexual encounters with my wife. The sight of her bare body re-evoked my worst jealous imaginings, and at times I could not bear her to touch me. He suggested that she should do everything she could to titillate me, whilst we were to debar ourselves from actual intercourse for a fortnight: I was adamantly to resist her advances. We were also to put aside set times of day for recriminating against one another: I was to shout and she was to throw things, four times per diem before meals. Although encouraging patients to practise habits they wish to be rid of is a currently fashionable method of treatment (known as paradoxical intention), the theoretical rationale behind it is obscure: it is vaguely described as an effort to bring un-wanted behaviour under one's own control, but there is nothing to suggest that it is actually helpful. Both for this reason and because neither of us could accept the artificiality of these devices, my wife and I were unable to carry out the advice proffered.

I am grateful both to the psychiatrist and to the social worker for their persistence in trying to help two such difficult patients. It may be that it is easier to help married couples whose problem is lack of communication than people like ourselves who suffer from too much communication of the wrong kind. There was little about our behaviour that an outsider could point out that we had not been over together *ad nauseam*. We knew or thought we knew how we should behave: our problem was that we could never put such knowledge into practice.

Our encounter with marital therapy lasted in all for about nine months, though we only fitted in about twenty sessions during this time. I continued to see the original consultant in charge of my case, at first two or three times a month but latterly at much longer intervals. He was always relaxed, sane and helpful: like the clinical psychologist, he treated even my silliest thoughts and fears with seriousness and gravity, never recriminated and never made silly jokes.

It would be pleasant to be able to report that having recovered from my second bout of depression my mood remained stable and I lived happily ever afterwards, a better and wiser man for the experiences I had undergone. Unfortunately, this did not happen. I underwent a further spell of mild euphoria and then descended into a more prolonged period of mild but miserable depression. I am of course incomparably better off than during the acute phase of the breakdown. My jealous imaginings no longer dominate my life to the exclusion of everything else, and I am able to work and concentrate.

The emotional tone of my life has, however, at least for the time being, changed out of recognition. Whereas previously I always seemed to be choosing between a multitude of fascinating things to do, I now cast around between unappealing alternatives in the vain hope of fastening upon something outside myself and my own situation that will capture my whole-hearted interest. I long for a return of the uncomplicated and uncontrived zest with which I used to pursue my daily activities, but no matter how much I force myself to engage in this or that pursuit, the zest does not reappear. Although many might envy my external situation, I can often find nothing in life to which to look forward – a feeling that characterizes depression. I suppose that I was once lucky and no longer am, I sometimes long for a return of the falsely optimistic and fragile mood of elation; it both annoys and puzzles me that I cannot think of a way of attaining a stable balance at the mid-point between the slow swings of mood that have dragged me in their wake since the breakdown. When I asked the clinical psychologist about the possibility of a complete recovery, he said: 'Most people get better, but they often have the feeling that there is something missing in their lives.' Despite the unstinting efforts of some of the most distinguished members of the helping professions, I have been unable to work out my salvation.

My wife and I have stayed together. In our joint encounters with psychotherapists, the one thing that never failed to unite us was their suggestions that we should 'seriously consider separating, at least for a time: try not to fantasize about it, but consider it very carefully.' Although we have often speculated about it, we do not know what invisible bonds have held us together through the storms of the last few years. Is it love? Hate? Pity? Unconscious masochism? Fear of the unknown? Or are we just clinging to the creature comforts with which we reciprocally supply one another?

I suppose I have learned some things from my experiences. I can understand the agony of mental distress in others in a way that I previously could not. I may have more insights into myself, but the insights have brought only pain, since I do not like what I see. Psychoanalysts would doubtless allege that the insights do not go deep enough to be helpful, but I remain sceptical of the idea that self-knowledge is for everyone a precondition of happiness and effective functioning. Periods of high endeavour such as the Renaissance, Elizabethan England or Ancient Greece have often been characterized by a singular lack of direct concern with the hidden springs of behaviour except in so far as they can be obliquely externalized in drama, verse and painting.

In my own case it is too early to know what will be the final outcome of the breakdown. In gloomier moments I repeat to myself the Greek proverb: 'Call no man happy until he is dead,' but such are the vicissitudes of human fortune that at other times I continue to hope and to strive.

The previous paragraphs were written two months ago: since then I have become immersed in writing the remainder of this book. I let the paragraphs stand as a reflection of what a minor depression feels like, but I am currently revising the book in a better mood than that in which some of it was first written. I seem to have found a quiet harbour from the restless ocean of despair and elation on which I have been tossed for the last few years. I wish I could feel that the haven was anything other than a temporary refuge.

8

The Nature of Mental Illness*

The remainder of this book sketches the current state of play in the field of mental illness. I shall describe and evaluate the many different methods of treatment available, both psychotherapeutic and physical. It is a topic of great complexity: indeed, it is almost as complex as human life itself. Some treatments were developed through important insights, others by sheer luck. Almost all the common human virtues and vices play a role in the story – humility and arrogance, kindness and cruelty, commonsense and downright silliness, sympathy and inhumanity, sincerity and falseness, generosity and cupidity, understanding and ignorance. Much of what I shall report is tragic, but some is richly comic. Wherever possible I shall illustrate my account by further experiences of my own or of those I encountered in my sojourn in hospital.

The classification of mental illnesses is itself a furiously contested topic. Although all classification must be based in the first instance on symptoms, the main point of it is to decide what will be the most helpful treatment. In physical illness classifying according to the causes of the illness, for example, a bacterial infection, a vitamin deficiency or a tumour, normally gives guidance as to the indicated treatment. We still have little certain knowledge of the causes of most psychiatric disorders, and only in recent times has it become apparent that different constel-

* Throughout the rest of the book, notes on the sources I have used are to be found on pp. 251 *et seq.*

lations of symptoms respond differentially to different methods of treatment. Hence, classification is largely based on clinical experience that a particular group of symptoms tend to occur together and are associated with a particular life history. Diagnostic fashion varies from country to country and within a country from one psychiatrist to another: it also changes over time. Guidelines suitable for international use have been laid down by the World Health Organization: the eighth revision of its International Classification of Diseases (ICD–8) appeared in 1965, but in regard to psychiatric illnesses it is already out of date, and a further revision is in preparation.

The major categories of mental illness are usually taken to be the psychoses and neuroses, but even here there is a great deal of overlap and it is not clear how far they should be regarded as lying on a continuum. Thus, the *British Glossary of Mental Disorders*, itself based on ICD–8, states: 'the distinction between so-called psychotic depressions and depressive neurosis appears to many psychiatrists artificial and sometimes impossible.' In general, the psychotic is out of touch with aspects of reality, whereas the neurotic, however badly incapacitated by anxiety or depression, is in contact with his environment and can recognize what is going on around him.

The psychoses are in turn divided into 'organic' and 'functional'. The organic psychoses are due to known malfunctioning of the brain or other bodily organs. This does not mean that the functional psychoses are not also due to physical disorders of the brain: we are merely less sure what the physical disorder if any is. The organic psychoses include mental illness caused by general atrophy of the brain (senile dementia), by infection of the brain, as in syphilis, by poisoning or nutritional deficiencies, and by overindulgence in drugs such as alcohol, barbiturates or amphetamines. A wide range of symptoms may be produced by such causes, and they may be short-lasting or persist for long periods of time. Amongst the acute psychotic conditions is delirium tremens, which rarely lasts more than a week: the patient is disoriented and confused and has bizarre visual hallucinations. Korsakov's psychosis is also usually caused by alcohol poisoning, but is a chronic condition characterized by an inability to retain anything in memory for more than a minute or so: the patient usually fills in the gaps in his memory by confabulating imaginary events.

It is possible that poisoning or faulty nutrition are responsible for more mental illness than can currently be traced to such causes. Ergot, a disease of rye, is known to have caused outbreaks of mental illness in previous centuries. Throughout the history of civilization, drugs have been used to produce bizarre mental states akin to psychotic conditions. Witches are known to have smeared their broomsticks with an ointment made from such plants as deadly nightshade and mandrake: they rode their broomsticks naked, and the ointment was absorbed through their external genitalia. Some of the substances contained in it, when administered to volunteers, have been found to produce an illusion of flying and sensations of panoramic vision.

The organic psychoses will not clear up unless the underlying cause is removed, whether it be a brain tumour, vitamin deficiency, infection or abuse of drugs. On the other hand, the symptoms of many organic psychoses can closely resemble those of the functional psychoses, and it is therefore essential to determine at the outset by giving a medical examination and taking a life history whether the psychotic symptoms are produced by the sort of physical causes adduced.

The two most common categories of functional psychoses are schizophrenia and the affective psychoses: the latter include severe depressive illnesses, conditions where depression and extreme elation alternate, and (more rarely) mania not accompanied by bouts of depression.

The onset of schizophrenia tends to occur early in life, and there is a peak in first admissions to hospital of people between twenty and thirty. Roughly one in every hundred suffers from it at some point in life. It is a common misunderstanding to suppose that schizophrenia refers to cases of multiple personality. It means the patient is cut off from reality rather than that his personality is splintered into separate components. Although the schizophrenic usually retains a clear state of consciousness, he may experience marked feelings of unreality. He often feels that his inmost thoughts are open to the inspection of others, and even that they are controlled by others. Hallucinations are common, and he may hear voices commenting on his every thought and action. He may be unable to follow any coherent train of thought, and his speech is often inconsequential and, to the ordinary listener, meaningless. He often seizes on irrelevant aspects of a situation or takes everything literally: in one hospital there was a door bearing the notice 'Please knock', and a particular schizophrenic patient carefully knocked on the door every time he passed down the corridor. The outward display of emotion tends to be flattened and shallow; or emotions may be trivial and the patient may giggle meaninglessly or preserve a self-absorbed smile. In some cases, artificial poses of the body are maintained for long periods of time and the patient may sink into stupor: this may alternate with severe but pointless spells of excitement. Schizoid states, resembling schizophrenia, may appear in neurosis and may also be induced by drugs, for example by LSD.

The affective disorders involve moods of either extreme depression or elation or an alternation between the two. Characteristically, they make their appearance later in life than schizophrenia and are more likely to show spontaneous remission. The account of my own depression conveys some idea of what it is like. Apart from feelings of utter despondency, worthlessness, guilt, and loss of self-regard, it may, as in my case, be accompanied by extreme agitation and anxiety. In addition there is usually a loss of appetite for both food and sex and there are difficulties in sleeping. In some depressives, thought-processes and bodily movements are greatly slowed down: they may adopt a glazed facial expression, and reply to questions only after a long interval and then in an almost inaudible voice. They may have delusional ideas and think that they are shunned by others, or in extreme poverty: if depression lasts long enough such ideas may come to correspond to reality. Occasionally sensory illusions may occur.

I have also given a description from my own case of what it feels like to be unduly elated. I underwent a period of hypomania, but in true mania, behaviour can be much more extreme. Patients may exhibit flights of ideas connected by only superficial links such as the sound of a word, which may produce a pun or a rhyme resulting in a complete change in the direction of thought. The excitement may be so uncontrollable that speech becomes wholly incoherent.

During the last twenty years, there has been great controversy over how to break down affective illness into different sub-categories: although many hundreds of papers on this problem have been published, no general agreement has been reached and the consensus of opinion changes almost from year to year. It is generally agreed that one basic division is into bipolar and unipolar affective illness. In bipolar illness (the classic manic-depressive syndrome), spells of depression alternate with mania or hypomania. The evidence for its being a discrete diagnostic category comes from three sources. First, there is a strong genetic predisposing factor – there is a high incidence of manic and depressive episodes in the ancestors and other blood relatives of patients suffering from clear-cut bipolar affective illness. Second, as determined by differences in the presence of certain chemicals in the cerebrospinal fluid, the brain biochemistry in bipolar illness differs from that of the normal population and of other depressives. Third, bipolar illness responds better to a particular drug (lithium) than do other forms of depression, and does not respond well to a further group of drugs (known as the tri-cyclic antidepressants) which are helpful in some other kinds of depressive illness.

Within the unipolar group of depressive illnesses there are many different possible ways of categorizing. Until recently it was common to divide them into endogenous and reactive depression, where it was assumed that the latter was set off by a personal misfortune such as bankruptcy or the loss of a spouse, whereas the former arose spontaneously, possibly through constitutionally-determined fluctuations in brain biochemistry. It was also thought that endogenous depressives had difficulty in sleeping in the morning whereas the reactive depressive finds it hard to get to sleep at night. More careful research has shown that there is little if any consistent difference in the sleeping habits of those placed in each diagnostic category, and that so-called endogenous depression is as often triggered by a personal misfortune as reactive depression. My own psychiatrist told me: 'It does not matter whether we call your illness reactive depression or endogenous depression, the treatment is the same.'

There are, however, some indications that there are different kinds of unipolar depressive illnesses: some may respond best to electro-convulsive shock, others to the tri-cyclic antidepressants, and within the latter group there may be differences in symptomatology between those who respond better to each of two different kinds of antidepressant, imipramine and amitryptiline. I was placed on the latter drug, which is often thought to be particularly suitable for depressions accompanied by marked agitation and anxiety appearing in middle age. Current research findings on these issues are frequently contradictory, but the above account should serve to convey the main issues. It is likely that considerable progress will be made over the next decade in uncovering more information about the biochemical bases of depressive illnesses and in devising a taxonomy that will be useful in determining the most appropriate treatment.

All the kinds of depression so far discussed are known as primary depressions. Secondary depression may also accompany many other forms of mental illness such as schizophrenia, hysteria, or obsessive-compulsive neurosis. In addition, it frequently accompanies or follows some kinds of physical illness such as viral pneumonia, influenza and glandular fever (mononucleosis). Depression is also a normal consequence of severe misfortune. It is thought that provided it does not degenerate into the incapacitating illness from which I suffered, the misery attendant on personal misfortune cannot be alleviated by anti-depressant drugs, nor can secondary depressions resulting from other forms of mental or physical illness. In practice, and in our current state of knowledge, the borderline between 'normal' depression and patho-logical depression warranting drug treatment is often hard to draw, despite the existence of clear-cut cases like my own where the reaction was out of all proportion to the triviality of the precipitating event.

Before leaving the subject of the psychoses, I shall give one more example of the way in which careful research can help not merely to establish meaningful diagnostic categories but in determining the most appropriate treatment. Diagnoses of schizophrenia are about twice as common in the United States as in England, and diagnoses of affective illness are correspondingly less common. When a team of British and American research psychiatrists agreed with one another on a set of explicit criteria for diagnosing schizophrenia, and used these criteria to assess patients admitted to hospitals in New York and in London, there was good agreement between the diagnoses made inde-pendently by different team members. Moreover, the difference in the percentage of patients in London and New York receiving the diagnosis schizophrenic largely disappeared. Many of the New York patients diagnosed by the hospital doctors as schizophrenic were not so classified by the research workers. Some were reclassified as manic-depressive. The group of patients admitted in New York with a diagnosis of schizophrenia but reclassified as manic-depressive is of particular interest. It was found that they had many more relatives who had suffered from manic-depressive disorder than the patients who were agreed by both hospital and research psychiatrists to be schizophrenic. Of more practical importance, they were not in general much helped by being given chlorpromazine (a drug widely used in the treatment of schizophrenia), but they were helped by lithium the drug most com-monly used to treat the bipolar type of manic-depressive. This is a nice example of the way in which refining diagnostic category can improve the treatment of the mentally ill.

As we have seen, the distinction between psychosis and neurosis depends largely on how far the patient remains in touch with reality and has insight into his own condition: the difference is often far from clear-cut. The most commonly recognized categories of neurosis are as follows.

The term 'anxiety neurosis' speaks for itself: it is characterized by excessive anxiety or panic permeating the patient's whole life. It is usually accompanied by such bodily signs of fear as palpitations and extreme shakiness. My own story illustrates the extent to which the same symptoms may appear in disorders that are treated as diagnostically different entities. The early stages of my depressive illness were marked by extreme levels of anxiety rather than by feelings of depression. However, whereas depressive illness can occur in middle age with little or no previous history of depression, severe anxiety neurosis usually only develops in individuals who have experienced high levels of anxiety or nervousness for much of their lives. Although one form of mental illness shades into another, the distinction is more than a mere quibble, since an anxiety neurosis is unlikely to respond to treatment by antidepressant drugs. Depressive neurosis, sometimes called reactive depression, is also a recognized category. Except in regard to severity, it would appear to differ little from depressive psychosis, and I have no idea whether in the statistical returns in which my case figured I was classified as psychotic or neurotic.

Thanks to Freud, perhaps the most famous example of neurosis is hysteria. In conversion hysteria, some bodily organ fails to function for psychological not physical reasons, or the patient may feel aches or tingles that have no organic basis. Such patients may develop paralysis of a limb, contorted postures, and may even have seizures that simulate those of an epileptic. They may also develop partial or complete blindness or deafness or lack of sensation in a limb. The principal way of distinguishing such conversion symptoms from similar symptoms caused by organic damage to the nervous system is that, in hysteria, the symptoms correspond to the patient's ideas about anatomy. She may develop total lack of feeling in the area covered by her gloves or stockings, but the regions of skin involved do not correspond to a part served by a single nerve that might have suffered injury. In a further kind of hysteria, 'dissociative states', the patient's consciousness may be limited to a single realm of experience. She may walk round in a trance paying no attention to the external world. It is common for patients subsequently to have no memory for what occurred in such fugue-like states. Hysteria is in fact now a rather rare form of neurosis, though it appears to have been common, particularly in women, in Victorian times, and many of Freud's patients were hysterics. Nobody knows why its frequency should have diminished. It often remits suddenly and with no obvious cause.

Neurasthenia also appears to have been commoner in Victorian women than it is today. It is characterized by extreme lassitude and irritability and is often accompanied by headaches.

A phobia is an unreasonable and intense dread of approaching a given situation or object. Many otherwise normal people, particularly women and children, have circumscribed phobias. Some of the commonest are fear of worms, snakes, insects, mice, thunderstorms, public speaking, air travel, and taking examinations. A severe phobia has much the same characteristics, but can be completely disabling. To take a typical case, a middle-aged woman was out shopping when she found herself violently attracted to a man standing next to her. The man made an indecent proposition; she panicked and ran out of the shop in distress. Subsequently, she developed a phobia of entering any shop, and found that the nearer she approached a shop the more terror she felt. She naturally avoided going near shops. Every time she withdrew from their vicinity she became calmer: hence, since it made her feel better, her avoidance of shops was reinforced and she learned to stay further and further away from them until eventually she could not venture out into the street. She had developed agoraphobia – fear of public places. The origins of most phobias are less clear. One girl on my ward, pale-faced and thin, had developed a terror of spiders. She was in continual distress, and so great was her fear of spiders that wherever she went she clutched to her bosom a tin of insecticide. She was unable to go to bed at night for fear of finding spiders in her room, and would tearfully entreat the nurses to enter it before her to make sure it was spider-free. She lived in a private Hell populated only by spiders, but as far as could be ascertained she had never had an unfortunate experience with a spider.

A further category of neurosis involves obsessive compulsions, and can be illustrated by another patient on my ward. He was a pleasant but shy and soft-spoken man of about forty-five. He muttered to himself, usually about things he feared he might have left undone or articles that he might have left out of place. It took him several hours to get into bed each night: he could not stop himself from checking the exact position in which he had left each item of clothing, and as soon as he tried to climb into bed he would feel over and over again a compulsion to go back and check again in case he had overlooked anything the previous time. Many obsessive compulsives are terrified of dirt, and will wash their hands at five-minute intervals. Again, many normal people develop annoying but not disabling compulsive rituals. They may systematically avoid walking on the cracks in the paving stones, or feel that ill luck will befall them if they fail to tie up their left shoe before the right or to put on their clothes in a certain order.

Not recognized in the World Health Organization's classification is a form of neurosis sometimes called 'existential neurosis', appearing usually in young people who may seem outwardly normal and even cheerful. They complain to their intimates, however, that they can see no point in life, they have no ambition, there is nothing they really want, and they may feel unsure of who they are. They sometimes have strong suicidal tendencies. My impression, based not on objective evidence but purely on personal experience, is that these feelings are becoming increasingly common in the age group sixteen to thirty, particularly among girls of the middle and upper classes who have faced little in the way of physical hardship or deprivation.

Another disorder, related to neurosis, that appears to be becoming more prevalent amongst young women is anorexia nervosa. I have already described one such patient on my ward. The sufferer is unable to eat and may starve herself to death. Some are unable to keep food down when they consume it, and some have extreme fluctuations in weight and may at one time have been obese. The illness is usually accompanied by amenorrhoea and severe depression or anxiety. It is possible that there is some physical pathology underlying anorexia nervosa.

It is usual to distinguish 'personality disorders' from neuroses, but once again the dividing line is difficult to draw. In general, personality disorders are less marked by anxiety or depression than the neuroses, and behaviour is less bizarre. Personality disorders are attributed to those who are excessively sensitive, hyperaggressive, too gloomy, too exuberant, too shy, very aloof, over-conscientious, too dependent on others or too passive. They should perhaps be regarded as lying midway between normality and a genuinely incapacitating neurosis. Many psychiatrists would like to dispense with this category. Psychopaths (known in America as sociopaths) are also classified as having a personality disorder: their behaviour is antisocial and frequently criminal, and it is characteristic that they are not restrained from committing such acts by any fear of punishment.

Dependence on various drugs is also treated as a clinical condition by the World Health Organization, and so are various forms of sexual deviation like homosexuality, transvestism, paedophilia and exhibitionism. In my opinion such behaviour should only be dealt with as a medical problem where it involves elements of compulsion: it is one thing to indulge in cross-sex dressing in the privacy of the bedroom, it is another to be driven to exhibit oneself in public or to give way to an uncontrollable impulse to seduce small boys. Perhaps in part prompted by the Gay Liberation movement, the American Psychiatric Association recently decided to delete homosexuality from its list of mental illnesses.

Returning to the neuroses with which we are primarily concerned, it should again be emphasized that they often do not appear in pure forms. Phobic or obsessive compulsive disorders are often combined with free-floating anxiety or with depression. Diagnostic categories are in fact only of use in so far as they indicate the need for different treatment or a differential prognosis.

Exact figures on the frequency of different kinds of mental illness are hard to obtain: they will in any case vary with changes in diagnostic fashion. A survey undertaken in London found that in the year 1962 fourteen people in every hundred consulted their family doctor at least once for some form of mental illness. Over twice as many women as men consulted for this reason: since half the patients complained of disturbances lasting for over a year, most of the problems were not of a trivial nature. Nine out of each hundred individuals surveyed were diagnosed as neurotic.

Depression and anxiety account for eighty per cent of chronic neurosis. Anxiety states are equally common in men and women, but twice as many women as men suffer from depression. About three per cent of chronic neurotics have phobias or obsessive compulsive disorders. Put like this, it sounds rather few, but in absolute numbers it represents a formidable total of human suffering. In Vermont, two people per thousand members of the population were found to be suffering from severely disabling phobias, of whom less than half were receiving any treatment. If we generalize these figures, it would mean that in the USA alone there are at any one time over four hundred thousand people whose lives are crippled by a phobia.

Although different estimates are made, depending on the criteria applied, in countries like Sweden, Britain and the USA between thirteen and twenty-six per cent of the population will at some time in their lives undergo a neurotic breakdown. About a further four per cent will suffer a psychosis, and yet others will have mental disorders of varying severity in other categories ranging from drug addiction to the milder forms of personality disorder.

There is one thing on which all investigators of the frequency of mental illness agree. When its prevalence is estimated by screening members of the population rather than by using figures based on the number in treatment, it is always found that a vast number of cases, perhaps the majority, go untreated. In two North American studies, one conducted in Manhattan, the other in a rural area of Nova Scotia, it was found that about twenty per cent of the population were seriously impaired by mental disorder: in both studies, only about eighteen per cent were judged to have good mental health. As we shall see, it is a matter for debate how severe a mental disorder should be in order for it to merit professional treatment, but such figures give some idea of the misery and loss of effective functioning attributable to mental problems.

9

The Origins of Mental Illness

Despite a hundred years of thought and research devoted to the problem, the origins of most mental illness remain obscure. The possible causes include inheritance, constitutional defects caused by physical trauma in the womb, the unnatural mode of living imposed by modern society, the stress of poverty, maternal deprivation or other unfortunate events in childhood, and personal misfortune. These factors are of course not alternatives – some or all could operate simultaneously, and they could play different roles in the etiology of different kinds of mental illness. The evidence is complicated and sometimes inconsistent: at the risk of some dogmatism, I shall review it briefly.

It is now certain that genetic factors can predispose to schizophrenia and to some forms of affective illness. In pairs of identical twins (who have exactly the same genetic make-up as one another), if one member is known to have schizophrenia the other twin develops the illness in about fifty per cent of cases; in non-identical twins and in pairs of ordinary brothers or sisters having half their genes in common, if one member of the pair has schizophrenia the other will be affected in about ten per cent of cases. Since about one per cent of the population develop schizophrenia, anyone who has the same genes as someone who is a schizophrenic is fifty times as likely to develop the illness as somebody with no close schizophrenic relatives, and anyone having half their genes in common with a schizophrenic is ten times as likely to become one.

In Denmark, very complete records of adoption are kept, and by using these an American investigator (Kety) has been able to show that the chance of developing schizophrenia depends on its prevalence in blood relatives, but is not increased by being adopted by a schizophrenic parent. Kety was also able to establish that trauma within the womb is not implicated in schizophrenia. He investigated half-brothers and half-sisters born to different mothers and found that if one was schizophrenic there was still an increased chance of the others suffering the same illness even where they had not shared the same womb and had been brought up apart.

I have spelled out some of the evidence for the genetic transmission of a predisposition to schizophrenia both because it is a good example of how careful research work can rule out alternative explanations and because it is still popularly believed that schizophrenia is caused by a bad upbringing. The evidence for the involvement of genetic factors in some kinds of depressive illness is just as convincing, and recent research suggests that they may be implicated, but to a smaller extent, in the genesis of neurotic disorders. Less work has been done on the possibility that psychiatric disorder may be caused by damage in the womb. Prematurely-born babies appear to be at greater risk of developing mental illness than those who go to full term, but this could be because the parents react differently to premature infants or because mothers prone to premature delivery may themselves be predisposed to mental illness, and hence the child inherits genes that may in turn render him or her vulnerable.

There is no evidence whatever to support the view that mental illness is caused by the way of life adopted by modern Western civilization. Research on its prevalence in different communities is hard to interpret because the rates found vary greatly with the criteria used to decide what counts as illness. Where comparable criteria have been employed, little variation has been found from one country to another. For example, in a study already described, it was found that in one district of London fourteen people in every hundred consulted their family doctor at least once for some form of mental illness. Nine out of every hundred were diagnosed as neurotic. A study of the inhabitants of an Ethiopian village produced almost identical results: fifteen in every hundred consulted a doctor for mental disorder over a twelve-month period, of whom nine in every hundred were thought to be neurotic. The prevalence of psychiatric illness among Ugandan university students was found to be virtually the same as among students at Belfast or Edinburgh.

The popular belief that there are simple societies living in harmony and free from mental disorder is a myth. To give but one example of research on the problem, two investigators set out to study one such society – the Hutterites – living in North America. They are an almost entirely self-sufficient farming community leading a simple life far removed from urban civilization. Anecdotal reports had suggested that they were an exceptionally happy, stable and well-adjusted people; in seventy-five years, there had been only one divorce and three separations in the community. The research workers therefore expected to find very little mental illness, but these expectations were not confirmed. Despite the absence of mental hospitals or psychiatrists, the rate of psychosis was found to be higher than in most urban communities.

It is more difficult to obtain evidence that bears on the question of whether mental illness has increased over time. One might expect an increase in rates of hospitalization brought about by the increasing availability of psychiatric services. The state of Massachusetts has kept particularly careful statistics on hospital admissions going back to 1840. When these were examined, it was found, against all expectations, that between 1840 and 1940 there was no increase in first admissions for functional psychoses in the young and middle-aged. There is no good evidence on whether the incidence of neurotic illness has changed through time. Nevertheless, on reading the biographies of those who have lived in former ages, whether it be Dr Johnson, Newton or Richard II, one cannot help being struck by the number who have exhibited the irrational and self-destructive character traits that would nowadays be classified as neurotic.

The evidence on the effects of bad living conditions caused by poverty on the incidence of mental illness is hard to assess. In general, rural areas tend to have slightly higher rates of psychosis than urban and slightly lower rates of neurosis, but the differences are not large. The lower social classes, particularly in urban areas, do exhibit more psychiatric illness of all kinds than do the middle and upper classes. It is not known how far this is the direct result of poor living conditions. Those afflicted by mental illness tend to move down the social scale and to drift into urban slum areas. Moreover, many who migrate into towns are driven to leave rural districts by poverty: they therefore start off living in poor districts. Anyone prone to mental illness is likely to remain there, whilst many of those who are functioning well will eventually move into better neighbourhoods. To the extent to which mental illness is inherited, the same considerations will apply to their children. Hence, a pool of the mentally incapacitated is likely to accumulate in lower-class districts.

Many, indeed most, schools of psychotherapy believe that it is primarily events in early childhood that predispose to mental illness. Plausible though it seems, there is again little evidence to support this contention. We have already seen that genetic factors are heavily implicated in schizophrenia and in much depressive illness. Since, however, even in identical twins, where one is schizophrenic the other is normal as often as not, these factors cannot be the sole cause. Many, including Laing, have supposed that a faulty upbringing can produce schizophrenia: in particular it has been suggested that parents who make conflicting demands on their children – by, for example, saying one thing whilst meaning another – can induce schizophrenia. Careful research on interrelations in the families of children who have subsequently developed schizophrenia has failed to provide much support for this notion: it is hard to detect any clear differences in the upbringing of schizophrenic children and normal children, and it may well be that what differences there are are caused by the unusual behaviour of the child affecting parental attitudes rather than the other way round. Laing's ideas on this problem were particularly unfortunate in that they added to the misery of a parent with a schizophrenic child the guilt of feeling personally responsible for the child's condition.

Nor does the loss of a parent in childhood appear to predispose to schizophrenia, though it may be a contributory factor in the development of depressive illness and neurosis. One study found that loss of a parent through death or separation was three times as common in adolescents consulting psychiatric services as in the normal population. Even a finding of this kind is equivocal, since death and divorce are more common in parents who are themselves mentally unstable, and hence the predisposition towards mental illness may still have been transmitted by genetic means.

George Vaillant, of Harvard University, has recently undertaken a particularly interesting study on the influence of the child's environment on mental health in later life. In 1940, detailed information was recorded on the life history and personality of one hundred and ninety-nine male students at an American liberal arts college. Thirty years later, Vaillant succeeded in locating most of these men and investigated their subsequent development. Although there was a tendency for a good childhood to be associated with good mental health in adult life, his findings contain some surprises. There was no association whatever between childhood factors and successful marriage or a happy sex life. Nor did those who had what would conventionally be thought of as a good and happy upbringing have more successful careers than others. Indeed, only five per cent of the men rated as having the best childhood appeared in *Who's Who in America* or in *American Men of Science*, whereas twenty-seven per cent of the remainder appeared in one volume or the other. This could be taken as supporting the Freudian notion of sublimation, but it could equally well merely mean that the impatient or aggressive child grows up to be an ambitious adult.

Both this study and several others have found that there is little association between neurotic traits in childhood and the development of neurosis in later life. The child who wets his bed or sucks his thumb, and the child who is fractious or painfully shy and withdrawn, are just as likely to grow up to be normal well-adjusted adults as the child who is happy, good-tempered and reasonable. Indeed, according to my mother I was myself an exceptionally well-adjusted child, at least until adolescence, and I have no reason to doubt her statement. If, then, defective rearing practices do contribute to adult mental disorder, their effects become manifest only after a long interval during which the developing individual may be completely normal. An association between broken homes and delinquency is well established, but the association with neuroticism appears to be weak and is hard to demonstrate. Though experience in childhood may play a role in predisposing to mental illness, the evidence currently available suggests that many authorities have exaggerated its importance.

Finally, there is abundant evidence that personal misfortunes and stresses in adult life can precipitate both physical and mental illness. One study found that forty per cent of patients had experienced at least one stressful event in the week preceding the onset of a schizophrenic episode, whereas the rate in the normal population was only twenty per cent. As in my own case, the onset of depressive illness is commonly preceded by personal misfortune. One of the most convincing studies on this problem comes from statistics on soldiers serving in the American army during the Second World War. The incidence of neurosis in a given army unit varied directly from week to week with the number of casualties suffered by that unit. Depression and grief are of course natural reactions to the death or loss through separation of a close relative or intimate friend. Not surprisingly, there are indications that people who do not exhibit this kind of reaction are emotionally shallow and do not form close attachments. Although personal catastrophe undoubtedly precipitates mental breakdown in some individuals, vulnerability varies greatly from one person to another, and we do not yet know the extent to which such vulnerability is determined genetically or by experiences in earlier life.

The factors predisposing to mental illness discussed in the previous pages are all more or less remote causes. The actual onset and course of a mental disorder is determined by happenings within the individual. We can regard such processes either as physical events occurring in the brain or as psychological processes often perhaps of an unconscious nature. The two views are not incompatible – they describe or explain the same phenomena in different terms. Whether we choose in any given instance to explain behaviour by adducing psychological reasons for it or by pointing to causal factors in the nervous system is a pragmatic issue and depends on the purpose we have in mind.

In schizophrenia and severe depressive illness, it is probably most useful to think in terms of there being physical defects in the brain. It is now certain that the biochemistry of the brain in some depressive illness differs from that of the normal brain, and there is mounting but still controversial evidence that disorders of brain biochemistry are implicated in schizophrenia. Many schizophrenics and severe depressives can be helped to function more adequately by drug therapy, whereas no known form of psychotherapy is of much assistance. This does not of course imply that we should cease to treat psychotics in as humane a way as possible and to give such comfort as we can by psychological means.

The status of neurosis is more complicated, and it must be emphasized that there is a continuous gradation between incapacitating neurosis and the 'normal' personality.

It is usually thought that we all have our cracking point. Soldiers or airmen repeatedly undertaking severe combat missions develop rates of neurosis unheard of in civilian life. We are all susceptible, though an event that one person can brush aside may cause a total collapse in another. It has recently been suggested that neurotic depression is a form of 'learned helplessness'. If the individual is subjected to a series of untoward events over which he has no control, or even if a single catastrophic event occurs, he may come to feel that he can no longer influence his environment, and give up the attempt: the result is depression. We do not know in detail what makes one person peculiarly sensitive to this misfortune, another to that, but it must surely depend on their personality as formed by their previous experiences and by the genes they have inherited. The importance of hereditary factors in determining personality should not be underestimated. Babies of Chinese descent born in a hospital in San Francisco were found to be more placid and less fretful from birth than those of European descent, despite the fact that neither group had had any contact with their mothers. Heredity and environment interact in complex and poorly understood ways to determine adult personality.

The most likely possibility, then, is that susceptibility to neurosis is determined by an unfortunate combination of environmental and innate factors: this does not mean that there is any innate defect, merely that one's innate endowment may not fit one for the environment one actually experiences. Hence, there may be no one right way in which to bring up all children – the best way may depend on the individual child's constitution. If neurosis is due to maladaptive learning, it might be possible to cure it by teaching the neurotic to behave and think in more adaptive ways.

All psychotherapy can be regarded as an attempt to do just this. The various schools differ only in the methods adopted. Moreover, all schools are agreed that neurosis results primarily from unfortunate experiences, though as we shall see they again differ widely about the nature of the experiences in question. It should, however, not be concluded that drugs and other physical methods of treatment have no role to play in the treatment of neurotics. The neurotic's experiences may have seriously upset his hormonal balance, and a vicious circle may be set up. If someone is desperately anxious as a result of maladaptive learning, there will be an increase in adrenalin in the blood and the raised adrenalin may in turn increase anxiety. The neurotic may be rendered incapable of doing anything to help himself until something can be done to reverse such physical changes. When I was in my most desperate state of panic and despondency, I could neither help myself nor receive help from any fellow-being. Only the restoration of a calmer mood, doubtless assisted by the antidepressant drugs, enabled me once more to strive myself and to begin to profit from what those around me were saying.

There is one important question that the above account leaves unanswered, namely, whether neurosis – and even psychosis – should be regarded as an illness. The issue is complex, and in recent years much debated: I shall postpone discussion of it until I have reviewed the many different methods of treatment. In the meantime, I shall continue to employ the term.

10

Freudian Theory and Practice

In the field of mental illness, the only obvious genius to date is Sigmund Freud, the founder of psychoanalysis. I first read his works when in my teens, and it was in part a fascination with his ideas that led me into psychology. He had two great insights. First, he realized explicitly that we are often unaware of our own motives. Several other psychologists, such as Pierre Janet and William James, antedated Freud in the stress they laid on the unconscious. Moreover, its existence had always been implicit in the writings of many novelists and playwrights, and indeed it is taken for granted in much of our ordinary conversation. We can all recognize that most people who hunt down smut and cry out for stronger laws against obscenity are not necessarily actuated just by a sincerely held belief in old-fashioned morality. Their behaviour makes it obvious that they themselves take a vicarious pleasure in the obscenities they discover: Freud might add that they are disguising their anger against their own libidinous urges by venting it upon others. It is, however, one thing to use a principle implicitly: it may take a genius to make it explicit.

Freud's second important insight was that it should be the task of scientific psychology to explain in detail all human behaviour. If some-one makes a slip of the tongue, it is not enough to say he did so because he was tired, we should explain why he made this particular slip and not that slip. Freud's answer was to suggest that the form that mistakes take, the dreams we dream and the symptoms the neurotic develops, are dictated by unconscious wishes, and to prove this point he produced a vast number of instances that could be credibly explained in this way.

The fact that Freud's explanations are couched in the same terms as our everyday thinking about people makes them easy for the layman to understand, and for this reason, among others, his ideas have been seized upon avidly by literary critics.

Anyone reading Freud for the first time is likely to be carried away, as I was, by the sheer plausibility of his style of writing. It was not until I began to study psychology in detail that I became aware of Freud's deficiencies. He insisted that his methods were scientific, but in practice his investigations of human personality have more in common with the work of a historian or an old-fashioned detective hunting down clues than with the way in which a scientist thinks. His theories lack predictive power, they are never stated in rigorous terms and he never attempted to devise objective tests for them. He deluded himself in thinking that his approach was scientific. It is, nonetheless, important to recognize that in his age there were no scientific techniques available for answering the questions he posed: for the most part this remains true today. Scientific truths are, however, not the only kind of truths: indeed, I often tell my students that if they are interested in human personality they would do much better to study the great novelists and playwrights than to wade through the banal technical literature on the subject.

I was myself interested in obtaining more rigorous explanations of behaviour than is possible in the field of human emotion and personality, and for this reason my own work has been directed towards aspects of psychology that are at present more amenable to scientific explanation, in particular to the problems of perception and learning. I still believe that it will be possible to approach in a scientific way the mysteries of the human personality only when we have acquired a much fuller understanding of the mechanisms involved in perception, learning and the use of language than we have at present. Freudians might – and some do – allege that my interest in these superficially simpler aspects of human behaviour is determined by a defence mechanism that prevents me from examining too closely the springs of my own conduct, but there is of course no way of knowing whether they are right, nor does it matter. Freud himself believed that an interest in scientific research originated from the child's frustrated desire to examine its mother's genital organs.

Although it is still difficult or impossible to construct rigorous scientific theories about human personality, this does not absolve us from the task of collecting and assessing evidence in as objective a manner as possible. As we shall repeatedly see, common sense and intuition are not enough, nor are clinical hunches: they may be useful starting points, but must be treated with caution until supported by objective studies. Freud's most important failing – and that of many of his successors – was not that he was unscientific in his approach, but that he did not gather systematic evidence and evaluate it objectively in order to validate or disprove his ideas.

Freud, then, attempted to explain behaviour by showing that if we postulate certain unconscious motives it becomes rational: hence he concentrated on instances for which there is no everyday-life explanation, such as mistakes and neurotic symptoms. He never realized that normal and rational behaviour – seeing or solving a puzzle or understanding a story – stands just as much in need of explanation. How is it that we can recognize an object, given that we never see it from exactly the same viewpoint or in the same lighting twice in a lifetime? The answer to such questions takes us a long way from common-sense thinking about people, and psychologists would not be satisfied with any answer that was not sufficiently precise and detailed to serve as a blueprint for a machine that would carry out these functions in the same way that people do.

In the case of dreams and mistakes, Freud allowed that a great variety of motives could play a part. He noticed for example that many of his patients on entering his consulting room would leave the door communicating with the waiting room open. They only did so when the waiting room was empty, and he interpreted this thoughtless gesture as a mark of defiance towards himself: he was not such a great doctor after all, since he had an empty waiting room. In order to prevent the patient 'behaving equally impolitely and disrespectfully during the consultation', Freud always 'gave their arrogance in leaving open the door a sharp reprimand'. He was always authoritarian, and became more so in the course of his long life.

On the basis of his clinical studies, he concluded that all neurotic symptoms were caused by frustrated and unconscious sexual wishes. He interpreted sexual drive rather widely, and included in it the desire for the pleasures of sucking the breast and of excretion. To this extended concept of sexuality he gave the name 'libido'. For Freud, neuroses arise because society restrains the untrammelled expression of libido:

he frequently reiterates his belief that 'all neurosis is due to frustration of the libido'. The morality imposed by society is incorporated by the individual as his 'superego', corresponding roughly to conscience, except that we are all conscious of our conscience whereas the superego may contain prohibitions of which we are unaware. The 'ego' includes everything of which we are conscious, and the 'id' contains the unconscious aspects of the libido.

The ego, according to Freud, is shielded from the promptings of the id by a series of mechanisms that play a role both in normal people and in neurotics. Libidinal urges that clash with the superego remain unconscious, and many episodes from the past, particularly from early childhood, may be 'repressed', that is driven into the unconscious, because they remind us of such forbidden libidinal urges. We also disguise our inner drives from ourselves by 'projection' – attributing them to others and then turning our anger at ourselves on them. Forbidden urges may find satisfaction by displacement of their object – hoarding money becomes a substitute for hoarding and playing with one's own faeces; ambition a substitute for sexual potency; and art, in which forbidden objects are symbolized, the sublimation of our libido. The painter's lush landscapes represent his mother's vagina, for which he has an unconscious longing. Freud's theories were nothing if not imaginative.

He thought that neurosis originated from conflicts in early childhood. All growing boys are said to wish to possess their mothers and to be jealous and afraid of their fathers. In his later writings Freud thought that all little boys' fear of their father took the specific form of an anxiety lest he cut off their genitals ('castration complex'), whereas little girls hate their mother because she has not given them a penis and long for their father because only he can give them one. Small boys may wish to kill their father, but because he is so powerful they disguise this wish from themselves by identifying with him. By imagining they are he, they can sleep with their mother in fantasy and obtain vicarious gratification whilst at the same time taking over his morality. Another way of resolving the Oedipal complex is for the child to identify with the parent of the *opposite* sex whose love the child is unable to gain. Putting oneself in the position of this parent results in making love in fantasy to the parent of the same sex: this in turn disguises the jealousy felt of that parent, but at the expense of giving rein to the homosexual side of one's nature. Freud thought that everyone was bisexual. Finally, he believed that we all pass through three stages of sexual development

– oral, anal and genital – and parts of the libido may become inappropriately fixed at the earlier stages of development.

Freud was never clear about the precise causes of neurosis. He thought it developed partly as a result of unfortunate experiences, partly because of a constitutional lack. The very experiences that made Leonardo da Vinci into a great artist and scientist could have rendered someone with a different constitution a hopeless neurotic. For the most part, the unfortunate experiences consist of departures from the methods of child-rearing current in Vienna around the turn of the century: mothers can wean both too early and too late, they can be too loving or not loving enough, toilet-training can be commenced too soon or too late.

Freud's views on child-rearing should be treated with caution. Throughout most of history, child-rearing practices have been totally different from those current today. Indeed until recently, most young children appear to have received little in the way of love and care. In the sixteenth century, the mortality rate among young children was so high that no mother or father could afford to become too emotionally involved with their offspring. Nearly one child in three died before the age of one. The survivors were often savagely beaten, locked up in the dark, taken to see hangings and corpses, and even mutilated by having their teeth ripped out to provide dentures or being castrated to supply testicles for magical potions. On the other hand, toilet-training was often non-existent, and children lived in their own excrement. In many periods of history, childhood masturbation was not frowned upon. Courtiers kissed Louis XIII's penis when he was a young child, and he was encouraged to explore the vaginas of ladies-in-waiting with his fist. The Ancient Greeks practised infanticide on a grand scale, and had anal and oral intercourse with young children. In Victorian times, British upper-class children were breast-fed by wetnurses and often had only the most formal and occasional contacts with their fathers. Neither the Elizabethans nor the Victorian upper classes were noticeably more neurotic than anyone else, though for whatever reasons they may have had idiosyncratic personalities.

In reading Freud it quickly becomes apparent that whenever he starts to trace the origin of neurosis or the method of cure through psychoanalysis his writing becomes opaque and his arguments more difficult to follow. If he was unclear about the origin of the neuroses, he is equally unclear about the method of cure. Freud believed that psychoanalysis worked by bringing the repressed libidinal urges into consciousness: once the patient recognizes that his libido is stuck at an oral or anal stage, or that it is fixated on inappropriate objects such as the mother or father, the libido is somehow freed to move on to a more adult stage or to fasten on more appropriate objects. To be effective, recognition of unconscious urges involves more than merely conscious assent to what the analyst says: a cure can be achieved only if the patient accepts his own psychodynamic make-up at some deeper level.

Freud pictured psychoanalysis as a battle to overcome the patient's own resistance to recognizing his repressed desires: they are repressed precisely because he is afraid of them, and it is natural that he should unconsciously strive at all costs to avoid recognizing them. In overcoming such resistances, the analyst acts as the ally of the patient and tries by encouragement and sympathy to bring them to light. In this endeavour, the mechanism of 'transference' plays an important role. Freud noticed that most patients become very interested and dependent on their analyst – they fall in love with him. In so doing, they act towards him in the ways in which they have responded towards other important figures in their lives, particularly their own parents. Hence what occurs in transference can reveal patients' unconscious feelings about their parents. Moreover, the patients' love for the analyst can be turned to good account, since they will strive to please him and this provides them with a strong motive for uncovering and accepting their own unconscious wishes. Freud himself described transference as a neurosis that supervened on the original neurosis, and it was only when the transference neurosis was in turn resolved that the patient would recover. It can only be overcome when the patient himself recognizes the nature of the transference, and with such understanding he ceases to be dependent on the analyst.

Most patients also undergo phases of 'negative transference' during which they hate the analyst: this is yet a further form of resistance – by hating and despising the analyst, the patient is able to reject his interpretations and thus avoid admitting to his own desires. In negative transference, patients are again repeating hostile attitudes to earlier figures of importance in their life – particularly, attitudes towards the parent of the same sex.

Freud would have had little difficulty in making sense of my own attitudes towards therapists in these terms. In general I liked and grew dependent upon the three older male therapists – the first analyst, the psychotherapist and the consultant. If we assume they were father figures to me, my liking for them simply repeats my early trust in my father. My dislike for the young analyst may have arisen because I unconsciously identified him with my younger brother, of whom I had doubtless felt a long-forgotten childhood jealousy. If I was disappointed in my mother's love, I may have resolved this by identifying with her, and my anger at the young analyst may also have served the purpose of protecting me from a knowledge of hidden homosexual urges. Finally, my fury at the woman doctor simply gave expression to my anger at my mother's rejection of me, whether real or imagined. All this is most plausible, but it will not escape the reader's attention that had I produced any other pattern of interaction with the different psychotherapists, it would have been equally easy to interpret in Freudian terms.

The reader should by now have formed some impression of what to expect if he embarks on a traditional Freudian analysis. The first few sessions are usually devoted to an assessment of whether the putative patient is a suitable case for treatment. Freud himself laid emphasis on the importance of such assessment. He believed it was useless to treat psychoses by analytic methods, and he thought that depression ('melancholia' as it was then called) was resistant to psychoanalytic treatment. He also stressed the importance of making sure that there was nothing organically wrong with the patient. Since his day, it has become common to emphasize that two qualities are needed in a patient if psychoanalysis is to have any hope of success. The first is intelligence: presumably unintelligent patients would be unable to follow the contortions of their own psyche (as envisaged by Freud), and this would render attempts at interpretation ineffective. Secondly, many analysts only accept patients with high 'ego-strength'. By this is meant patients who are in touch with reality and give evidence of a certain amount of willpower.

One can readily agree that determination is a *sine qua non* of a successful analysis: it is a protracted, expensive and painful process. Nevertheless, it is difficult or impossible to distinguish between patients with a strong ego and patients who are not very ill: everyone agrees that a determination to recover is clinically a hopeful sign, and it could be thought that in selecting such patients analysts are in fact treating only those who will recover of their own accord.

Traditional Freudians insist on the patient lying on a couch. Its use arose from a historical accident. Freud's first essays into psychotherapy were based on hypnotism, and it is easier to hypnotize someone lying down and relaxed. Freud gives several reasons for the desirability of continuing the use of the couch. He writes that he disliked being stared at for eight hours a day, but he is quick to add clinical reasons which, had they been adduced by one of his patients, he would doubtless have described as rationalizations. He believed that for transference to be put to the best possible use the analyst himself should remain as shadowy and indistinct as possible: by so doing, he could encourage patients to respond to him in the way they had previously responded to important figures in their life. The patient is thus enabled to project onto the dim figure of the analyst the charateristics of his own parents or siblings. In addition, the couch encourages relaxation, and thus helps the patients to think dreamily and to voice irrational trains of thought.

Freud laid great stress on irrational thought-processes: when the ego is in full control they are unlikely to occur, and the id reveals its workings in dreams, mistakes, reveries and disconnected thoughts. These are the clues to the unconscious workings of the mind, and any Freudian analyst will at an early stage in treatment instruct the patient to withhold nothing, however trivial or irrelevant it seems. He will also concentrate on the patient's dreams, though even here the repressed desires manifest themselves only in disguised form: the 'censor' defends the ego from their direct expression. Hence the dream material needs much interpretation to reveal its true meaning. When I was under analysis I sometimes dreamed of sleeping with every member of my family – mother, father and brother: perhaps my censor fell asleep along with me.

Most patients find it very difficult to capture and reveal their stray thoughts, and may require several sessions before they learn what is required of them. In my experience, it is particularly difficult to state in all honesty one's own feelings about the analyst. These are bound to contain hostile elements, and one assumes that even analysts have their *amour propre*: moreover, most of us have a strong inhibition against deliberately hurting others' feelings except in anger. In addition, I always felt that apart from the altruistic motive of not wanting to be beastly to one's analyst, there is a more selfish reason for not saying exactly what one thinks: he is normally in a better position to hurt you than you are him. The doctrine that patients should be completely honest in reporting their feelings about their psychotherapist is widely held even by non-Freudian therapists: I suspect that it is rarely observed.

II

Evaluation of Freud

No brief description of Freudian theory and practice can hope to capture the full range of Freud's thought: he himself, particularly in the *Introductory Lectures*, is much his own best expositor. It should be remembered that in the course of his life he revised his theories many times and never attempted a careful synthesis and systematic statement. I have ignored much of his wilder theorizing developed late in life when he became very pessimistic about mankind. In his last years he laid great stress on the death wish – Thanatos – as opposed to Eros, love. He saw much of human activity as an attempt to die or to hurt oneself, though he thought that the organism was trying to die in its own good time. The addition of such a motive to the operation of the libido makes interpretation easier but more uncertain.

One must ask what is the standing of Freudian theory and practice today: I write 'theory and practice' advisedly, since it is important to separate the two. It could be that Freud's theories about human motives and the development of the personality are correct whilst the therapy has no value: it is also possible that his theories are nonsense whilst the therapy works – neurotics might, for all we know, be helped by being presented with mythical stories about the origin of their conduct. Freud himself was well aware of the dichotomy between analytic theory and practice, and he thought that he would be remembered more for his insights into the development of personality than for his therapeutic methods.

The kindest verdict one can return on the theory is that it is not proven. Freud's arguments are often curiously illogical. Thus, many children's dreams are clearly wish-fulfilments, as when Freud's own daughter Anna dreamt of the strawberries and cream she was not allowed to eat in the daytime: but Freud leaps from the fact that some dreams are wish-fulfilments to the unwarranted conclusion that all are. It would be just as logical to argue that because some dreams clearly express fears, all do, though in some the fears appear in a disguised form. Again, some neuroses clearly revolve around sexual anxieties, but to conclude that all do, no matter how disguised the libidinal problem, seems quite unjustifiable. Like other higher animals, man is born with many drives, and these include a desire for knowledge and mastery over his environment as well as the bodily urges. Neuroses can certainly be triggered by the frustration of such ambitions, and there is no more reason for concluding that all ambitions represent disguised sexual urges than for thinking that sexual wishes themselves arise from a desire for dominance. It is of course true that neurotic anxiety – or indeed anxiety of any kind – is inimical to normal sexual functioning, but it is also inimical to normal intellectual functioning and can play havoc with one's appetite for food: some eat to comfort themselves when anxious, others, particularly young women, may starve themselves to death.

Freud's theories are so flexible and imprecise that it is difficult to have much faith in any of his detailed interpretations. In both dream symbolism and in neurotic symptoms, one thing can always be replaced by its opposite. 'An element in the manifest dream which is capable of having a contrary may equally well be expressing either itself or its contrary or both together.' The mother can stand for the father, the breast for the penis, the scrotum for the womb. An Oedipal complex can be resolved by identification with the same-sex parent, which in later life may manifest itself either by rampant homosexuality or in the disguise of severe disgust at homosexuality. Freud also allows the opposition of many psychic forces: id and superego, Eros and Thanatos, the masculine principle and the feminine principle, self-love (narcissism) and love for others. What are we to make of passages such as the following?

> ... the life instincts or sexual instincts which are active in each cell take the other cells as their 'object' ... they partially neutralise the death instincts ... while the other cells do the same for them, and still others sacrifice themselves in the performance of this libidinal function. The germ-cells themselves would behave in a completely

'narcissistic' fashion, . . . The germ-cells require their libido . . . for themselves, as a reserve against their later momentous constructive activity.'

When you read a Freudian case history, it all sounds very plausible, but if you stand back from the material it immediately becomes obvious that the same case could be interpreted in many different ways even in Freud's own terms.

Of course none of this means that Freud is definitely wrong: it suggests only that there is no reason for subscribing to his beliefs, and in such circumstances it is more usual to dismiss theories than to suspend judgement. The reasons why so many people continue to have faith in psychoanalysis will be examined below.

A few brave souls have attempted to validate Freudian theory by objective means. It is possible to relate age of weaning or age of toilet-training to later personality: Freudians would expect early weaning or early toilet-training to result respectively in oral or anal characteristics. The passive oral personality is marked by such traits as love of eating and drinking, pessimism, guilt and dependence and the anal by obsessional traits such as orderliness, cleanliness, meanness and obstinacy. The majority of studies find little or no relation between personality and such features of early childhood. Some studies have yielded results directly opposite to Freudian predictions, and about the same number have produced findings in the expected direction.

At least fifty experimental studies have been undertaken to test the Freudian concept of repression. Both neurotics and normals have been exposed to material that on Freudian theory might be expected to arouse anxiety, and subsequently tested for whether recall is less good than for neutral material. A recent survey of this field concludes: 'In view of the amount and consistency of the data accumulated to this point . . . the continued use of the concept of repression as an explanation for behaviour does not seem justifiable.' It is of course open to Freudians to say that because of the different ways in which people can cope with traumas such as early weaning, it is impossible to test Freudian theory by looking for personality differences due to such factors; they can also argue that the processes underlying repression are so complex that they cannot be uncovered in artificial situations; but one can only doubt the validity and usefulness of a theory that cannot be submitted to objective testing.

A few years ago, it looked as though some support for Freud might be forthcoming from studies on the effects of disturbed homes, but as we have seen the results are open to more than one interpretation, and they do not confirm any of the details of Freudian theory. Nor can Freudians draw comfort from studies of monkeys brought up in deprived conditions. It is true that if reared in total isolation monkeys are severely abnormal when adult, but they are comparatively normal when brought up without a mother or father but with the companionship of monkeys of their own age. I have already commented on the fact that in many periods and for many classes of mankind, parental affection was the exception rather than the rule. It is likely that early upbringing does affect later personality, though perhaps not as much as was thought a few years ago. Growing children may well learn methods of satisfying their needs which carry over into later life, but it seems unlikely that their most important satisfactions revolve around the weird sexual fantasies that Freud ascribed to them.

If Freudian theory is too narrowly conceived, too illogical, and too lacking in any kind of empirical support to be acceptable, there is a presumptive case against the therapy derived from the theory. It might be expected that it would be a simple matter to find out whether neurotics who undergo psychoanalysis have a higher cure rate than those who do not. In practice, this is no easy thing to discover. Here are some of the difficulties.

Most neurotics recover in the course of time whether or not they are treated. Estimates of recovery rates differ wildly, but it would appear that between a half and two thirds are either better or much improved within two years of the onset of their illness. To make sure that analysis is having a beneficial effect, it is necessary to assign patients at random to analysis or to some other form of treatment or to no treatment at all. If a patient has faith in analysis, this becomes impossible or unethical.

Second, many analysts select their patients, but if as I have suggested they tend to treat only those most likely to recover, such selection will result in a higher recovery rate in patients undergoing analysis than in those who do not, regardless of any possible benefit of the analysis.

Third, the drop-out rate for patients under analysis is very high: most studies have found it to be in the region of fifty per cent. If it is the more severely ill who cannot endure the pain of a protracted analysis, then once again if drop-outs are not counted, the odds are being unfairly weighted in favour of analysis.

Fourth, who is the arbiter of what constitutes a recovery? Certainly not the analyst, who is likely to be biased, and possibly not the patient himself, who may lack insight into his condition as I did when I became elated. Perhaps one should rely on the judgement of a second therapist who sees the patient both before treatment is finished and after it has ended, or even on the judgements of the patient's family and friends, though there is a danger that they may themselves be too involved in the patient's neurosis to be able to judge impartially. A more objective criterion that has sometimes been used is ability to return to work.

Fifth, if it were shown that patients treated by analysis recovered more rapidly than patients not given psychotherapy, this demonstration would still not validate psychoanalysis as such. It would be necessary to show that recovery was brought about by the actual methods used by analysts and not merely by the opportunity to have sympathetic discussions about one's problems regardless of the specific nature of those discussions and the specific interpretations imposed. It would, moreover, be necessary to show that recovery was not due solely to the patient's faith in analytical methods: it has been repeatedly found that neurotic distress can be alleviated at least temporarily by any method of treatment in which the patient has faith, for example swallowing pills containing a harmless substance that does not affect the brain, like sugar or starch: such pills are known as 'placebos'.

Finally, investigations of the effects of analysis are lengthy and time-consuming. One needs to know not merely whether a patient has recovered but whether the recovery is sustained over a period of years. The patient may move to another town, he may refuse to cooperate in a follow-up inquiry or it may simply be impossible to trace him.

For all these reasons, it is very hard to assess the efficacy of analysis – or of any other method of psychotherapy. This difficulty does not excuse the shoddiness of most of the studies that have been performed. In many of the papers published on this topic, analysts have taken it upon themselves to judge whether or not a patient has recovered, they have failed to provide data on what percentage of patients have dropped out, and have failed to use control groups of patients matched for severity of illness but not treated by analysis.

Most of the research on the efficacy of psychoanalysis is, therefore, difficult to interpret. Although, for the reasons given above, many studies on the effects of psychoanalysis are loaded in its favour, there are about as many studies showing either no effects or even adverse effects as there are reports of some objective benefits. In one study, analysts themselves were asked about their cure rate. Although they claimed that over eighty per cent of patients who completed analysis were helped by it, in only twenty-seven per cent of cases did they succeed according to their own account in removing the symptoms for the treatment of which the patient had originally entered analysis.

If analysis does have beneficial effects, they are at best slight and uncertain. Two years ago David Malan, a prominent British analyst and a member of the leading British centre for Freudian analysis, wrote: 'The evidence in favour of dynamic therapy in the ordinary run of neuroses and character disorders – for which after all, this form of therapy was developed – is weak in the extreme.' In the same paper, he writes: '[Research on] the most influential and ambitious of all forms of psychotherapy, that based on psychoanalysis, has yielded almost nothing – a matter for shame and despair – until it has been saved at the last moment by the Menninger Foundation's report.'

Malan's last remark is extraordinary, and is hardly borne out by the contents of the report. The Menninger Foundation is one of the main bastions of psychoanalysis in the United States, and the report in question summarizes investigations of the treatment by analysis of forty-two patients over a period of eighteen years. On turning to the report, we find that the authors display a commendable candour. They say that they found it impossible: '(1) to list the variables needed to test the theory [of psychoanalysis] ... (3) to choose and provide control conditions which could rule out alternative explanations for results; (4) to state the hypotheses to be tested; or finally (5) to conduct this research according to the design.' Their main conclusion is that patients with a sound personality ('strong ego-strength') will prosper regardless of the method of treatment, whereas patients with weak ego-strength will not benefit from psychoanalysis. The authors even write that their findings 'raise the question to what extent psychoanalysis may be considered the ideal treatment for patients who need it least, that is for those with initial high ego-strength'. In other words, it may be that analysis is unhelpful regardless of whether a patient's ego-strength is high or low.

12

Popularity of Freud

Many analysts are themselves sceptical of the value of psychoanalysis in speeding recovery from neuroses. Why then do they continue to practise? They adduce several reasons. When I challenged my own analysts with figures on recovery rates, they both made the same reply. One said: 'For every shrink in the south-east of England making people better, there are six in Manchester fouling people up.' The other answered: 'There are only six good analysts in London – the rest often make people worse.' There is in fact evidence that some analysts are better than others – a finding that is hardly surprising. The evidence suggests that analysts – and other psychotherapists – exhibiting towards their patients 'non-possessive warmth, genuineness and empathy' do better than therapists who do not exhibit these qualities: it seems not unlikely that at least some neurotics may be helped by a genuine expression of human sympathy, and it remains open to question whether it is the expression of this sympathy that is helpful rather than the probing into the patient's subconscious, particularly as other methods of psychotherapy are, as we shall see, at least as effective as psychoanalysis. Indeed, if sympathy is desirable in psychotherapy you are least likely to find it from a traditional Freudian. The master himself wrote: 'I cannot advise my colleagues too urgently to model themselves during psychoanalytic treatment on the surgeon, who puts aside all his feelings, even his human sympathy.'

The second line of defence on which analysts fall back is that the lack of success of much analytic treatment is the fault not of the analyst but of the patient. Only some patients are suitable for analytic treatment, and at present we do not know who these patients are. To quote again from Malan's article: 'I am also convinced that what analysts have never faced up to is that there are many types of patient, whom we continue to treat with never diminishing hope and ever increasing denial, who are not helped by our methods. It has been the failure to face this that has for so long stood in the way of our showing that, with other types of patient, our work may be uniquely effective.' It is presumably only by continuing to practise analysis on those suitable and unsuitable for it that there is any hope of isolating the characteristics of those who might be helped.

Many analysts are in fact beginning to face up to the fact that analysis is not a suitable treatment for many patients. For example, the Medical Director of the St Louis Psychoanalytic Institute recently wrote: 'In many individuals the limitations of their own psychopathology or the therapeutic capacities they bring to the treatment situations make it necessary for other [i.e. non-analytic] approaches to be introduced.' It is characteristic of the curious thought-processes of many analysts that he should blame the limitations of the patient rather than of the therapy.

A third reason given by analysts for ignoring the evidence on the lack of efficacy of the treatment is that they are not merely interested in effecting cures: they are trying to bring about some character change, including the acquisition of self-knowledge, and the nature of this character change is so elusive that it cannot be specified, much less detected, by the use of objective methods. With this argument, I have no sympathy. Any neurotic who finds himself in the desperate state of misery in which I existed for five months does not want to have his character changed, he wants to recover and to be able to function normally. Unless analysts believe they can achieve this aim, they should not practise on neurotic patients, though there would seem little harm in continuing to offer analysis to people within the normal range who wish to change their characters in this unspecified way.

Indeed, both in Britain and in North America, there appear to be many more normal people undergoing analysis than there are neurotics. Analysis is much more widely practised in America than it is in Britain, particularly in large urban centres such as New York and Chicago. It has been suggested that much analysis is akin to prostitution, in that instead of paying for sex, the patient buys synthetic friendship – 'Rent-a-Friend'. Anyone seeking analysis for this reason would again do well to avoid traditional Freudian analysts, and should perhaps bear in mind the reply of one analyst to the question of what would happen if a normal person came to him: 'Even though he were normal at the beginning of the analysis, the analytic procedure would create a neurosis.'

We should not be too surprised that many analysts continue to believe in the usefulness of a method of treatment for which there is no good evidence. The history of medicine abounds with examples of treatments that were useless – and often lethal – and that were employed for many decades by practitioners with an honest but misguided faith in their curative value. As I shall later show, many treatments given today both for mental and physical illness make patients worse, not better. For psychological reasons, however, the analyst is likely to be more predisposed to cling to his faith in his method than are most doctors in theirs.

First, he will normally have submitted himself to the expense, time and pain of analysis. There is abundant evidence that where we have made a sacrifice to obtain some object, we come to value it: we cannot afford to admit to ourselves that we have made the sacrifice in vain. Hence, to abjure analysis, the psychoanalyst not only has to give up a profitable method of making a living, he must admit to himself that he has made a costly mistake. It is small wonder that few are prepared to make this admission – though some, to their credit, have and are now practising better attested forms of psychotherapy. Although doctors also have a long and arduous training, they are less likely to be committed to one particular method of treatment: if a drug is found not to work, it requires less moral courage to admit the mistake and substitute another than it does for an analyst to forswear his whole procedure.

Second, patients constantly confirm the analyst's faith in his own theories by producing the sort of material he most wants to hear, that is to say material that agrees with his own view of the origin of neurosis. By expressing interest or approval, the analyst rewards his patients for talking about topics he thinks are important. Many analysts including Freud himself go much further than this. The master writes: 'The mechanism of our assistance is easy to understand: we give the patient the conscious anticipatory idea (the idea of what he may expect to find) and he then finds the repressed unconscious idea in himself on the basis of its similarity to the anticipatory one.' In his writings, Freud stressed over and over again that it was only with the help of suggestions made to him by the analyst that the patient could hope to uncover his unconscious desires. 'There are some patients who need more of such assistance and some who need less; but there are none who get through without some of it.' Despite Freud's numerous protestations to the contrary, many may suppose that far from discovering things in his own mind for himself, all the patient does is to rediscover material already placed there by the analyst, and embroider it in ways pleasing to the analyst. For these reasons Freud's patients may well dream (or at least report) Freudian dreams, Jung's dream Jungian dreams and Adler's dream about power suitably symbolized. The patient shapes himself in the image of his analyst –

> The Aethiop gods have Aethiop lips
> Bronze lips and curly hair
> The Grecian gods are like the Greeks
> As tall blue-eyed and fair.

Each analyst gets the patients he deserves: they reflect back to him his own ideas, and hence confirm them.

There are two more minor reasons why analysts preserve their faith. Psychoanalytic theory acts as an ingenious device for propping up their own self-esteem. All analysts can and do put down anything the patient says that is critical of themselves merely to an expression of hostile impulses towards his parents or other figures of importance in his early life. They frequently extend this notion into everyday life, and are so busy thinking up the psychodynamic reasons why other people say things that they rarely take what is said – particularly if it is threatening to their own beliefs – at face value. Freud himself was guilty of this irritating trick: he frequently said that he would not reply to his critics because no rational argument would convince them: he thought the only reason anyone could have for not accepting psychoanalytic theory was their resistance to acknowledging that some of the processes postulated were operating in themselves. This argument is of course self-defeating: if one takes it seriously, one can only speculate about the traumatic events in Freud's early life that led him to uphold such a bizarre body of beliefs as an adult. The unconscious motives, Freudian or otherwise, for holding a given belief are wholly irrelevant to its truth or falsity. I used to tell my colleagues that provided they produced good scientific work their motives were nobody's concern but their own: the work stands in its own right, whether it is produced out of a love of knowledge, a desire to be promoted, a longing for the Nobel prize, the wish to prove a colleague wrong, or the displaced infantile lust to examine one's mother's genitals.

Finally, most neurotics recover whether or not they are analysed, and the fact that the majority of the analyst's own patients recover will fortify him in his faith that his particular method works. Those who fail to recover will sooner or later drop out of analysis, and the analyst can close his case notes by writing 'terminated analysis prematurely'.

It is not surprising then that analysts should retain their faith in their methods. It is perhaps more surprising that so many of the general public should continue to believe both in the theory and practice of analysis, but it is again possible to discern several reasons for its popularity. Many of Freud's own beliefs fit in with the current *Zeitgeist*. They can be and often were, at least in some strata of society, taken as providing a licence for unbridled sexual activity. If the most basic aspects of personality derive from the sexual urge, and if frustrated libido makes us ill, it is natural to let it rip. Freud himself often warned against this interpretation of his theory. Moreover, he took a rather censorious attitude towards the perversions in which he included many kinds of sexual activity, such as kissing the partner's genitals, that are today regarded as completely normal. Nevertheless, his theories can be seen as justifying all forms of sexual deviation: if our upbringing is responsible for the direction our sexual urges take, why should we hold ourselves responsible for them? I myself had a Puritanical upbringing, and I can remember the sense of relief with which I read Freud in my late teens. It should be remembered that Freud started publishing towards the end of the Victorian age, when many must have suffered guilt about masturbation and extramarital sex. He undoubtedly helped then both to lift the taboo on talking freely about sex and also to remove some of the guilt associated with sexual urges. It is difficult to know how far he is popular because his ideas fitted in with a changing climate of opinion, how far he actually helped to create this climate.

A second reason for Freud's popular success is the sheer imaginative power of his theorizing. As Eysenck puts it:

'Freud was a great novelist and dramatist himself; his theories are like a medieval morality play, with heroes, villains and monsters rushing about in all directions. Here the "ego", "id" and "superego" have their three-cornered fight; there the censor battles with the forces of the "unconscious"! Watch the celebrated "Oedipus complex" burrowing its way to the surface! See "sublimation" and "displacement" at work! Watch Eros battling against Thanatos! There is a tremendous cast, and their antics are astounding. The whole action of the play is centred on sex – what could be a greater draw than that?'

We should add to this that much of Freud's own writing has the compulsion of a detective story. In case after case, we watch the great sleuth hunting down the clues to the wicked activity of the unconscious mind. Close on the trail of the id, he follows the same tortuous paths of reasoning as Sherlock Holmes or Hercule Poirot, and despite the many bafflements en route we can read happily on, secure in the knowledge that in the last chapter he always gets his complex.

Apart from his talent for drama, Freud was a remarkably persuasive expositor of his own ideas. He was particularly good at anticipating criticism, and took great pains to disarm it: indeed there are few criticisms that can be made of his theories and methods of reasoning that he did not explicitly set out himself. The following passage is typical:

'But you will now tell me that, no matter whether we call the motive force of our analysis transference or suggestion, there is a risk that the influencing of our patient may make the objective certainty of our findings doubtful. What is advantageous to our therapy is damaging to our researches. This is the objection that is most often raised against psychoanalysis, and it must be admitted that, though it is groundless, it cannot be rejected as unreasonable. If it were justified, psychoanalysis would be nothing more than a particularly well-disguised and particularly effective form of suggestive treatment and we should have to attach little weight to all that it tells us about what influences our lives, the dynamics of the mind or the unconscious. That is what our opponents believe; and in especial they think that we have "talked" the patients into everything relating to the importance of sexual experiences – or even into those experiences themselves – after such notions have grown up in our own depraved imagination. These accusations are contradicted more easily by an appeal to experience than by the help of theory. Anyone who has himself carried out psychoanalyses will have been able to convince himself on countless occasions that it is impossible to make suggestions to a patient in this way. The doctor has no difficulty, of course, in making him a supporter of some particular theory and in thus making him share some possible error of his own. In this respect the patient is behaving like anyone else – like a pupil – but this only affects his intelligence, not his illness. After all, his conflicts will only be successfully solved and his resistances overcome if the anticipatory ideas he is given tally with what is real in him. Whatever in the doctor's conjectures is inaccurate drops out in the course of the analysis; it has to be withdrawn and replaced by something more correct. We endeavour by a careful technique to avoid the occurrence of premature successes due to suggestion; but no harm is done even if they do occur, for we are not satisfied by a first success.'

Note the skill with which Freud makes concessions to his opponents – 'the objection . . . cannot be rejected as unreasonable' – only to trounce them at the expense of taking for granted the very point he is trying to prove. 'After all, his conflicts will only be successfully solved and his resistances overcome if the anticipatory ideas he is given tally with what is real in him.' Note the disarming cunning of that 'After all' – so reasonable, so persuasive. And finally, the *coup de grâce*; 'Anyone who has himself carried out psychoanalyses will be able to convince himself . . .' In other words, no one except a practising psychoanalyst can possibly judge the theory – a theme that recurs repeatedly in Freud and his successors: it sounds plausible but it is a shabby argument, and we should resist taking anyone's word on trust, whether he is a lawyer, a doctor, an architect, a historian or a psychoanalyst. Finally, observe the subtle reference to technique: 'We endeavour by a careful technique . . .'; it sounds scientific but it is not – Freud's techniques are nowhere spelled out in detail, and indeed he says himself that the techniques could only be learned by experience.

Moreover, Freud made a brilliant use of telling analogies – more so, I think, than any other advocate of a cause whom I have ever read. Here is another instance of his persuasive style:

'Now, however, you think you have me at your mercy. "So that's your technique," I hear you say. "When a person who has made a slip of the tongue says something about it that suits you, you pronounce him to be the final decisive authority on the subject. 'He says so himself!' But when what he says doesn't suit your book, then all at once you say 'He's of no importance – there's no need to believe him.'"

'That is quite true. But I can put a similar case to you in which the same monstrous event occurs. When someone charged with an offence confesses his deed to the judge, the judge believes his confession; but if he denies it, the judge does not believe him. If it were otherwise, there would be no administration of justice, and in spite of occasional errors we must allow that the system works.'

Finally, Freud was a great synthesizer: he rests his case not merely on his experiences with patients on his couch, but on many acute observations about incidents from everyday life, particularly dreams and mistakes, on evidence from anthropology, myth, drama and religion, and upon a re-examination of the lives of famous figures such as Leonardo da Vinci. He was somewhat of a polymath, and appears to have had a retentive memory for everything he read. He tries in fact to make sense in his own terms of the whole of human existence, and there is a temptation to be awestruck by the size of the edifice at the expense of failing to notice whether it is built of bricks or cardboard.

Freudian theories then can, wrongly, be interpreted as being in tune with our current sexual mores, and they appeal to our sense of drama and liking for comprehensive explanations. Moreover, the ideas are for the most part easy for the layman to follow, since the arguments are couched in everyday language and the technical terms are no obstacle to understanding. Anyone can quickly learn how to interpret the actions of those around him in Freudian terms, and the reasoning involved is so elusive that nobody can prove him wrong. Making such interpretations has become a parlour trick for novelists, biographers and literary critics, and the trick has much the same fascination when well done as Freud's own detective work in his case histories. It is small wonder that Freud in particular and psychodynamic theory in general still have a large following despite the lack of evidence for their validity.

Perhaps one is surprised at Freud's popularity only because in any age there is a tendency to believe that currently held beliefs are rational. In this respect we are, however, little different from our forefathers who believed in alchemy, necromancy and phrenology. In the Victorian age it was widely held that masturbation led to insanity, and this is stated as a self-evident truth in medical textbooks as late as the early years of this century. Indeed, the persistence of such myths is startling. The government of the People's Republic of China recently circulated its citizens with a tract condemning masturbation and explicitly stating that it leads to weakness of the nerves, whilst a survey conducted as recently as 1960 showed that fifty per cent of the medical students in Philadelphia thought that masturbation led to insanity.

Given that there are no sound reasons for believing in most of the dogma of psychoanalysis, we can still ask how far Freud's influence has been for good, how far for harm. On the credit side, the psychoanalytic movement certainly played a role in opening up important areas of human behaviour to discussion and investigation, though there were others, unconnected with analysis, such as Havelock Ellis, who were also instrumental in bringing this about. Moreover, by attempting to specify the causal origins of mental illness, Freud and his successors played a part in persuading society to stop blaming the mentally ill and to treat them more humanely: this movement was, however, well under way when Freud first started practising. On the debit side, we must place the experiences of all the poor wretches who have endured to no purpose the pain of an analysis, and the fact that the mystique of analysis may have prevented psychologists from attempting to develop more effective procedures for dealing with mental illness.

Finally, many, if not most, analysts seem to take themselves very seriously: it is rare to encounter an analyst with a sense of humour. Seriousness of purpose is not in itself a fault, but like Freud himself few analysts are prepared to admit the possibility that they might be wrong, and some appear to think that they have privileged access to the only road to the truth about mankind. The chairman of a session at the International Psychoanalytic Congress held in Vienna in 1971 remarked that 'psychoanalysts have a unique contribution to make owing to their privileged access to the psychological processes of human functioning'. Such arrogance is merely a source of irritation to many, but it can be the cause of extreme agony in some.

Most hospitals both in Great Britain and North America can instance cases of women who were treated for frigidity by analysts only to discover eventually that they had a vaginal lesion; or of men who underwent the pain and expense of an analysis to cure depression or agitation, only to discover that their thyroid glands were not functioning properly. Anyone in doubt about this aspect of analysis should read *The Victim is Always the Same*, a book written by a neurosurgeon, I. S. Cooper. It describes the fate of four children suffering from a rare neurological complaint known as dystonia musculorum deformans, which produces horrifyingly painful muscular contractions that force the sufferer into hideously contorted postures. All four were unfortunate enough to fall into the hands of psychoanalytically oriented psychiatrists.

One of these patients was a boy called David. His right hand was so contorted that he could not use it for masturbation, and this was interpreted by the analyst to signify castration anxiety; his illness forced him to stick out his stomach whilst he walked, and this was taken as an imitation of his mother when she was pregnant with his younger sister; he walked with his bottom stuck up in the air, and the psychoanalyst naturally saw this as an invitation for a sexual assault from the rear. David was told that he identified himself with women and was attracted to men. In time he came to believe all the nonsense with which the analyst fed him. This must surely be a classic case of how easy it is to interpret any symptoms in Freudian terms – and how easy it is to be wildly wrong. Despite the fact that the brain disease from which he suffered becomes progressively worse unless operated upon, he was discharged from the psychiatric hospital with the diagnosis 'Conversion hysteria: condition – much improved'.

Another case was that of a little girl who was seven years old when she fell into the clutches of a psychoanalytically oriented psychiatrist. In the words of the girl's mother:

'And we told [the doctors] that we had had an episode – it was the only thing we could think of – about a year before, where a little boy in the neighbourhood had been pulling the girls' pants down, and all of a sudden they had this big kick on, and said, "This is it." They started, you know, thinking it was probably a sex problem . . .

'They brought out all three of us – my husband, Janet, and myself – into the room. And they sat there and they started talking about Janet taking her bath and playing with her brother. And all she did was sit there and cry, and I leaned over just to touch her with my hand and they told me to take my hand away. And they just kept on talking about what she knew about intercourse. And all she did was sob the whole time . . .

'And afterwards I got mad, and I said, "What right have you got to – you know – I'm her parent and I think I have the right to tell her about sex and the way I feel." They said I was a puritan and had puritan ideas on sex. All Janet did was sob. They sat there and accused her of playing with her brother in the bath-tub. I don't know what Janet told them when we weren't there. Janet added nothing to the conversation but tears.'

The psychiatrist believed that Janet was adopting a hysterical posture to gain attention: he kept her in a room on her own for a month, during which time she was made to do things for herself, though she was in such a state of agonizing muscular spasm that she could hardly drag her body across the floor to get the food that was brought to her at intervals. A third child, Susan, was treated in a similar way: the analyst laid the blame for her condition on the parents, and treated the girl with inhuman cruelty; the mother was almost driven to suicide by remorse and the marriage nearly broke up over arguments about whether or not to carry out the therapist's orders to stop helping their daughter in her agony and to make her do things for herself.

It is of course true that anyone with an arrogant faith in his own methods can produce suffering of this sort. Many surgeons have made the reverse mistake of operating on patients presenting hysterical symptoms. Nevertheless, some analysts seem peculiarly prone to this species of arrogance despite the fact – or perhaps because of it – that there is no reason to suppose that analysis is helpful. My own advice to anyone suffering from a mental illness would be to avoid analysts, but if you must seek an analyst, try to find one whom you find sympathetic: there is no evidence that being made to feel worse ever made anyone feel better.

13

Varieties of Analysis

Because of his historical importance and because the majority of analysts in practice today are basically Freudian, I have considered Freud at some length. This chapter portrays a few of his successors, and the sort of treatment to expect from members of the many different schools of psychoanalysis still flourishing. All analysts share the belief that neuroses are the outward expression of frustrated and unconscious urges and that neurotic patients can be helped by giving them insight into their unconscious mental life. Each of Freud's more significant successors emphasized a different set of unconscious wishes, and although this has resulted in a rather broader view of neurosis, many analysts practising today are just as dogmatic about the importance of the particular set of motives on which they have seized as was Freud himself in his insistence that sex was the root of all evil – and good.

The most renowned of Freud's associates was C. G. Jung, a Swiss Protestant who had in fact developed many of his own ideas before he met Freud. He was at first warmly welcomed into the Freudian fold if only, as Freud put it, to save psychoanalysis from 'the danger of becoming a Jewish national affair'. Freud broke with Jung in 1913, mainly because Jung rejected sexual frustration as the underlying cause of all neurosis and sexual drive as the motive force behind all human endeavour. Jung is reported, probably apocryphally, to have said: 'After all, the penis is only a phallic symbol.' In 1910, Freud had told him:

'Promise me never to abandon the sexual theory . . . We must make a dogma of it, an unshakable bulwark.' When Jung, in some surprise, asked why, Freud told him that it was a bulwark against 'the black tide of mud . . . of occultism'. Freud also said: 'I cannot risk my authority.' The development of psychoanalysis has perhaps been marked by more doctrinal schism and intolerance than that of any other movement in history, with the exception of the Christian religion. Freud, however, did not have the power to burn Jung at the stake, and contented himself with never letting his name cross his lips again.

Unlike Freud, Jung wrote badly and obscurely. Moreover, he made little attempt to build systematic theories but threw in new bits and pieces as he thought he developed new insights. His writings are marked by a strain of mysticism: he believed that dreams could foretell the future, and he claimed to have had many paranormal experiences himself. For example, when he had a heart attack, he dreamt that his doctor would die in his place and the doctor duly did so. He accepted other paranormal phenomena, such as clairvoyance and psychokinesis, attempted to prove the truth of astrology, and derived inspiration from the writings of alchemists and Gnostics, an early Christian heretical sect. He also believed in God.

Despite this mystical strain, Jung made some highly practical discoveries. He invented word association as a method of arriving at 'complexes': he found that if patients were asked to give associations to a list of words, the time taken increased if the word was emotionally laden for them. He even used this method to trap criminals, and was one of the first to experiment with measurements of changes in the electrical resistance of the skin for the same purpose. He can therefore be credited with the invention of the lie-detector. He was also the first to distinguish clearly between introversion and extroversion. The introvert has 'a hesitant, reflective, retiring nature that . . . shrinks from objects, [and] is always slightly on the defensive.' The extrovert on the other hand has 'an outgoing, candid and accommodating nature that adapts easily to a given situation, quickly forms attachments and will often venture forth with careless confidence into unknown situations'. Jung recognized that both propensities can exist in the same individual and that the same person may indeed oscillate, as I appear to have done, between introversion and extroversion.

Possibly influenced by his early work with schizophrenics, Jung believed that many persons inhabited the same body, indeed he fractionated the mind into many more components than Freud himself.

Every man was supposed to contain an 'anima' – the feminine inside of himself, and every woman an 'animus' (her masculine tendencies). Falling in love, according to Jung, results from projecting the anima (or animus) onto the beloved: anyone in love is in fact in love with a part of himself and is blind to the true qualities of the object of his love. Again, everyone carries around with him his 'shadow', the personification of everything that is evil within him, of which he will normally strive to remain unconscious. In an attempt to disown one's own shadow, it is projected onto others – preferably onto people unlike oneself – and this results in prejudice towards outgroups, for example racial prejudice. Everyone develops a 'persona', or mask, which is the image they exhibit in public as a result of the roles they play: if this differs markedly from the true self, much psychic energy can be used in maintaining it and neurosis can result.

One of Jung's more far-fetched ideas was the notion of 'archetypes'. He thought that many of our ideas and images were derived from 'the collective unconscious': we are born with them, and they do not come from experience. Jung developed this notion because he was much impressed by the similarities between some of his patients' dreams and the myths of other civilizations. For example, an uneducated patient asked him whether he could see the sun's penis, from which a great wind came, and Jung subsequently discovered that exactly the same image appears in the Mithraic religion, a cult emanating from the East and practised in the Roman empire. He thought that a child's images of its parents derived at least in part from archetypes – archetypes for example of the good and the bad mother as typified by the Virgin Mary and an evil witch. The animus, anima, and shadow were all, at least in part, archetypal, and derived from the collective unconscious of mankind. The archetypes could affect our conscious ways of thinking but they appear more directly in dreams, when they may give us good advice.

Jung believed that modern man had lost touch with his archetypes, which in previous civilizations were directly represented and accepted in the form of myths. To be healthy and to discover the true self, one has to get in touch with the unconscious elements of the self and in particular with the archetypes. Jung quotes with approval a letter from a patient describing how he came to his true self:

'Out of evil, much good has come to me. By keeping quiet, repressing nothing, remaining attentive and by accepting reality, unusual knowledge has come to me and unusual powers as well, such as I could never have imagined before. I always thought that when we accepted things they overpowered us in some way or other. This turns out not to be true at all . . . So now I intend to play the game of life, being receptive to whatever comes to me, good and bad, sun and shadow, for ever alternating and in this way also accepting my own nature with its positive and negative sides.'

The idea of accepting all sides of one's nature, discovering the true self, becoming an individual ('individuation' in Jung's terms) or a 'real person', reappears in more recent therapeutic movements, particularly in Gestalt and existential therapy. It has of course also appeared often enough in the past: Shakespeare wrote: 'This above all, to thine own self be true', though he may well have had his tongue in his cheek, since the advice is put in the mouth of a silly old buffer. I have recounted how I rejected the more emotional and more feminine sides of myself – my 'anima': had I been treated by a Jungian analyst, he would doubtless have seized on this aspect of my life.

Jung himself suffered a mental crisis in his thirties when he felt that life had no significance, and much of his subsequent thinking seems to be a search after a meaning for existence. Some of his latter-day followers have tried to strip his ideas of their mystical element, but when they are so stripped most of them appear rather banal and they fail to provide a reason for living. It is of course true that the majority of mankind have believed in some form of myth or religion, and that their lives may sometimes have been enriched thereby. Nevertheless, one cannot alter one's intellectual beliefs in order to obtain emotional gratification. No matter how much I would like to believe in an afterlife, I cannot accept it at an intellectual level – the alert Freudian will doubtless detect my death-wish at work again.

Anthony Storr, an analyst with a Jungian training, who practises in London, has pointed out that Jung's own beliefs about the development of the self can be seen as rather egocentric. For Jung, salvation lay in obtaining access to the parts of oneself rather than in satisfactory personal relationships: even love is devalued to the projection of one's own animus. Notwithstanding his mysticism and his egocentricity, however, he should be given credit for widening the scope of analysis and for certain insights, such as the development of the persona, that have influenced the thinking of many other psychotherapists.

Until recently, Jungian analysis was more popular in Britain than in the United States, but there are now training institutes in New York, Los Angeles and San Francisco. Although I have not followed this convention, it is usually referred to as 'analytical psychotherapy' rather than as 'psychoanalysis'. Jungians place less emphasis on the sexual origins of neurosis than do Freudians, and are usually more interested in bringing to light and resolving current conflicts than in tracing them back to events in early childhood. They believe that neurotic conflicts can be uncovered by paying close attention to dreams, in which the less conscious side of one's personality shows itself. Most modern Jungians are a good deal less mystical than Jung himself.

Adler's system is more eclectic than those of Freud or Jung and is correspondingly harder to describe. It is also nearer to common sense. A psychiatrist reproached Adler after a lecture by remarking: 'You're only talking common sense,' to which Adler replied: 'I wish more psychiatrists did.' He thought of people as being always engaged in the mastery of some task involving the pursuit of goals usually not far removed from consciousness. The neurotic had either picked the wrong goals, adopted poor means of achieving them or was in some way mis-perceiving reality, for example by seeing everyone as hostile to him. Adler is most popularly known for his concept of 'the inferiority complex'. In an effort to master social relations, people may come to wish to feel superior to others. In areas where they may have reason to feel inferior, they frequently overcompensate: the short man may compensate by chasing girls and boasting of his sexual exploits, the unintelligent by loudly despising intellectual activities, and so on.

Much Adlerian theory has a modern ring to it, and in some ways it resembles the most recently developed method – behaviour therapy. He saw the therapist's task as giving the patient insight into his own goals and his methods of achieving them – his 'life-style'. Insight alone, however, is not enough: the patient must learn with the therapist's help to change his goals where they are not sensible for him and to adopt better methods of reaching them based on a more realistic perception of the world. Adlerian therapy is more directive than either Freudian or Jungian. The therapist may set his patients tasks to carry out and may attempt to train them to behave more appropriately by, for example, showing more – or less – aggression in dealing with others. Adler thought it important to recognize one's own strengths and weaknesses in order to select goals that are suitable for the individual. He also stressed the importance of interpersonal relations and of seeing other people as they are. His ideas may not sound very exciting, perhaps because they are so near to our everyday modes of thinking, but it is no small achievement to have pursued a common-sense approach to the problems of the neurotic at a time when Freud and Jung were creating their spectacular theoretical edifices.

More directly in the Freudian tradition were his daughter, Anna Freud, and Melanie Klein, both of whom worked in London. They undertook the analysis of children as well as adults: since they thought they saw neurosis in very young children, they attached more importance to the pre-Oedipal stage than did Freud, that is, to events in the first two or three years of life. In America, Reik also thought this the most important period for the formation of the personality and attached great importance to the way in which the patient had been mothered. Neurosis could be induced both by negligent mothering and by a surfeit of mothering. In particular, Reik thought the 'Jocasta'-type mother a prime cause of neurosis: such mothers are characterized by having an unfulfilled love life with another adult, so that they direct all their love and concern to their child but will not allow the child to break away and become independent. The Reikian therapist attempts to uncover the complex of repressed material and emotions centred upon the mother.

Freud himself had taken an unflattering view of women: he regarded them as castrated men, and thought they all suffered from penis envy. Hence, as adults they look up to men and adopt a passive role faced with the possessors of this powerful organ. One of the first to challenge this view was not surprisingly a woman analyst, Karen Horney. She originally worked in Berlin but emigrated to the United States in 1932 and was so impressed by the cultural differences between Germany and America that she came to believe that neuroses were the product of society's expectations of the developing person. American society, starting with parental influences, expects boys to be aggressive and ambitious and girls to be meek and compliant. According to Horney, the neurotic adopts the ways of behaving expected by society instead of being able to respond flexibly as the occasion demands. The neurotic is unable to act spontaneously and there is a conflict between society's expectations and his true self.

Horney called attention to the aspiration of many American women to be the ideal wife and mother and to the anguish and loss of self-esteem resulting from failure at this difficult task. She also pointed out that the American ethos of success was bound to produce many neuroses, since it is in the very nature of success that not everyone can attain it; those who try and fail become a prey to envy of others and hatred of themselves. Neurotics resist having their false picture of themselves stripped away, and find it difficult to accept themselves as they really are, but only by so doing can they hope to actualize themselves. The therapeutic process therefore attempts to overcome this resistance, to persuade the patient to accept his real self and to develop the best aspects of it.

Hornevian therapy has become immensely popular in the United States: 23,000 applications for treatment were made to the Karen Horney clinic in 1972. The fees charged are graduated to the patient's ability to pay. Horney started two important and subsequently influential trends. She saw neurosis as being caused by society, and she believed in self-actualization, the discovery of the real self, which she thought always contained good elements capable of development. Her ideas contain the seed of the concept of alienation, which today has become a cant word in therapy.

It is likely that there are elements of truth in all these theories, but this does not mean that the proposed methods of treatment are effective. Many other analysts have propounded ideas that are delightfully barmy, and are worth describing for some light relief. Rank, for example, believed that all neurosis originates in the 'birth-trauma'. The pain of being born and the shock of leaving the comfort of the womb and being exposed to the cold realities of the outer world leaves the individual with a lasting unconscious desire to return to the womb. The cure consists of persuading the patient to relive this terrible experience with the help of the love and support of the therapist. The patient is encouraged to 'work through' his fear of asserting his own identity and separateness, a fear derived from the experience of birth. The resolution of the transference, when the patient is ready to function without the therapist's help, is equivalent to the resolution of the birth-trauma.

Apart from his narrow and somewhat implausible view of the origins of neuroses, Rank differed from Freud in emphasizing that the analyst can only help the patient if he provides him with love and empathy, and this aspect of Rank's treatment reappears in several more recent and now more popular varieties of dynamic therapy. Rank may also indirectly have influenced the originators of one of the currently fashionable and more zany therapies, that based on the primal scream. Invented by a Californian psychologist, Arthur Janov, this form of therapy has the attraction of extreme simplicity. He thought that from early infancy we all acquire a primal pool of pain, and that the only way to overcome the resulting tensions and anxieties is to summon up the pain and give vent to the primal scream. Primal therapists encourage their patients to stand around, usually in groups, screaming and shouting abuse of their parents.

Perhaps the analyst who in recent years has become the greatest cult figure is Wilhelm Reich. Born in 1897, he also parted company with Freud and was subsequently expelled in successive years from the Communist Party and the International Psychoanalytical Association. He emigrated to America in 1938, and by the time of his death in 1957 had become something of a folk hero. His ideas, especially in later life, were a curious combination of mysticism and pseudo-science. He believed that all neurosis arose from sexual repression – particularly from toilet-training, punishment for masturbation, and sanctions against sexual freedom in adolescence. He thought that from the age of fifteen onwards everyone should be encouraged to have sexual intercourse freely, and that marriage was an unnatural and undesirable institution. He claimed that sexual attraction could not last: he liked to be precise, and gave its natural term as four years. His desire for precision also led him to state that 'biologically speaking the healthy human organism calls for three to four thousand sexual acts in the course of a sexual life', a figure that will strike many as distinctly low in the present era of sexual potency.

Reich was one of the first to stress the importance of orgasm for women, and in consequence has earned the esteem of the women's liberation movement. Although the young admired him for his promulgation of sexual freedom, he was himself in many ways curiously Victorian. He refused to accept homosexuals as patients, saying: 'I will have nothing to do with such swine,' and according to his third wife he was happy to live up to his own standards of sexual freedom himself while forbidding her the same licence. He never left to go on a trip without making her promise fidelity, and was savagely jealous.

He thought all life was sustained by a form of vital energy which he termed 'bio-energy'. He repeatedly claimed that the presence of this energy could be detected under the microscope, with thermometers and with Geiger counters. The energy existed in packets called orgones, which were blue in colour, oscillated continuously and had size but no mass. In the healthy individual, the life force was discharged periodically in the form of an orgasm. In a proper orgasm, the individual became united with the cosmos, but unfortunately modern man was sick and few people were able to have proper orgasms: too often sex was an expression of anxiety rather than of true desire.

Reich is perhaps best known, or most notorious, for his invention of the orgone box, a device intended to accumulate orgones from the atmosphere and concentrate them on anyone lucky enough to be sitting in it. He claimed not only that bio-energy helped to cure neuroses but that patients who sat in his orgone box could also be cured of cancer and psychosomatic illnesses. The United States Food and Drug Administration placed an injunction on the distribution of orgone accumulators on the grounds that Reich's claims for their efficacy were fraudulent. He refused to obey the injunction, and in 1955 was sentenced to two years' imprisonment for contempt of court. In prison he was diagnosed as suffering from paranoia and was transferred to a psychiatric penitentiary, where he was declared sane. He died shortly thereafter of a heart attack. In America, some states also declared his books pornographic, and they were seized and burnt. His supposed martyrdom at the hands of the US government only served to increase the appeal of his teachings.

Reichian therapy was directed to enabling neurotics to have more satisfactory orgasms. He thought muscle tension an obstacle to the ideal orgasm, and attempted to reduce it both by direct manipulation of the patient's body and by forcing the patient to concentrate on his own facial expressions and to change them. By all accounts, he treated his patients harshly, and pointed out their neurotic defences and weaknesses in no uncertain terms: one of his own disciples referred to his 'cruel and penetrating technique' and thought that many of his patients were crushed by him. Reichian analysis is still practised both in Britain and in the United States; his followers all subscribe to the importance of the orgasm, but each tends to use his own method of helping patients to reach it.

The flavour of dottiness that surrounds Reich can be brought out by a personal experience of my own. In 1954, out of idle curiosity, I visited a community of Reich's disciples. They lived in a commune some time before this style of life became as fashionable with the young as it is today. The commune occupied several Nissen huts in a pine wood on the edge of a deserted airfield. Leaving my car outside a gate bearing the name 'Communitas', I walked through the trees towards the nearest hut. On the way, I stooped and picked up a pinecone. A window shot up and a voice bellowed: 'Put that down – it's mine.' Evidently, their ideas about sharing all property were not working out too well. Nevertheless, I was received with kindness and given a cup of tea.

The commune had been founded by eleven adults – five men and six women. They were vague about the number and the parentage of the children, but there appeared to be about thirty or forty running about naked and unkempt. Walking round the grounds, I was puzzled by the fact that one strip of runway had been carefully weeded and levelled – the other runways were long since disused, and were covered with weeds and cracks. The inhabitants, so they told me, had received a message from the master (Reich) that if they tended a strip of runway they might expect a visit from a flying saucer. I asked whether they were looking forward to this visitation and they replied: 'Of course – the flying saucer will contain Martians dressed in green, and they will bring with them a free issue of orgones, enough to last us for years.'

They also proudly showed me their orgone box, conveniently placed next to an excessively large double bed. It was made of layers of plywood, zinc, steel wool and other substances thought by Reich to accumulate orgones from the atmosphere. It was about five feet high and big enough to accommodate an adult sitting down on a chair. I regretfully declined their invitation to spend half an hour in the box, largely because in order for the experience to be efficacious one had to sit in the nude, and the temperature in the hut was little above freezing. I explained that my middle-class morality would prevent me from taking advantage of the accumulation of orgones with any of the assembled women who offered themselves, and honour was satisfied on all sides.

The group with whom I was talking (four women and a man) had told me that they had an exceptionally good library of the works of Reich and his disciples, and I expressed an interest in seeing it. They explained, rather shamefacedly, that although they had originally intended to share everything there had been a schism in the commune over a doctrinal point: the remaining four men and two women were in a separate building, so was the library, and the two groups were not on speaking terms. They pointed out the building, where I was again received with kindness and was given an opportunity to inspect the library. The second faction explained to me with sadness that they were excluded from the orgone box and described the suffering they were undergoing as a result. Since the first group had more academic inclinations than they, it would have been a better arrangement if they had occupied the hut with the orgone box while the others had had access to the library. I was reminded of W. S. Gilbert's tale of the two castaways who divided a desert island between them to their mutual disadvantage:

On Peter's portion oysters grew – a delicacy rare,
But oysters were a delicacy Peter couldn't bear.
On Somers' side was turtle, on the shingle lying thick,
Which Somers couldn't eat, because it always made him sick.

Dotty though Reich undoubtedly was, some of his ideas were in advance of his time, particularly the stress he laid on the female orgasm and his insistence on the quality rather than the quantity of orgasms. Nevertheless his therapy seems to have little to recommend it.

One of the most flourishing schools of analysis today is that of 'existential analysis'. It is a curious compound of the ideas of Freud and Jung and the existentialist philosphers such as Heidegger and Sartre. It was founded by a Swiss psychiatrist, Binswanger, in the late Fifties. His works do not make easy reading, as is illustrated by the following not atypical extract about a young girl called Lola who caught typhoid and subsequently developed various phobias including the fear that something terrible would befall her:

'It is self-evident and follows from the total mode of existence that, in the case of Lola Voss, her existence had deserted itself and had succumbed to an alien power in a much higher degree than in any of the earlier cases. It does not maintain itself any more in designing its own authentic potentialities, but is constantly sucked into the whirl of inauthentic possibilities of being, that is, such as have not been chosen by it but imposed upon it by a power alien to the self. In other words, it exists only as something "thrown", or in the state of "thrownness". But thrownness is still part of existence. Hence, the "alien power", although alien to the self, cannot be considered as alien to existence, as something outside or above it. Thrownness means, rather, the seduction and temporary reassurance, the alienation and entanglement of existence in general. It is, in our case, definitely distinguished from thrownness in the sense of constant addiction, an addiction to the everyday power of the "they", of being possessed by it.'

It is difficult to understand the ideas behind existentialist analysis, let alone to encapsulate them in a few words. Much stress is placed on man's freedom to choose and on trying to make the patient accept that he is responsible for his actions but is always free to act wisely. The person you are depends upon the choice of actions you make, and depending on your choices you are always in the course of becoming another person. Existentialist therapists emphasize the totality of experience of a person without trying to interpret it: they encourage patients to be open to their own experiences. Everyone is said to be 'thrown' – as in a die, certain aspects of their existence are determined for them by the circumstances of their birth and surroundings. It is everyone's task to find their 'authentic self', and much play is made with the concept of self-actualization: failure to live up to one's authentic self results in inescapable guilt and neurosis.

Most existential analysts believe that the therapist must never deceive his patient in any way: he must act towards him with genuineness, spontaneity and love. One may wonder how it is possible for an existentialist therapist to act with genuine love towards a patient he dislikes, but this conflict apparently rarely arises, since such therapists are fortunate in that they claim there is something lovable in all men – once you get to know them. The emphasis on the paramount importance of the quality of one's own experiences and on the doctrine of universal love has caught the spirit of some movements recently fashionable amongst the young, such as the flower people and the hippies. To someone in the throes of a severe breakdown, however, existentialist doctrines can be very threatening – particularly the emphasis on self-actualization and taking responsibility for one's own actions. Among others who have been influenced by existentialist ideas are Rollo May and Abraham Maslow in the United States and Peter Lomas in England.

In the above account of different schools of analytic therapy, I have of course omitted many important figures. I have said little about the neo-Freudians like Sullivan, Fromm or Erik Eriksen, who whilst adopting a basically Freudian position put more emphasis on interpersonal relations and slightly less on the dynamic processes occurring within the id. I hope, however, that I have said enough to give some idea of the diversity of the different approaches and of the flavour of each. Many of the practitioners of the different schools follow Freud in believing that nobody should write about a particular brand of analysis unless they have experienced it, but if this precept were followed rigorously it would make comparison difficult, since few have the time, money or fortitude to endure one let alone many versions of analysis.

It should be apparent that most schools of psychoanalysis offer not merely the promise of a cure for neurosis but a view of the nature of man. Each strives to interpret human existence in terms of its own, usually rather narrow, conception of the meaning of life. Moreover, analytical theories tend from Freud onwards to reflect the preoccupations of the middle classes who form the great majority of analysts' patients. All schools – except for those that are merely barmy and those that are so mystical as to be virtually unintelligible – may have captured aspects of the truth about man's condition, but no school begins to grapple with the true complexity of man. By fastening on one aspect of the human personality, each presents only a caricature, and none grapples with the richness of human existence. Indeed, it is likely that the reasons for breaking down are as multifarious as the goals that different people pursue, and it is curious that, with the possible exception of Adler, no analysts have recognized this possibility.

14

Analysts and Their Patients Today

Those with the leisure to do so have often puzzled over the meaning of existence: many find it difficult to live without subscribing to a cause, whether it be a religion, a patriotic campaign, or a more sectarian movement like women's liberation. For some members of the moneyed classes, particularly in America, psychoanalysis has itself come to provide a meaning for life: it is small wonder then that intensely mystical beliefs play a role in several kinds of analytic theory.

It is, however, one thing for those enjoying comparatively good mental health to seek analysis as a substitute for religion; it is an altogether different matter for the neurotic to enter analysis in the hope of finding a cure for his misery. A danger inherent in all forms of psychotherapy is that the therapist will consciously or unconsciously impose his view of life upon the patient. In view of their love of dogma, psychoanalysts are particularly guilty of bringing such pressures to bear. In choosing an analyst, it is therefore important for the patient to take into account the analyst's beliefs, yet few patients exercise the same care in selecting an analyst as the analyst does in choosing his patients.

If you happen to be religious, there is little point in seeking treatment from an analyst who thinks that belief in God is itself a neurotic symptom. According to Rogow, who conducted a careful survey, many American analysts think that analysis has failed if on termination the patient still believes in God. If you are a woman and a feminist, you will only be irritated by an orthodox Freudian analyst, since Freud ascribed a passive role to women. In the USA, the women's liberation movement is currently engaged in drawing up a list of 'feminist' psychotherapists recommended for their adherents. If you thirst for worldly success and worldly goods, you are unlikely to obtain anything but sorrow and guilt from an existentialist analyst who will attempt to focus your thoughts on your inner experiences. Yet most patients select an analyst almost at random, on the recommendation of a doctor or a friend, with no effort to discover whether his beliefs are compatible with their own.

Some who seek analysis are unclear about the distinction between psychoanalysis and psychiatry. Psychoanalysts of almost all persuasions subscribe to one rather narrow method of psychotherapy that relies for its success on making the patient acknowledge and accept his unconscious wishes. As we shall see later in the book, there are other kinds of psychotherapy – the attempt to help the mentally unwell by discussing their problems – than analysis, and a few analysts, particularly in the States, are becoming cognizant of other methods of treatment and use them where they feel it is appropriate.

Psychiatrists are medically qualified and specialize in the treatment of mental and emotional disorders. As part of their training, they learn how to administer physical methods of treatment, mainly drugs and electroconvulsive therapy. Nowadays, they also receive some training in the principles of psychotherapy. The extent to which they give psychotherapy themselves, the kind they use, and how much they know about it depends on the peculiarities of the hospitals at which they were trained and on their own predilections. In Britain all consultant psychiatrists are members of the Royal College of Psychiatrists, and in the United States virtually all reputable psychiatrists are members of the American Psychiatric Association. In many American states, however, a medically trained doctor may call himself a psychiatrist without having a sufficiently extensive training in the subject to merit recognition by the American Psychiatric Association.

It is small wonder that many members of the public are confused about the distinction between the two professions, since in practice there is considerable overlap. In the USA the main professional psychoanalytic body is the American Psychoanalytic Association, which insists that only medically qualified doctors are eligible for a trainee analysis and for membership. Freud himself did not regard a medical training as a prerequisite for practising psychoanalysis, and some of his own non-medically trained disciples like Rank were refused membership when they emigrated from Europe in the Thirties and Forties. There are, however, a number of other psychoanalytic organizations in North America which are not affiliated to the American Psychoanalytic Association, most of which do not require a medical qualification before granting recognition as an analyst.

The history of psychoanalysis in America repeats the series of schisms that occured in Europe during the early years of the movement. Rank was cast into the wilderness by the American Psychoanalytic Association; Alexander, Grinker and others in turn broke away from that body to found the American Academy of Psychoanalysis; Karen Horney founded her own institute, but her associates Sullivan and Fromm in due course broke away from her. There are in addition many smaller bodies not recognized by the American Psychoanalytic Association and based on the teaching of analysts who disagreed with Freud, like Adler, Jung, Reich and Reik.

Because of the insistence of the American Psychoanalytic Association that all its members should have a medical degree, many of the analysts in practice in the States are also psychiatrists. Contrariwise about one psychiatrist in ten is a trained analyst. Moreover, between about 1930 and 1960, Freudian analysts had a major influence on American psychiatry, and many American psychiatrists not themselves trained as analysts subscribe to psychoanalytic doctrines.

The situation in Britain is rather different. Few psychiatrists there have had a psychoanalytic training and many of those who have are largely engaged in private practice and do not hold positions as consultant psychiatrists attached to a hospital. Since the major psychoanalytic body in Britain has never made a medical qualification a prerequisite for membership, the majority of analysts in Britain are not medically trained, or where they are medically trained have no training in psychiatry.

Both in North America and in Britain, almost all reputable analysts have been trained at one or other of the psychoanalytic institutes. The most essential requirement is thought to be a training analysis in which the student himself passes an average of about six hundred hours undergoing analysis: he spends three sessions a week on the couch for over four years. The analysts who give such training analyses have reached the top of their profession, and their relationship with their trainees must be a curious one. On the one hand, the trainee is expected to reveal his innermost life, but on the other he is presumably striving to show that he is not too neurotic to become an analyst himself. As one training analyst put it:

'The training analysis is not a good analysis because the trainee is on probation, you know, he is being looked over . . . and he can't fulfil the role of the patient. But his second analysis, after he's been accepted and been working with patients who have pulled at something in him that gets disturbed, that analysis can be a good one. Then you can really learn a lot. I think that most of the good analysts have had repeated analyses, but I don't know how many. It's not talked about.'

In addition to undergoing a personal psychoanalysis, the would-be analyst also attends lectures mainly on the theory and practice of analysis, and he undertakes the analysis, under supervision, of a few patients. Psychoanalysis has been described as a treatment with undefined aims, which works by unknown means, and whose effectiveness is unproven: all are agreed that in order to practise it a prolonged and expensive training is necessary.

Nevertheless, not everyone who claims to be an analyst has been through this rigorous training. In Britain and in most American states, anyone can legally set up a brass plate outside his front door reading 'Mr S. Freud – Psychoanalyst'.

There are few studies of what makes people choose psychoanalysis as a career. Doubtless a desire to help the mentally distressed plays a role, though there are other ways of achieving this. Of the analysts known to me, many initially became interested in the subject because they were dissatisfied with themselves and clutched at analysis as a way of helping themselves whilst at the same time assuring a reasonable income. In America, a few analysts may make as much as $100,000 a year, and the cynical may think that this in itself is an adequate reason for adopting this career. In Britain, fees vary from about £5 to £12 for a fifty-minute session. In the United States there is considerable variation in the fees paid. Many analysts adjust their charges to the income of their patients and some, for instance in the Hornevian clinic, may treat poorer patients free. In a study conducted by Rogow, it emerged that psychoanalysts in general earn more than psychiatrists. Two out of thirty-three analysts investigated said they earned more than $60,000 a year, and thirty per cent earned more than $50,000: his study was conducted eight years ago, and earnings today would be considerably higher.

It is characteristic of analysts that they provide a therapeutic rationale for the fees they charge. Some claim that the high fee is not for their own benefit but for that of the patient. The willingness to pay high fees reflects a patient's commitment to the therapeutic relationship; it becomes a tangible token of the patient's trust in his analyst. Moreover, the higher the fee, the less likely a patient is to break an appointment knowing that he will have to pay whether he attends or not. A few analysts charge the full fee even when a patient gives advance notice that he is unable to attend a session with good cause, for example physical illness. The rationale is that analysis is unpleasant for the patient and he may unconsciously develop reasons for avoiding sessions, including minor illnesses, unless the fear of losing money is used as a deterrent. Finally, the more fees a patient has paid, the more he will feel he has to lose if he breaks off analysis prematurely. Analysts are almost certainly right in supposing that the higher the fee the more the patient will value the treatment; in general, the greater the sacrifice made in order to take part in some activity, the more it is valued. Nevertheless, one cannot help wondering whether analysts have probed their own motives sufficiently carefully when they assert that the high fees are entirely for the benefit of their patients.

I have described how both my analysts pressed me to continue analysis, and this is a recurrent theme. A budding analyst who was an acquaintance of mine was told bluntly on joining a practice of New York psychoanalysts that his career depended not on the patients whom he could initially attract, but on his ability to keep them in analysis. Analysts do of course have a genuine faith in their own treatment, and in applying persuasion to remain in treatment – they doubtless sincerely believe that they are acting in the patient's interest. The patients, however, often become extraordinarily dependent on their analysts, and are not in a position to take sensible decisions: one can debate the ethics of bringing pressure to bear on patients to do something that may or may not be for their own good, but will certainly benefit the analyst.

Freud himself was aware of the problem created by patients becoming addicted to analysis and making it a way of life; one of his papers is entitled 'Analysis terminable or interminable'. Some modern analysts, for example Balint and Malan in London, have introduced shortened forms of analysis and limit treatment to fifty or a hundred sessions. They focus on the attempt to remove only the patient's most upsetting symptoms.

Despite Freud's warning, there are some analysts who specialize in 'second analyses'. They would do well to bear in mind the words of a training analyst:

'Alexander's idea was that we should avoid fostering dependency by making appointments irregular, by cancelling occasionally, by giving the patient vacations so that he's on his own and sees what he can do. That way he experiments with life and then we know what successes and failures he has. Alexander thought that drawing out the length of an analysis was for the benefit of the analyst, not the patient. And Alexander was right. When anybody comes to me and says he's been in analysis for ten years, I'll wager anything he hasn't learned anything in [the last] five years.'

The practice of analysis is perhaps not as painless as it may seem to the patient who tends to view his analyst as being immune to ordinary human foibles. In the words of another training analyst:

'Okay, you want to be an analyst, you want to go through training even though it's a horrible experience, means you're going to have your childhood perpetuated for another seven or eight years, going to be treated with all the indignities, going to be brainwashed, made to conform. Okay. But for Christ's sake don't do full-time analysis, because when you get to be 45 years old and you've been sitting there day in and day out listening to this tuss of ten, twelve patients, you're going to be so bored to death you'd like to cut your throat. Also, you won't know anything else to do, you won't have any skills, you won't have done any research, you'll be a pretty goddamned dull tool.'

It is not known what if anything makes a good analyst: in the words of one report, successful analysts have 'psychologically accessible latent femininity and correlated passivity'. Studies have been undertaken of the characteristics of American analysts, and as a group they tend to be liberal in their politics: in Rogow's survey ninety-five per cent of analysts were found to have voted for the Democratic party in 1964, and six in ten claimed they would have no objection to their daughter marrying a Negro – a proportion much in excess of that found in the general population.

There are at present about two thousand members of the American Psychoanalytic Association, but it is estimated that there are over ten thousand practising analysts in the United States, since there are numerous breakaway movements. The corresponding institution in the United Kingdom, the British Psychoanalytic Society, has only about three hundred members, and there cannot be more than a few hundred practising analysts in Britain.

On both sides of the Atlantic almost all analysts treat mainly private patients. A full analysis is too expensive and too poorly validated for it to be generally accepted within the National Health Service in Great Britain or within state hospitals in the United States. Both in Britain and America, however, many psychiatrists and psychotherapists who are not fully-trained analysts make some use of psychoanalytic concepts. Analytically oriented therapists, sometimes with minimal qualifications, are to be found in many clinics on both sides of the Atlantic. At one British university, it is a standing joke amongst students that if you go to the Health Centre for treatment of a broken toe, the first question asked is whether your mother trod on it when you were a baby.

Now that other and more promising treatments are available, the heyday of psychoanalysis is almost certainly over: according to a report which appeared in 1967 in the newsletter of the American Academy of Psychoanalysis, 'fewer candidates are applying for psychoanalytic training than ever before and the quality of the applicants leaves much to be desired'.

Whether or not psychoanalysis has a future, it must be remembered that it could never provide the solution to the problem of mental illness, if only because of the expense and time that treatment takes. A single analyst can only treat between eight and twenty patients simultaneously. The opportunity to have psychoanalysis has always been one of the doubtful privileges of the leisured classes; the concentration on obtaining insights into the self sought in various ways according to the school to which the analyst belongs makes it a self-indulgent and elitist activity. It is not without significance that when Rogow sent out his questionnaire to analysts, only one in three claimed to interview members of the patient's family, and only one in a hundred ever saw friends or colleagues of the patient. One analyst commented:

'Sometimes there is a kind of paradox in that people, individually, are helped by analysis, but their families are less helped. I think this is because analysts pay so much attention to the individual patient they aren't aware of the acting-out the patient does in working through his conflicts. So the effect on the spouse and kids is kind of left out, and the analyst may not even hear about it.'

There will probably come a time when psychoanalysis is itself regarded as one of those curious aberrations of the mind to which man is periodically prone. Each age invents its own delusional systems.

15

Other Forms of Individual Psychotherapy

Analysis is only one form of psychotherapy: over the last thirty years or so, several other methods have been developed. In practice there is no clear-cut distinction between some forms of analytic therapy and other kinds of psychotherapy: there is a continuous gradation of types of therapy ranging from classical psychoanalysis to behaviour therapy. Some of the newer treatments have been developed by clinical psychologists, and it is important to be clear about the distinction between psychoanalysts and psychologists.

Clinical psychologists take a university degree in psychology and then follow a specialized postgraduate training in clinical psychology, in the course of which they attend classes and treat patients under supervision. Until recently, they took little part in therapy. Their role lay mainly in the development of 'objective' tests that were used in the assessment of patients. Some of these tests have proved their value, but others have been found to be worthless. For example, the famous Rorschach test, based on patients' associations to ink-blots, has no validity and no predictive power: it is, however, still used, particularly by analysts.

Since the early Fifties, clinical psychologists have become more involved in the administration of psychotherapy, a development resisted by medical doctors both in America and in Britain. In the USA the medical profession gave evidence against psychologists becoming recognized under state law, and in England many psychiatrists in hospitals refused to allow clinical psychologists to take any part in treatment: some still do. In North America, clinical psychologists, unlike analysts, are now certified or licensed in almost all states. In general, certification means that the psychologists so certified are recognized by the state as bona fide practitioners of psychology: others may still practise privately. Where a licence is required, no one can practise as a psychologist within that state without being licensed to do so. Psychologists do not need a licence to practise in Britain, but unless properly qualified they cannot obtain positions in hospitals, and since there is only a handful of clinical psychologists in private practice in Britain, this means that even there almost all practising clinical psychologists have received a formal training in the subject.

In Britain, the role of the clinical psychologist depends very much on the psychiatrist with whom he works. Where the psychiatrist has some faith in the usefulness of clinical psychology, psychologists will be consulted over all stages in the treatment of the patient and will themselves take an active part in such treatment. Otherwise the psychologist will play a subservient and frustrating role. Even in hospitals where clinical psychology is highly valued by most of the doctors, I have known psychologists express extreme frustration at the fact that the last word over any case is the psychiatrist's, and they may see months of hard work with a patient undone because he decides to adopt a procedure that they feel is ill-advised. The position in the hospital service is somewhat similar in North America, but there the medical profession in recent years has come to accept the importance of psychology: indeed some of the major psychiatric clinics are actually directed by a clinical psychologist who may even be responsible for appointing doctors – a situation not yet approached in Britain, where the medical profession has been slower to relinquish this kind of vested interest.

To understand the approach of the clinical psychologist, it is necessary to add something more about the nature of modern psychology. It is a vast subject, of which psychoanalytic theories are a tiny fragment. Budding clinical psychologists learn at university about the whole area of psychology, most of which is not directly concerned with the problem of mental health. Psychology itself can be divided into 'basic' and 'applied': the basic psychologist attempts to investigate and understand the workings of the mind and brain without necessarily considering how his findings may be applied for the benefit (or detriment) of mankind. The applied psychologist attempts to apply the findings of basic psychology to help (or to manipulate) people. The relationship between applied and basic psychology is not unlike that between engineering and physics.

Basic psychology has many branches – the broadest are experimental and social. The experimental psychologist studies topics like perception, learning, reasoning, and the use of language. He may try to solve such questions as how we are able to judge with reasonable accuracy the distance that objects are away from us: this may sound rather simple, but the problem of how we construct in our heads a representation of the real three-dimensional world from the two-dimensional patterns of light that impinge on our eyes turns out to be staggeringly complex. It can be studied in normal people (and indeed in animals), and advances in basic knowledge may help the applied psychologist working with people having visual disorders. The second major branch of pure psychology is social psychology, which embraces the relationships between people, as well as the development of human personality and human emotions.

The main fields of applied psychology are educational, industrial and clinical. The educational psychologist's primary concern is with remedial procedures for children who are academically or emotionally backward, though some educational psychologists attempt to develop and test new and, they hope, improved methods of teaching. The industrial psychologist applies the findings of experimental and social psychology to industrial problems: for example, he may use our knowledge of how vision works to design more easily-read dials for aircraft, or our knowledge of interpersonal relationships to improve managerial structures. The clinical psychologist may work with the mentally retarded or with neurological cases, or he may work with people who are mentally ill.

It is only clinical psychologists working with psychiatric patients who directly concern us here. They have a more broadly based knowledge of the human mind than do psychoanalysts, and in consequence are likely to be more eclectic in their approach and less ensnared by dogma, though there are unfortunate exceptions. Moreover, clinical psychologists are likely to be the only members of a team who have received training in the difficult problem of how to evaluate the efficacy of new methods of therapy, and this should be regarded as one of their most important functions. Their knowledge of the disappointing results of many objective studies of different types of psychotherapy should make them cautious about rash claims for new methods.

In addition to psychiatrists, psychoanalysts and clinical psychologists, two other professions administer psychotherapy – social workers and psychiatric nurses. In America, psychiatric social workers usually have a university degree, and have received some postgraduate training in social work. In Britain they more usually have a diploma in the subject obtained through technical colleges, though some are also trained at universities. The depth and value of the training of social workers varies widely and depends very much on the idiosyncrasies of the institute at which they were trained. Some may be given a psychoanalytic orientation, others may be trained in some of the other techniques of psychotherapy to be discussed in this and the following chapters. At progressive hospitals, nurses are becoming more and more involved in psychotherapy, and it is being given more emphasis in the training of psychiatric nurses. Many clergymen also give psychotherapy, with or without formal training. Finally, a large number of laymen with little or no training practise their own forms of psychotherapy on a gullible public, particularly in the USA.

Psychotherapy – talking with the patient – can have three rather different objectives. First, getting to know the patient and his preoccupations is a necessary preliminary to deciding what further methods of treatment to use; for example, what should be the detailed aims of therapy, or whether to treat the patient by physical methods such as drugs or ECT. Second, it can be purely supportive: the therapist, by listening sympathetically and by making encouraging noises, may try to alleviate the patient's current distress without attempting intervention to bring about a 'cure'. In the case of depressive illnesses such as my own, most patients recover with the passage of time, but it is important to do something to make their life more endurable in the meanwhile, and for suicidal patients such support may actually save life. Third, psychotherapy may be aimed at bringing about a remission of symptoms – a 'cure'.

It is not obvious how psychotherapy is supposed to effect such cures. Many non-analytic schools of therapy use rather vague terms and seek to foster 'personal growth' or (Gestalt therapy) 'wholeness' or 'integrity' of the self. It is true that many neurotics, including myself, in the course of their neuroses behave in very childish ways, but whether one becomes childish as a result of the neurosis or develops the neurosis because one is in some sense not grown-up is an open question. Other schools of thought regard neurosis as the result of underlying conflict between motives, and the therapy takes the form of trying to help the patient resolve his conflicts.

★   ★   ★

It is widely agreed that neurotics in general lack personal esteem and self-respect, and one of the few objective results in the whole field of psychotherapy is that recovery from a breakdown is associated with improvements in self-regard. Hence, most therapists will attempt to build up a patient's self-esteem, if only by showing that they are genuinely concerned for the patient and really 'care' about him.

This approach to therapy was carried to its extreme by Carl Rogers in the United States. In the late Forties he founded a new movement called 'non-directive' or 'client-centred' therapy, in which the therapist merely listens to the patient and reflects back at him what he says: the therapist expresses his concern but does not make interpretations, nor does he give any direct guidance. Rogers was one of the first clinical psychologists to break with the psychoanalytic tradition and develop his own therapeutic style. He also broke from the medical tradition and regarded neurosis not as an illness but as on a continuum with the difficulties that affect us all. For this reason he referred to those he treated not as 'patients' but as 'clients'.

Rogers's therapy has a complex theoretical superstructure, though many of his ideas appear to be derivative from such predecessors as Jung, Horney and Reik. He thought that the primary human drive was towards self-actualization: throughout life people have a need for deeper and more creative experience. Out of the need for richer experience, the growing person comes to develop the concept of himself as distinct from the outer world. He learns that his self-concept is enriched when others have a high regard for him, and hence the need to be liked develops out of the need for self-actualization. This drive for approval can distort the perception of the self: in order to please other people, someone may suppress aspects of himself unacceptable to others, and also strive to develop false qualities of which they approve. Neurosis arises because the neurotic distorts both his behaviour and his perception of his self in directions calculated to obtain others' esteem. He is hence prevented from actualizing his true self, and anxiety arises.

Rogers thought that successful therapy was based on three crucial factors, all of which concern the therapist's attitude to the patient. First, the therapist must accept the patient unconditionally as he really is by providing 'unconditional positive regard': in this way, the patient is helped to accept his true self. Next, the therapist must be completely genuine and honest in everything he says, in order to demonstrate to the patient that it is possible to accept one's true feelings. Finally, he must understand and empathize with the patient's feelings. Since the aim of the therapy is to make the patient accept and develop his true self, and since only he can know that self, the therapy is 'non-directive' and is centred on the client. The three qualities of the successful therapist have been summarized in the acronym 'CARE', standing for Communicated Authenticity (genuineness), Regard (warmth) and Empathy (understanding). Rogers believed that the actual therapeutic techniques used were of little consequence. All that mattered was for the therapist to display CARE. He even wrote that his own client-centred technique was 'by no means an essential condition of therapy'.

Rogers's views pose a number of problems. He is not very specific about what constitutes self-actualization, perhaps because different people will actualize themselves in different ways. He adopts a distinctly Panglossian view of human nature – everyone is good at heart if only they can discover it. Cultivation of the self can be regarded as an elitist and selfish doctrine. Most people do not have the leisure for self-actualization – they are too busy trying to earn enough to pay the rent. Finally, the therapy can presumably only be practised by those rare individuals who, like Rogers himself, can be totally accepting of others and who believe that at heart everyone is good.

As a clinical psychologist, Rogers set out to test the effectiveness of his treatment. He and his colleagues tried to measure the personality of therapists and to discover whether those rated as being warm, empathic and genuine did achieve more success than those not exhibiting these virtues. The results are only mildly encouraging. In a most carefully conducted study, it was found that schizophrenics treated by Rogerian therapy did no better than control patients receiving no treatment. Moreover, the patients treated by therapists rated high on CARE did no better than those treated by therapists with poor ratings on these qualities. Schizophrenia is of course particularly resistant to any form of psychotherapy, and results obtained with mildly neurotic patients and with delinquents are slightly more positive. A preponderance of these studies suggests that therapists exhibiting non-possessive warmth, genuineness and empathy do achieve slightly better results.

Perhaps the most dramatic demonstration to date that the effects of psychotherapy depend upon the characteristics of the individual therapist is a study carried out by a New York psychiatrist, David Ricks. He investigated the effects of treatment by two different therapists on twenty-eight boys attending a child guidance clinic. All patients were treated, most of them for schizophrenia, when they were aged about thirteen or fourteen. Fifteen were treated by a therapist whom the boys themselves had a very high regard for: they had in fact given him the name 'Supershrink'. The remainder were treated by a therapist whom Ricks refers to as therapist B.

Of those treated by Supershrink, only four were found to be suffering from schizophrenia in adulthood, whereas eleven of those treated by the other therapist received this diagnosis as adults. Ricks examined the protocols made by the therapists at the time of treatment, and concluded that although they were both psychoanalytically orientated, they differed in the following ways. Supershrink made fewer psychoanalytic interpretations of behaviour and concentrated more on giving the boys support: he encouraged them to be autonomous and to take responsibility for their own actions more than did therapist B. He also met the boys' parents more often and gave them more direct guidance. Therapist B allowed himself to be caught up more readily in his patients' depressions, and seems to some extent to have fostered depression by telling the boys how depressed they sounded. Supershrink also gave more practical advice on attending camps, obtaining jobs and so on than did therapist B. It would of course be unwise to place too much reliance on an isolated study of twenty-eight children, but the differences in therapeutic style and outcome are suggestive.

Unfortunately, it is often unclear whether the differences in therapists' effectiveness are caused by the good therapists making patients better or by the bad therapists making them worse. Truax, who has conducted a great number of such studies, comes to the alarming conclusion that: 'The implications for the [psychotherapist] are relatively straightforward. First, the odds are two out of three that he is spending his energy, commitment, and care for mankind wastefully; he is either ineffective or harmful. Two out of three of his colleagues, he can be quite certain, are ineffective or harmful.'

Many of the studies undertaken on the importance of CARE are open to a further objection. Extracts from tape-recordings of the transactions between therapist and patient are played to independent observers, and therapists are rated on how far they display CARE. Since therapists are likely to display more warmth, empathy and genuineness to patients who show signs of responding to treatment, it is sometimes difficult to be sure whether recovery was promoted by CARE or whether CARE was induced in the therapist by signs of recovery. Despite these objections, and despite many discrepant findings, it seems likely that therapists showing CARE do more good – or less harm – than therapists not showing

CARE. There is a moral: no patient should continue in treatment with a therapist whom he dislikes or who appears to dislike him.

Since non-directive therapists do little in the way of interpretation, it is possible to simulate with a computer program, albeit in rather a crude fashion, the way in which they talk. Such a program was written at the Massachusetts Institute of Technology. On one occasion, it was left loaded on the computer in error and a computer salesman wishing to use the computer from a remote terminal found himself conversing with this program through a teletype without knowing what had happened. He wanted to demonstrate the computer's performance to potential customers. The following dialogue ensued.

Salesman: Do you think I can use the computer this morning?
Computer: Why do you ask?
Salesman: I might be able to make some additional telecomp sales.
Computer: Why aren't you sure?
Salesman: My prospective customers have never seen a demonstration of the system.
Computer: Does this mean very much to you?
Salesman: Of course it does.
Computer: You seem very positive about that.
Salesman: This is ridiculous.
Computer: What do you mean this is ridiculous?
Salesman: Is there any reason why I can't use the computer now?
Computer: Tell me more about your prospective customers.
Salesman: Please dial me up on 491-1850.

The program was of course considerably more obtuse than most non-directive therapists, but it does catch the flavour of such therapy.

A second major school of psychotherapy is known as 'Gestalt therapy'. As a recent verse has it:

> 'That brings us round to Frederick Perls
> Whose penchant for pinching the bottoms of girls
> Made lechery a therapeutic style . . .
> When has there ever before been a doctor
> Who charged his patient while he foctor?'

Perls, the founder of Gestalt therapy, took a medical degree and then trained as a psychoanalyst in Germany and Austria, where he subsequently worked with brain-injured soldiers. He emigrated to South

Africa, where he served as a psychiatrist in the British Army, and in 1946 moved to the United States to work in private practice. There are now many Institutes of Gestalt Therapy up and down North America.

Gestalt therapy has nothing to do with the movement in experimental psychology known as 'Gestalt psychology'. This school flourished in Germany and subsequently in the United States in the first half of this century, and was concerned primarily with perception. The Gestalt psychologists emphasized that perceptual experiences are 'wholes' – they are more than the sum of their parts. The way in which we see something falling on a given part of the eye is determined by everything else impinging on the eye at the same time. For example, a brightly-lit piece of coal may send the same amount of light to the eye as a piece of white paper in poor light, yet we continue to see one as black and the other as white, provided surrounding objects in the visual field give us clues to the lighting conditions.

Perls transposed some of the ideas of Gestalt psychology into the field of psychotherapy. His theorizing, is, however, so vague as to be worthless, and one has the feeling that his use of Gestalt terminology as applied to human personality and emotions is a gimmick. He believed that neurosis arises because the personality is fragmented and is no longer an integrated Gestalt. The healthy person can form good Gestalten – he can organize his experiences in meaningful ways. When someone is reading they are conscious only of the meaning of the text: it becomes a good figure against a background of other sensations of which the reader is only dimly aware. Neurotics are unable to organize their experience meaningfully into figure and ground in this way, and have become unaware of large areas of their experience. Perls placed great emphasis on being aware of one's environment – both the appearance of objects in the world and the feelings of others. Gestalt therapists also attempt to train patients to become aware of their own feelings and bodily sensations. Great stress is laid on the 'here and now', on concentrating on what is happening within and around one at the present point in time: neither the past nor the future exist, only the present.

Perls was suspicious of verbal expressions, and like Reich tried to make the patient aware not just of what he was saying but of the tone of voice used, the expressive movements of his body, the presence of bodily tensions and so on. He thought there were five layers within the neurotic personality. The outward layer consists of 'game-playing' – the neurotic plays games or roles, and attempts to live up to a false conception of himself. If this layer is stripped off, the 'phobic' layer is revealed, in which the patient is afraid of his true self, concerned about his failures and governed by moral imperatives ('shoulds' and 'should-nots'). Beyond this is the 'impasse' in which the patient feels empty and without meaning in his life. Next comes the 'implosive' layer in which the neurotic turns his thoughts inwards: he uses his psychic energy to examine himself instead of interacting with the world. The final layer, which when uncovered signifies a return to health, is the 'explosive'. The patient reassesses his own feelings and can express himself openly and spontaneously whilst interacting fully with the world around him.

The silliness of Perls' theorizing, much of it apparently based on unconscious verbal puns, can best be illustrated by a quotation:

'What is the opposite of existence? The immediate answer would be nonexistence, but this is incorrect. The opposite would be anti-existence, just as the opposite of matter is antimatter. As you know, scientists have managed to create matter out of energy. What has this to do with us in psychology? . . . There are no 'things'. *Nothingness* in the Eastern languages is *no-thingness*. We in the West think of nothingness as a void, an emptiness, a nonexistence. In Eastern philosophy and modern physical science, nothingness – no-thingness – is a form of process, ever moving.'

It will be apparent that there is little new in Perls's thought – he borrowed ideas from Freud, Reich, Sullivan, the existential psychologists and many others, and then applied the window-dressing of a terminology partly invented by himself and partly borrowed from the Gestalt psychologists.

Perls himself was a bombastic bully, though he was capable of a facile charm when occasion demanded: he used his position as a psychotherapist to have sexual intercourse with those of his women patients whom he fancied 'in the here and now' – *viz.* his consulting room. In this way he doubtless tried to assist his women patients to strip themselves down to the explosive layer. A minority of his followers appear to have inherited these traits – a tendency to bully and exploit patients for their own ends. Gestalt therapy is often very aggressive: the therapist challenges everything the patient says in an attempt to make him concentrate on the present and dig down to his true feelings. He tries to strip away the patient's defences and to prevent him acting passively. He may forbid him to use the word 'it' and other detached verbal expressions, and will constantly accuse him of playing games in order to hide his true self. An outbreak of anger or tears from the patient is taken as a sign that he is beginning to recover his feelings.

Although Perls and his followers were vague in their theorizing, they did invent a number of specific tricks to help the patient develop fuller awareness. The patient may be told to talk to a pain in his own body, act out parts of his dreams, pretend to be an inanimate object or address an empty chair while imagining his father or some other important figure in his life sitting in it. I shall instance further gimmicks of this sort when I describe the encounter group movement, in which Gestalt therapy has been highly influential.

With its emphasis on immediate awareness, the importance of the here and now, and the person's own responsibility for his actions, Gestalt therapy forms part of the humanistic movement in psychotherapy. No effort has been made to test its efficacy: the emphasis on subjective experience as the measure of all things has made its practitioners reluctant to submit their techniques to objective testing. The aggressive nature of much Gestalt therapy and its emphasis on self-actualization can make it very threatening to anyone at all seriously depressed or anxious. At such times it is particularly difficult to live up to someone else's idea of what you should be like.

Indeed at one point in my own depression I attempted some of the exercises recommended by Gestalt therapists. I tried to 'make up sentences about what [I was] immediately aware of, beginning them with "now" or "at this moment" or "here and now",' but I continued to be depressingly aware only of my own jealous obsessions. I tried thinking of 'pairs of opposites' and reversing the roles of everyday objects; I tried 'paying attention to some visual object' and 'noticing how it clarifies itself by dimming out the space and objects about it', and attending to my own bodily feelings – itches, aches and tensions. I was, however, unable to see the world in a new way or to feel empathy with inanimate objects like stones and tables; in my depressed condition I thought to myself that my failure signified that I was an even more hopeless human being than I had imagined. I recalled that I had always had poor powers of visual recognition, particularly for people. Indeed, I once followed a singularly attractive girl in the street only to discover on overtaking her that she was my wife, a discovery that induced a strange mixture of pleasure and disappointment. The result of my brief brush with Gestalt methods merely made me feel more inadequate than ever.

At present, Rogerian and Gestalt therapies are perhaps the two most widely practised forms of non-analytic psychotherapy. There are innumerable others. 'Transactional analysis', espoused and popularized by Berne, tries to make patients understand that most of what they and others say should not be taken literally: the content of many conversational interchanges reflects attempts to impress, please, dominate, or otherwise manipulate others. Moreno invented 'Psycho-drama', in which patients act out roles in an effort to make them understand better their own motives and the position of others. 'Hypno-therapy' is also still practised: under hypnosis, suggestions are made in an attempt to improve the way the patient feels and behaves or his underlying motives are probed. In addition, there are various forms of group therapy, and there is much therapy that is either wild enough to be reported for its amusement value or so bogus that it should be recorded as a warning to the public. The next two chapters will be devoted to these topics. It will have been noticed that there is much overlap in the ideas of the different schools of analysis and other forms of psychotherapy, and indeed there are many practising therapists who draw their techniques and views from a wide variety of movements.

16

Group Therapy

Group therapy appears to have been first used in Britain in the Thirties. It arose in part out of the idea of a therapeutic community – a milieu in which the patient could learn how to interact with others. It is now practised by therapists of almost all theoretical persuasions, with the exception of orthodox Freudians, for whom it is not a suitable method because of their emphasis on uncovering the history of the individual. The optimal number of patients in a group is usually thought to be about eight. Many therapists believe there should be two therapists present: apart from giving two points of view, they can observe and interpret one another's behaviour in the context of the dynamics of the group.

One obvious advantage of group therapy is that it saves the therapist's time, but a plausible rationale has been developed for supposing that at least for some patients it may be a better method of treatment than individual therapy. Irvin Yalom of Stanford University, one of its leading exponents, lists ten advantages of group over individual therapy, of which the most important are as follows.

Most neurotics are pessimistic about their future: only if they can be given hope will they start to strive themselves towards recovery. By including within the same group patients at different stages of recovery, those who are most seriously ill may see from the example of others that recovery is possible. Members who are getting better often describe the course of their recovery to new members. This can be much more reassuring than being told by a therapist that you will recover, when there is a tendency to think: 'He's only trying to reassure me as part of his job: he doesn't really believe I will get better.' The success of Alcoholics Anonymous may in some measure be due to this factor.

Many neurotics feel that their wretchedness is unique: they become isolated and lonely and then compound the problem by blaming themselves for their own sorry state. Once in a group, they can see that they are not that out of the ordinary. They can also share their miseries more readily with others equally unhappy, since they do not run the risk of being looked down upon. It will be recalled that patients in the hospital I attended feared to confide their problems to their own friends. Yalom points out that many normals, as well as neurotics, harbour secrets that they feel would make them despised if others knew them. As an experiment he requested members of groups of normal people (so-called 'T-groups') to write down their most guilty secret on a piece of paper, and he then read out the secrets without revealing whose secret was which. He was struck by how commonly the same kinds of guilty secrets were produced – feelings of inadequacy, worries about being unable truly to love anyone or to feel deeply, and shame about deviant sexual longings or actual sexual practices. Any therapist knows that everyone has committed cruel or dishonest acts of which he is ashamed, but the demonstration from other patients that we are all guilty of the same sins must be a much more effective way of relieving guilt than any reassurance from a therapist.

In a successful group, patients may help one another both by sympathy and by interpreting one another's behaviour. Feelings of uselessness and worthlessness predominate in most neurotics: if a patient can help others it may go some way to restoring his own self-esteem.

Most neurotics have poor relationships with other people. They may lack social skills, not understand how others see their behaviour and misinterpret the behaviour of others towards them. In the course of group therapy, they may learn from others that they avoid looking at the person to whom they are talking, or that they are bores, or overbearing. Yalom instances a patient who in conversation went into endless minute and often irrelevant detail in everything he said: until the group pointed this out, he had been unable to understand why people shunned his company.

Within the safety of a group, the patient may also be able to experiment with new ways of responding that he would never try out on his own friends. Most people, particularly neurotics, are often afraid to show their true feelings for fear of making fools of themselves. If a patient can give expression to his feelings before the group and finds that he is still accepted, the experience can be both cathartic and liberating. Yalom has referred to this as 'the corrective emotional experience'. He asked patients who had recovered if they could recall an incident in group therapy which for them formed a turning point. Two kinds of incidents were commonly mentioned. In the first, the patient had expressed anger or had condemned something said by another patient; he had been surprised that his forthrightness, instead of provoking a catastrophe, had been calmly accepted. He had learned either that his expression of anger was irrational and inappropriate or that his previous avoidance of saying anything that might give offence was irrational. Secondly, some patients recalled incidents in which they had openly expressed liking for other members of the group and were surprised to find that they were not derided or rejected.

In summary then, the group makes possible the open display of previously secret thoughts or feelings: if these are accepted, the experience is often beneficial. It is also possible to learn how others see one. Most people have some objectionable habits, but the neurotic may think that everything he does is objectionable: within the group he may learn that only some of his behaviour is objectionable, and be able to concentrate on his good points while modifying the behaviour to which others object. Ideally, he will develop a realistic respect for his own virtues and be able to carry over his new ways of behaving into situations outside the group.

On the basis of interviews with recovered patients, Yalom constructed a list of sixty factors that could be found helpful in group therapy. He then asked recovered patients to place these factors in order of importance in so far as they affected their own recovery. The ten most important were:

Discovering and accepting previously unknown or unacceptable parts of myself.

Being able to say what was bothering me instead of holding it in.

Other members honestly telling me what they think of me.

Learning how to express my feelings.

The group's teaching me about the type of impression I make on others.

Expressing negative and/or positive feelings towards another member.

Learning that I must take ultimate responsibility for the way I live my life no matter how much guidance and support I get from others.

Learning how I come across to others.

Seeing that others could reveal embarrassing things and take other risks and benefit from it helped me to do the same.

Feeling more trustful of groups and of other people.

It is clear that a convincing case can be made for the *potential* benefits of group therapy: the question remains of how often these benefits are realized in practice. Some groups may function along the ideal lines indicated by Yalom, with members being supportive towards one another whilst at the same time accurately appraising each other's good and bad points. In many other groups, however, the members may remain hostile towards each other: they may use the group as an opportunity to dominate or to act out their own aggression, and far from supporting one another's weaknesses they may actively deride each other. If the group has a potential for doing good, it has an equal potential for doing harm. Much presumably depends on luck – on the detailed composition of the group – and on the therapist's own skill in creating a cohesive and supportive atmosphere. Yalom found that patients popular with the group in the sixth week of therapy had a better prognosis than unpopular patients: group therapy may help you if you are likeable, but could be damaging if you are not.

The reader will recall that the group meetings I attended in hospital bore little resemblance to the ideal depicted by Yalom. There has in fact been no good research comparing the efficacy of group therapy to individual therapy or even to no therapy at all. It is probably not a suitable method of treatment for those who are desperately ill – when I first entered hospital I was unable to sit through group sessions, since I could not control my anxiety.

The basic techniques of group therapy are of course now widely used with people who would not be classified as neurotic. In the early Sixties, the method was taken up by industry and was known as the 'T-group'. Executives and salesmen attended T-groups in order to learn how to improve their skills in dealing with others: the theory was that they would learn how others saw them, modify their bad habits and also become more sensitive to others' feelings and hence be more effective in their jobs. When a businessman returns from such a group, he is sometimes at first rated as more effective by his colleagues, but any beneficial effects seem to dissipate rapidly, and no effects are measurable after six months or a year. Nobody has attempted to assess whether T-groups produce more or less short-term benefits than other changes in routine like a skiing holiday, a weekend in the country or an ocean cruise. About as many who attend T-groups are harmed by them as are helped: the biggest organization conducting such groups is the National Training Laboratory, whose headquarters are in Washington, and they report one per cent of their clients suffer 'serious stress and mental disturbance' as a result of attending T-groups. Many more suffer less serious emotional upset.

More recently, encounter groups have become enormously fashionable: it is estimated that in the United States one adult in three has participated in this craze. There are now a great variety of such groups, and people have diverse motivations for attending. They may wish to explore themselves, to improve the ways in which they relate to others, to experiment with methods of behaving that they do not normally use, to make friends, to feel part of a group, to use the group as a chance to take out their aggression on people whom they will not see again, to obtain a sexual kick, find a marriage partner or satisfy their curiosity about what happens in such groups.

The founders of the encounter movement were Perls, Rogers, and another clinical psychologist called Schutz, and its Mecca is Esalen, at Big Sur, California. Although all kinds of encounter groups exist, the movement as a whole is dominated by the ideas of Perls. Great emphasis is placed on the expression of the emotions, however transient or trivial; on becoming aware of one's own and others' true selves – often achieved by aggressively telling other members of the group what one thinks of them, whether it be good or ill; and on the value of opening oneself up to immediate experience and feelings. Participants are taught by the leaders to ignore the verbal content of each other's remarks and to concentrate only on the feelings behind them. Intellectual remarks or the expression of opinion as against the expression of feeling are anathema to most leaders of encounter groups, and are regarded as a defence against one's true feelings – 'mind-fucking', in the schoolboy language adopted by Perls and many other leaders. According to Perls, 'a good therapist does not listen to the bullshit the patient produces, but to the sound, to the music, to the hesitations'.

Numerous techniques have been developed to persuade the members of encounter groups to wean themselves from mere verbalization and to act out their emotions. Schutz starts the proceedings off by asking members to say whom they like and dislike and why. Members may be asked to spread themselves out on the floor and try to experience sensations suggested by the leader; they may be instructed to feel one another's bodies, concentrating on the nature of the sensations obtained. They are encouraged to confront one another – at first perhaps just by standing in pairs staring into one another's eyes, later by such techniques as occupying the 'hot seat' or 'making the rounds'. A patient in the 'hot seat' is told by each of the other members in turn exactly what they think of him. The reciprocal process is making the rounds: when a member has made a remark about the group as a whole, he may be asked to make it individually to each member of the group in turn, showing in what way it is applicable to each. Another method is the 'stay-with-it' technique. A member who expresses some unpleasant feeling, for example disgust at the sight of someone else's body, may be asked to stay with the feeling – to preserve the disgust as long as he can and to talk about it: by so doing he is supposed to assimilate his unpleasant feelings and learn that they are part of himself, instead of running away from them.

In some encounter groups, nudity is *de rigueur*, and the participants are ordered to hug one another. Some use drugs to heighten sensory awareness of the here and now, others encourage group sex. One Gestalt encounter group devoted to 'marriage enrichment' at a respected Canadian university has become a simple vehicle for wife-swapping. Many encounter groups are not counted as successful until all the members have at one time or another been reduced to tears, others involve physical punch-ups. The American Psychiatric Association's Task Force on Encounter Groups found evidence of many instances of physical injuries. Marathon encounter groups lasting for forty-eight hours rely on sheer fatigue to break down normal methods of reacting, feeling and sensing.

Most encounter groups do not claim to offer psychotherapy. Although they are not primarily intended for the mentally ill, many disturbed individuals do attend: if you are neurotic and have been brainwashed by current psychotherapeutic fads into believing that neurosis results from the inability to express your feelings and to relate intimately to others, encounter groups may seem a quick and easy solution to your problems. They can, however, be disastrous for the mentally disturbed. Not everyone reacts well to being told exactly what others think of him. Many encounter groups are led by charlatans with no training in psychotherapy: they may be in the business for financial gain, as a means to express their own aggression, to exploit group members sexually, or because their own existence is emotionally shallow and they need the synthetic emotional highs provided by the encounter game.

Bruce Maliver, a clinical psychologist with wide experience of the encounter movement, wrote an excellent book on the subject. He says: 'To my knowledge, not one of the current encounter game stars holds a certificate from a program specializing in conventional psychotherapy.' He also states that at least one well-known leader, Martin Shepard, was expelled from a training programme in psychotherapy for sleeping with a patient. The American Group Psychotherapy Association has concluded: 'If encounter were a drug, it would clearly be banned from the market.' If a comparatively reputable organization like the National Training Laboratory itself admits to producing psychotic reactions in one per cent of its clients, it can well be imagined what the risk of psychosis or breakdown is in participants in groups run by less skilled leaders openly encouraging aggression between members. Many suicides are on record directly produced by attendance at encounter groups. Whether or not they were caused by the methods used, there have been at least three at Esalen.

Moreover, the available evidence suggests that even the mentally robust gain little or nothing from encounter groups. The most careful study to date was undertaken at Stanford University. In evaluating the results, it should be remembered that there were observers present at all sessions: hence, the leaders were likely to be on their best behaviour. The investigators compared changes in students who attended groups with changes in students who did not over the same period of time. They estimated that about ten per cent of students attending suffered serious psychological damage as a direct result: the proportion was higher in those groups run on the highly aggressive lines favoured by Perls. When interviewed immediately after participation, three quarters of those attending thought they had been helped by the experience, but six months later only about a third thought they had been helped. Moreover, as seen by their friends, fewer changes for the better and more changes for the worse were noted in students who had attended encounter groups than in control students who had not attended.

In summary, attending encounter groups can harm you: they may make you feel better for a short time, but they are likely to make you more obnoxious to your friends.

The encounter movement emphasizes the value of experiencing strong and unusual sensations and emotions, and attempts to manufacture them by synthetic means in situations where they may be totally inappropriate to their context. As Braginsky and Braginsky write:

'By providing, as Koch notes, a convenient psychic whorehouse for the purchase of a gamut of well advertised existential "goodies", authenticity, freedom, wholeness, flexibility, community, love, joy, encounter groups simply distort and coarsen our sensibilities. Manipulative gimmicks, a simplistic lexicon and psychic striptease replace the intelligent, sensitive struggle of man attempting to come to terms with himself, with others and with the world.'

Encounter groups can be seen as a way of purveying the group emotions experienced in other countries and other times through fertility rites, military rallies, wakes, public hangings and religious ceremonies. They differ in that they serve no extraneous aim other than the whipping up of emotion, and the emotions are directed from one member to another rather than focused on some external purpose. It may or may not be true that in the Western world most people give too little expression to their feelings, and that they lack the opportunity that intimate friendship provides for unburdening their souls. There is in fact little evidence in literature that men in other ages felt the need to discuss their innermost thoughts with those around them, though several religions, like Catholicism, have a place for institutionalized confession.

The atmosphere of many encounter groups appears to resemble the hysteria of some of the revivalist sects that flourished in America in the Twenties and Thirties. At their best they provide a harmless source of diversion for many, at their worst they produce suicide, psychoses, and divorce. Moreover, they encourage authoritarian and intolerant attitudes in that in the hysteria of the moment the leader and most members are unwilling to tolerate the opinions and wishes of the minority who do not subscribe to the same set of beliefs: members not prepared to enter into the spirit of the group are often treated with derision and spite. Baring one's soul to strangers or taking part in group sex are fine for some, but this does not excuse the bullying of members reluctant to participate in such activities.

Encounter groups foster a synthetic and artificial approach to human relationships, the cultivation of which outside the context of a group with common aims and interests seems a desperate and pointless undertaking. Moreover, the intimacy generated within groups is likely to be shallow and irresponsible compared with normal friendships evolved through close and continued association with those with whom we live, work or spend our leisure hours. Finally, the encounter movement underestimates the intellectual and creative side of man. It may be that some people can feel fulfilled merely by giving vent to the expression of the self, but many undoubtedly need to follow goals outside themselves, and the apostles of encounter offer no such goals.

17

The Wilder Shores of Therapy

Along with the growth of the encounter movement, there have recently appeared several zany forms of individual psychotherapy. I have already mentioned 'primal therapy', where the cure consists of screaming away your pain in a group. Bioenergetics, invented by a psychoanalyst called Alexander Lowen, carries some of Reich's ideas to their logical conclusion. In order to observe and correct muscular tension and bad posture, he often treats his patients in the nude. He believes that most patients both desire and fear bodily contact, and to remove this conflict the therapist touches, massages, and cuddles the patient. There are now many other practitioners of bioenergetics, which is sometimes known as 'cheap thrills therapy': sessions may culminate in sexual intercourse or other forms of sexual exchange between patient and therapist.

Yet another technique is known by the acronym ASCID – Altered State of Consciousness Induction Device. This invention is supposedly copied from a swing used by medieval witches. The patient is strapped in and rocked around with the intention of producing 'deep trips' and visions. Perhaps, however, the prize for the most bizarre form of psychotherapy yet invented should go to Bindrim. The inventor of nude marathon groups, he has more recently devised a form of therapy known as 'crotch-eyeballing'. He notes that the crotch is the central locus of three kinds of hang-up – difficulties in toilet training, guilt about masturbation, and adult sexual problems. His method of overcoming these problems is to have two naked patients spread-eagle a third on the floor with his or her knees up and legs held wide open: the remainder of the group gather round and stare long and hard at the 'offending target organ'.

It is sad to think that the encounter movement and many of its zany offshoots were in fact fostered by a school known as 'humanistic psychology', whose avowed aims were to restore the dignity of man, which, it was alleged, had been attacked by the deterministic approach of scientific psychology on the one hand and of psychoanalysis on the other. The founder of humanistic psychology was Abraham Maslow, who in 1967 tried to dignify his ideas by setting them out in twenty-eight propositions which combine pomposity, silliness and vagueness in about equal proportions. Some extracts follow:

'Proposition I. Self-actualizing individuals (more matured, more fully human), already suitably gratified in their basic needs, are now motivated in . . . higher ways, to be called "metamotivations".

'Proposition II. All such people are devoted to some task, call, vocation, beloved work.

'Proposition V. At this level the dichotomizing of work and play is transcended.

'Proposition X. Less evolved persons seem to use their work . . . as a means to an end.

'Proposition XII. These intrinsic values are instinctoid in nature . . . The illnesses resulting from deprivation of intrinsic values (metaneeds) we may call metapathologies.'

As Braginsky and Braginsky point out, few people can aspire to meta-motivation: 'The assembly line worker who is bored with his job (not "devoted to beloved work"), who looks forward to weekends when he can go fishing (he 'dichotomizes work and play") who, nonetheless, works as much overtime as he can in order to earn enough money to send his oldest daughter to college (he "works as a means to an end") is suffering from "metapathology" and is presumably a "less evolved person" ' than someone who devotes himself to the 'beloved task' of writing bunkum.

Although the encounter movement has attracted an undue proportion of quacks and charlatans, it should not be supposed that among the various forms of psychotherapy it has a monopoly of them. In 1972 the New York State Attorney brought an action against Albert and Maya Wood, the proprietors of the Long Island Institute for Emotional Disorders. The action was successful and the Institute was closed down.

During the case, the history of the Institute emerged. Albert Wood had been a plastics salesman, and subsequently sold books on psychology and psychiatry for a New York publisher. He was caught thieving from his employers and was sacked. He then decided to become a psychotherapist, and accordingly listed himself in the telephone book as 'Albert D. Wood, Ph.D., Psychological Counselling'; at first he used a room in his house as a consulting room. Having no Ph.D., his only qualifications for psychological counselling were an introductory course on psychology taken in his first year at university and his experience as a salesman of books on the subject. Nevertheless, his business thrived, and he subsequently bought a three-acre estate on Long Island and started the Long Island Institute for Emotional Disorders, run by himself and his wife; she too granted herself a doctorate on the basis of having spent one year in junior college studying home economics.

By 1972 the Woods were earning $500,000 a year. They had branched out from individual therapy for adults, and now treated retarded children and ran group therapy sessions. In addition, they conducted a school for training in psychotherapy and offered unaccredited doctoral degrees costing $5,940 each. This also secured them the unpaid services of thirteen trainee therapists who treated members of the public as a requirement for their sham Ph.D.s. One of their patients committed suicide, and his wife subsequently brought a legal action claiming that through fraud and misrepresentation they were responsible for her husband's death.

Enterprising amateurs are also found in Britain, though the existence of the National Health Service makes it harder for them to find patients. As a result of the newspaper articles I published on my own breakdown, I received several offers of help from such lay therapists. One was written by a woman claiming to be a SPECIALIST IN MIND* AWARE*NESS' (her asterisks). She wrote (without change of punctuation or spelling):

'My Accurate 'ANALYSIS does not rely on questions; but is based on The Fundamental Principals [*sic*] upon which we are all created.

'My assessment is correct and effective; Scientifically told reliable and lasting. and speedy two sessions; one to estimate the other to see if MY Way is adhered to.

'Should you wish to KNOW Yourself' or should I say your 'Better Self? Perhaps you could write to me, and make an appointment either at your business or the above address; either on a wednesday or if you are very booked up; on Sunday; IF no result no fee . . .'

I had other equally kind offers. A gentleman describing himself on impressively headed paper as 'Psycho-Therapist' wrote disarmingly: 'Although (and perhaps because) I am in the "unqualified" sector of psychologists, I continually see and help patients with exactly those symptoms which you mention.' He was kind enough to enclose his own diagnosis of my case: 'The basic cause of your breakdown is certainly repressed sexual guilt, probably arising from a masturbation contact with boys or a boy between the age of 11 and 14.'

After pointing out the errors made by conventional psychoanalysts and psychiatrists, he added: 'Had I treated your case, I would have expected a recognisable though slight improvement in 3 weeks, marked improvement in 6 and boredom (you not me!) indicating recovery in 10 weeks. Termination of treatment in about 16–18 weeks, about 15 visits in all.'

From his description of his successes with other patients, I could have saved myself much misery had I only known of his existence, though at the expense of emerging from my treatment slightly bored. On his headed paper, there appeared the impressive initials 'M.N.C.P.', standing for membership of a body with the awe-inspiring title 'National Council of Psychotherapists'. On investigation, it turned out that this body is an association of lay therapists who hold meetings from time to time. In its rules, it is stated that the only qualification for membership is that two members of the Council 'shall vouch for the candidate's fitness for membership'. Interestingly enough, another rule states: 'Scientologists, including all who are training, practising, instructing, administrating or are in any other way connected with the Scientology movement or with the practice of Dianetics are ineligible for membership.'

Some of the other rules of the body are also of interest:

'All members undertake to refer patients to medical doctors, where there is even the slightest reason to suspect physical illness.'

'No member shall use his special position of confidence with any patient to procure payments of money beyond his standard fees, bequests in wills, sexual intercourse or any other unusual favour of advantage or benefit to the therapist and consequently of harm to the patient.'

It would be interesting to know what Freud would have made of the curious *non sequitur* contained in the last clause.

Another rule requires that: 'Members shall not indicate they have medical qualifications or are doctors, either Ph.D. or otherwise, unless they are so qualified, but this clause shall not prevent their using the letters L.N.C.P. or M.N.C.P. if they so wish' – standing respectively for licentiate and member of the council. The initials M.N.C.P. should not be confused with M.R.C.P., a set of initials much coveted by medical doctors in Britain, since it stands for Member of the Royal College of Physicians. Although I am sure that the members of this body act in good faith, their rules indicate what can be expected of many other lay therapists.

It may be of course that many lay therapists do just as well as the professionals: indeed if the ability to exercise warmth, empathy and genuineness is all that matters, they are as likely to possess these qualities as anyone who has undergone a training analysis or taken a doctoral degree in clinical psychology. Moreover, there are cases on record of psychiatrists who have ordered ECT for patients and produced a recurrence of epilepsy because they failed to take a proper medical history; of analysts who have driven female patients to suicide by sleeping with them and then abandoning them; and of psychologists who have treated patients with brain tumours for supposed mental illness, thus preventing them from seeking proper medical advice in time to deal with the tumour.

Nevertheless, you run less risk of being exploited if you seek treatment from a qualified psychiatrist or a certified psychologist than if you seek it from a layman, if only because members of professional bodies, if detected in malpractice, risk losing their licence or certificate. Many practioners of psychoanalysis have had no formal training; before signing up for analysis it is worth finding out whether the analyst was trained at one of the major institutes and checking his credentials with that institute.

18

Behaviour Therapy

In the late 1950s a new form of psychiatric treatment came into being – 'behaviour therapy'. This method was developed and is practised mainly by clinical psychologists. The treatment involves the paradox that it is at the same time much the closest to common sense, whilst being based on the scientific findings of experimental psychology. Instead of viewing neurosis as the outcome of dynamic and unconscious processes, the behaviour therapist sees it as the result of having learned maladaptive habits. The method of cure is simple and direct: the therapist attempts to teach the patient new and more suitable ways of responding, using our knowledge of the learning process, particularly the principle of reinforcement. This principle, with which the name of B. F. Skinner is usually associated, states that all animals, including man, tend to repeat behaviour emitted in a given situation if that behaviour is followed by 'reward': a reward is any consequence that is pleasurable. This proposition was in fact first enunciated clearly by Thorndike, an animal psychologist who worked in America around the turn of the century, but Skinner has acquired a popular reputation by repeating it loudly and often and by upholding its application as the panacea for all human ills.

Behaviour therapy has many precursors. In the days of the Roman Empire, Pliny the Elder applied aversive conditioning in the treatment of alcoholism. One of the first systematic attempts to employ behaviour therapy was made by Joseph Wolpe in South Africa in 1958: in England, Eysenck became a spokesman for it, and much of the early work in the field was done at the Maudsley Hospital in London, with which he is associated. In the 1960s the technique spread throughout the United States and Canada. In 1960 there were five papers published on the subject in learned journals: today there are about three thousand a year. These figures may be compared with the number of psychoanalytic papers published, which has remained constant over the last fifteen years at about one thousand five hundred a year. Behaviour therapy is widely practised today, and the ideas behind it have influenced therapists who would not themselves claim to make direct use of its methods.

I have already illustrated the largely unsuccessful use of behaviour therapy to alleviate my lack of concentration and my obsessions, and to reduce my smoking. The area in which its use is best validated is in the treatment of phobias.

Little is known about how phobias develop. The case already described of a woman who developed agoraphobia after receiving an indecent suggestion from a young man in a shop is clearly susceptible to a psychodynamic interpretation: her subsequent fear of shopping may have represented a fear of her own promiscuous sexual urges, and in withdrawing from the situation she may have been avoiding exposing herself to the temptation to throw herself into the arms of good-looking strangers. Not all phobias seem to be like this. For example, in one of Freud's most famous cases, a five-year-old boy, 'Little Hans', developed a phobia of horses; he had in fact been badly frightened when he saw a horse bolt and when a friend of his was bitten by a horse. Freud through the medium of the boy's own father was able to convince the wretched lad that he had an Oedipus complex and the horse represented the feared figure of the castrating father.

It should be noticed that, as in the case of the agoraphobic woman, once a phobia gets a grip it feeds upon itself: the more the sufferer withdraws from the feared situation, the more reward she obtains by so doing and the less possible it is for her to discover that no harm would ensue if she entered it. Behaviour therapy for phobias is in essence simple: the patient is persuaded to approach the dreaded object, discovers that no harm befalls her, breaks the vicious circle, and overcomes the phobia. In practice, four rather different methods of treatment have been developed.

The oldest and best known is 'systematic desensitization'. It is based on two principles discovered in the course of work with animals. First, the startle response to an alarming stimulus can be greatly diminished if the stimulus is initially introduced at such a low intensity that no startle ensues, and if it is then very gradually increased in strength. The animal is thus enabled to tolerate a very intense stimulus that in the absence of training would have produced a massive fear response. Second, it has been found that animals may overcome their fear of an object if they are induced to approach gradually closer to it by rewarding them with food or some other pleasurable experience: this technique is known as counter-conditioning.

In preparation for treatment, the patient is first taught, as I was, progressive relaxation. Next, the therapist, in interviews with the patient, establishes a hierarchy of the situations that cause the phobic reaction, running from those of which the patient is only mildly afraid up to situations that produce intense levels of anxiety. In the case of spider phobia, the hierarchy might range from seeing an old spider's web with no spider present, through a small spider at a distance, up to allowing fearsome-looking spiders to crawl over one's body: there would also be many intermediate cases. After these preliminaries, the patient is instructed to relax and the therapist asks her to imagine the lowest – i.e. least fearful – item on the hierarchy. This procedure is repeated until she can tolerate imagining that item without anxiety and whilst remaining completely relaxed. The therapist then proceeds progressively through the whole hierarchy, reverting to less fearful items whenever the patient experiences any discomfort on the presentation of a particular item. The treatment normally requires between twenty and thirty sessions, and once the patient can tolerate in imagination the most dreaded scenes in the hierarchy she is encouraged to approach the situation that arouses the phobia in real life.

A second method is known as 'flooding'. The patient is asked to imagine from the outset the scenes of which she is most terrified: for example, allowing large hairy spiders to crawl all over her body. This normally arouses extreme fear, but the patient is asked to keep on imagining the terrifying scenes until the fear subsides. The method has the danger that if the patient cannot bear to continue until her fear subsides, the reduction in fear when she stops imagining the terrifying scenes will actually reinforce avoidance of the object of the phobia and may make it worse rather than better. Where the patient is able to endure until the fear begins to subside, the method works at least as well as systematic desensitization. Nowadays flooding is often carried out whilst the patient is calmed by tranquillizing drugs. This greatly reduces anxiety, and recent reports suggest that flooding under drugs is at least as efficacious as without.

'Modelling' is a third method; it takes advantage of the fact that we all tend to model our behaviour on those we respect. The therapist first tries to persuade the patient that her fears are irrational by demonstrating that the phobic situation is in fact harmless. He then places himself in the situation to show that no harm comes to him and induces the patient to copy him. This sort of treatment is again usually accompanied by graduating the fear-provoking stimuli and in successive sessions persuading the patient to approximate closer and closer to the situation that she originally found most terrifying. One of the women on my ward suffered from agoraphobia: she was particularly afraid of cemeteries and funerals and her life had been incapacitated for years, since she dared not catch a bus or go into the streets for fear of catching sight of a cemetery or funeral. Several times a week she was led by a behaviour therapist to a nearby cemetery, and she was taught to approach closer and closer to it and finally to enter. She had been through a protracted and expensive analysis to no avail, but by the time I left hospital she was much better able to cope with her problem. In practice modelling is often combined with desensitization or flooding.

The fourth, and newest, behavioural method of treating phobias has more general application and I shall leave discussion of it until the end of the chapter.

There is now unequivocal evidence that both desensitization and flooding can help to cure phobias. In several studies their efficacy has been directly compared with that of dynamic therapy and has been found to be superior. In most experiments the total number of sessions has been of the order of twenty, and proponents of dynamic therapy can of course reply that this is not enough to allow their method to work. Even if this were true – and no systematic study has ever shown that psychoanalysis has any effect on phobias – a method that is less expensive in therapists' and patients' time is clearly preferable. The dynamic therapist could also allege that behavioural methods of treatment will simply be followed by 'symptom-substitution': if symptoms are caused by deep conflicts or by frustrated libido, the conflicts will produce another set of symptoms if the phobia is removed. The evidence directly contradicts this view: when phobias and other symptoms have been alleviated by behaviour therapy, it has invariably been found that the condition of the patient improves in other respects as well. He – or she – tends to have less general anxiety, to sleep better and to function better all round.

I do not want to give the impression that all phobias can be cured by behaviour therapy: at present they cannot. In general, the stronger the phobia, the more difficult it is to cure, and if it is accompanied by other symptoms such as extreme depression, withdrawal or generalized anxiety, it may be impossible to persuade the patient to cooperate with the therapist well enough to allow the method to work. The suffering of the girl with a phobia of spiders was not relieved during my stay on the ward: in fact she spent nearly twenty-four hours prostrate on the floor in a corner of the room, and had to be removed to another ward.

Many people, particularly women and children, have phobias that are not completely disabling but which can be a nuisance: they may, for example, have unreasonable fears of worms, thunderstorms or public speaking. Carefully controlled experiments have been performed on treating such minor disabilities, and it has been found that behaviour methods not only work but work better than any other method tested, such as counselling or analysis. In one of the most impressive of these experiments ninety-six students who complained of fears of speaking in public were assigned at random to different treatment conditions, and to a no-treatment condition. All treatment was conducted by traditional psychotherapists who believed that the most effective technique was to give the patient 'insight' into his problem. These psychotherapists were trained   give behaviour therapy, and although they themselves did not believe in its efficacy, even as practised by them it turned out to be superio to their own methods. When allowed to use their own technique, the result was better than giving no treatment at all, but was no better than a 'placebo' method that involved merely showing patients encouragement.

The progressive development of behavioural methods for the treatment of phobias over the past seventeen years is impressive. Instead of the random and untested evolution of theories based on clinical hunches that characterizes the history of psychoanalysis, hypotheses have been put forward about the causative factors responsible for inducing improvement and have been carefully tested and refined by experiment. In 1966 a psychiatrist at the Maudsley Hospital using systematic desensitization brought about a mean reduction of .9 points on a 1–5 rating scale in the strength of patient's phobias. In 1974 the same psychiatrist working at the same hospital and with similar patients used a flooding technique conducted on groups of patients and produced a mean change of 2.8 points. Not only had the treatment improved in its efficacy by a factor of three, but far less therapist time was spent on the second batch of patients: whereas in 1966 the therapists spent an average of sixty to seventy hours per patient, in 1974 they spent an average of only 3.3 hours.

Anyone whose main symptom is a phobia should seek help at least initially from a behaviour therapist. In addition, many people with minor phobias of such things as flying or public speaking could benefit from treatment. Systematic desensitization has been described as 'the first psychotherapeutic procedure in history to withstand rigorous evaluation'. It is, however, becoming clear that flooding and modelling are in general even more effective methods than desensitization.

Behaviour therapy has also had marked success in the treatment of obsessive-compulsive cases. Such patients develop rituals that can totally incapacitate them. On sitting down at their desk, they may spend several hours checking that everything is exactly where it should be, and they often wash themselves over and over again. The theory behind the treatment is that the patient has developed an irrational fear of leaving some piece of ritual undone: since he always goes through his ritualistic checks or compulsive acts, he can never find out that omitting them will not produce untoward effects. Since, normally, no harm befalls when he obeys his compulsions, he is reinforced in his belief that they are necessary to ward off evil. If he can be persuaded to omit his compulsive acts, he has a chance of learning that they are unnecessary. Using the techniques of progressive relaxation and modelling, and by attempting to get the patient to expose himself in real life to the situations that bring on his compulsive rituals – wearing dirty clothes, touching sticky food, or looking at objects out of place on his desk – whilst allowing no opportunity to carry through the rituals, behaviour therapy has had some success with such obsessions, as proven by well-controlled studies: once again, when an obsessive patient reduces his compulsions there is an all-round improvement in his condition, and no symptom-substitution appears.

Behaviour therapy has been used in the treatment of many other forms of neurosis, but despite its promise its efficacy has not yet been properly validated for neurotic illnesses other than phobias and obsessive compulsions. Depression is still very resistant to treatment by this or any other method. Psychologists try to induce depressive patients to undertake some task that will 'take them out of themselves', even if they can only concentrate on it for a few minutes at a time: it has been shown that such treatment does produce a temporary elevation of mood, but the effects are usually short-lasting, and it is not known whether the treatment actually shortens the term of the illness. It has been repeatedly found that if one symptom can be eliminated, there is often a halo effect producing alleviation of other symptoms. It was with this in mind that the clinical psychologist in the hospital attempted to train me to recover my concentration.

Many behaviour therapists believe that neuroses can either originate or be perpetuated by other people rewarding or punishing the sufferer inappropriately. Freud himself postulated the concept of 'secondary gain', whereby a neurosis could be perpetuated because the symptoms served some function other than their original psychodynamic role. For example, someone who dislikes his job may, without knowing it, continue in his neurotic behaviour to avoid a return to work: it is well established that, in the USA, neurotics without disability insurance go back to work after a breakdown sooner than those who are so insured. The tearful or fractious child may be trying to gain attention, and the neurotic woman may use her neurosis to keep her husband away from bars and extract sympathy. Florence Nightingale suffered from neurasthenia and spent much of her life in bed: it was probably the only place in a Victorian household where she could find peace from the daily round expected of middle-class women and could concentrate on her reading and writing, and devotion to administration.

For these reasons, behaviour therapists dealing with neurotic patients will often make a point of seeing the patient's family, friends and colleagues. Attempts are made to persuade his associates to reward him for behaving well: for example, a husband might be encouraged not to express too much solicitude when his wife complains of a headache, but to be particularly nice to her whenever she acts in a brighter way. Behaviour therapy is often combined with talking therapy, in which the patient is encouraged to express his current conflicts and an attempt is made to help him resolve them. Much treatment of this sort relies heavily on common sense, and is comparatively unsystematized, though the common sense is often supplemented with ideas introduced from developments in the theory of learning. For instance, a husband who is prone to sulking may be told to sulk only on a special stool placed in his garage, and to repair there every time he wishes to sulk in the hope that sulking may be brought under the control of this one stimulus, and hence be reduced in other situations. It will be recalled that the marital therapist tried to use a similar technique with my wife and myself.

*   *   *

Apart from its use in the classical neuroses, behaviour therapy has been applied to many other problems. As a further instance, we may consider the treatment of alcoholics on my ward. They were all voluntary patients and knew that if they took any alcohol they were likely to be summarily discharged: they would therefore have wasted the agonies of withdrawal experienced during the first days or weeks after admission. This in itself was a strong incentive not to drink. Various methods were used to give them control over their urge to drink. For example, part of their treatment was to enter with another alcoholic a pub in the nearby village and to order and drink non-alcoholic beverages. Many patients failed this test – not by breaking down and drinking, but because having arrived at the pub they felt they dared not go in for fear that they would be unable to resist ordering something alcoholic.

Apart from the application of such direct behavioural methods, the alcoholics gave one another considerable support through group therapy. Some became extremely cheerful after the first five or six weeks, and treated the hospital as a free holiday camp. Their normal length of stay was about twelve weeks. Most stuck it out until they were discharged in the hope that they were cured: the remainder either discharged themselves too soon or drank persistently during their stay until it became clear that it was impossible to keep them for the sake of the other alcoholics. About seventy-five per cent stuck it out and left hospital cured of their addiction – for the time being. Unfortunately, follow-up studies show that even patients who have gone through the full course of treatment have a tendency sooner or later to resume their drinking habits. Alcoholics Anonymous has developed common-sense methods of assisting alcoholics that bear a strong resemblance to behaviour therapy.

The same considerations apply to the use of behaviour therapy to cure other addictive habits like obesity or smoking. Usually the method has some initial success: patients lose weight or reduce or stop smoking. Reports of average weight losses of up to thirty-five pounds are not uncommon, but this is not a great achievement in a woman weighing two hundred pounds at the start of therapy, and there is often a tendency to put on weight again as soon as therapy ceases.

Some of the methods used in weight reduction are of interest: again they are based on experimental findings. Stanley Schachter of Columbia University has found that obese people tend to eat more food than normals when they are tempted by the sight of readily accessible food, but if they have to make an effort to obtain food they eat less. In addition, fat people suffer less discomfort than those of normal weight if they are not allowed to eat at regular mealtimes, particularly if nothing happens to remind them of food. Schachter suggested that eating behaviour in the obese has come under the control of external stimuli instead of being regulated by internal stimuli signalling hunger.

Prompted by these findings, behaviour therapists encourage obese patients to bring their eating behaviour under the control of a limited set of external cues to which they will not be too often exposed. In particular, they are recommended never to eat anywhere except sitting down at a dining room or restaurant table. They are also taught to chew each mouthful with great care, to savour the food as much as they can and to avoid all other activities such as reading or watching television whilst eating. They are instructed to finish each mouthful before commencing the next and to leave an interval between mouthfuls. During therapy, their weight is of course constantly monitored, and they are reinforced with praise for weight-loss. Although derived from experimental findings, these methods again have a ring of common sense, and if only partially successful they are certainly more efficacious than the attempt to persuade patients that they overeat because their libido is fixated at an oral stage.

I have already discussed methods used to reduce smoking. Again, despite some initial success, the rate of recidivism in heavy smokers is very high. It is common to find that of those who attend a smoking clinic run on behavioural lines, over half can be induced to stop completely for several weeks. When follow-up studies are undertaken a year or so later, all but a few are usually found to be smoking as heavily as ever. Although behaviour therapy appears to help in the treatment of addiction, it is as yet no panacea.

A further instance of the use of behaviour therapy on my ward was the treatment of a patient with anorexia nervosa. She was a rather handsome upper-middle-class woman in her mid-forties, with blue-grey hair; she was fastidious about her appearance but since she ate almost nothing she was in a skeletal-like state. It was this woman who, as I explained earlier, was constantly begging food from other patients and hoarding it in her room: she would also carry morsels of food away from the table to ward off night starvation, but they remained uneaten. At one point in her treatment, and of course with her own agreement, she was confined to her room and all privileges were withdrawn including contact with her family, access to television and the reception or sending of letters. She was weighed once a day, and whenever she gained weight some privileges were restored: when she lost weight, they were again removed. She discharged herself prematurely, and I do not know how successful the treatment was. This is a crude application of the effects of rewards and punishments on behaviour: it appears to work in some cases though by no means all, but anorexia nervosa is a dangerous condition, and difficult to treat by any method.

Rewards and punishments have also been used for such problems as homosexuality, transvestism, exhibitionism and various forms of fetishism. The homosexual is shown pictures of nude men and women in suggestive poses: those of men are accompanied by shocks, those of women by some pleasant stimulus such as a favoured morsel of food. Patients are also encouraged to masturbate while fantasizing images of attractive women or while examining *Playboy*'s girl of the month. Again the method is crude, but there are a few studies that suggest it may work in some instances. Appropriate sets of slides together with the apparatus for delivering shocks are commercially available in the United States. At psychological conferences, the stands of firms exhibiting such slides are a favourite attraction both for heterosexual and gay psychologists: on such occasions no shocks are delivered.

When my literary agent read an early draft of the above paragraphs, she was horrified that behaviour therapists should seek to impose their own view of what constitutes normal sex by attempting to change patients' sexual proclivities in this way. This is a common misconception of the activities of the behaviour therapist. Even in these enlightened times, there are many homosexuals who at a conscious level would much prefer to be heterosexual. Some are tortured by moral scruples, others would like to have children and a normal family life. No behaviour therapist with any common sense would attempt to change the sexual habits of a patient against his will. Apart from its being unethical, it is wholly impracticable, since the methods of behaviour therapy demand the whole-hearted cooperation of the patient. Only after a very full discussion, in which alternatives are explored, should a behaviour therapist agree to help the patient to change his desires in this way. The alternative is of course to help him reduce any anxiety he feels about his habits and to accept and fulfil his own nature as it is: many behaviour therapists to this end keep directories of gay clubs and act as marriage bureaux for homosexuals.

Most neurotics have difficulties in their personal relationships. Some behaviour therapists tackle this problem head-on by giving extensive coaching in social skills. Patients are rehearsed in the appropriate way in which to ask a girl to go out with them, or on how to approach their boss in order to request a rise in salary. One form of such therapy is 'assertive training', in which the patient is taught to act in a more assertive and aggressive fashion. Since low self-esteem is associated with feeling inferior to others, it is thought that by learning to stand up to others the patient's self-esteem may also be improved, and there is some objective verification for this belief.

So far I have discussed only applications of behaviour therapy that are made with the full consent of the patient. When the patient seeks help voluntarily, it is always important to obtain agreement between patient and therapist on the precise aims of therapy and on the methods to be used, and my own discussions with the clinical psychologist in hospital were typical in this respect. In America many behaviour therapists actually draw up a written contract between therapist and patient before treatment begins: the contract specifies the objectives and methods of treatment. In institutional settings, however, particularly with patients confined by law, it is possible to apply behavioural methods without the patient's consent.

The best-known examples are 'token economies', which have been used, particularly in the USA, in the treatment of long-stay mental patients – usually psychotics. Such patients often suffer as much from being institutionalized as from their mental disorder. It becomes difficult to disentangle how far the maladaptive behaviour of a patient who has spent years on a psychotic ward is due to his original illness, how far it is due to the apathy induced by institutionalization. The patients live in conditions of extreme monotony, and because they are freed from taking decisions and become accustomed to being cared for by others, they may lose all sense of responsibility. Long-stay patients may cease to care for their appearance or comfort, develop slovenly eating habits and sink into apathy.

Attempts have been made to help by introducing 'token economies'. The patients can earn tokens by behaving in more responsible ways, for example by washing themselves, cleaning their teeth, making their beds, helping other patients, or performing hospital chores like washing dishes, waiting at table, sorting laundry, or gardening. The tokens can be exchanged for goods or privileges, for sweets, cigarettes, access to television or a chance to talk with the hospital staff. There is evidence that some token economies have helped patients to become more respons- ible, but the administration of such programmes is complicated and requires all the hospital staff to be trained in the technique: indeed it has been said that the use of token economies is falling into disrepute since it is 'in danger of being ruined by amateurs'.

Moreover, the method has dangers of its own. In order to set up a system of rewards, it is often necessary to deprive patients of other methods of gaining whatever is used as a reward. Hence, although staff may see patients as working for rewards, the patients themselves may feel that they are working to escape from a punishment they have done nothing to deserve: in consequence, they may become alienated from the staff. Furthermore, the system can never be any better than those administering it, and the power to give rewards can always be misused to persuade patients to do things that are patently for the good of staff members but are not so obviously for the patient's own good. Although this can sometimes happen, I would reject the general criticism that such systems are always set up only for the convenience of the institution or of society: a mental patient who is unkempt and besmeared with faeces not only has little self-respect but makes it difficult for other people to be kind to him. Persuading him to adopt more sanitary habits is in his own interests, if only because it will predispose others to treat him better.

Perhaps a more important reason for not using coercive methods of behaviour therapy is that, according to several recent studies, its benefits do not generalize beyond the initial situation. A patient who brushes his teeth or helps another patient because he wants to earn a token is unlikely to continue such activities once he is in a free environment and tokens are no longer forthcoming. Everything we know about learning suggests that as soon as the rewards are withdrawn, the behaviour will simply 'extinguish'; when patients are discharged from institutions run on token economy lines, this has often proved to be the case. The answer may lie not in abandoning attempts to set up token economies but in attempting to work out ways of providing patients with endogenous motives for continuing to behave in ways that will benefit them on discharge.

There has been a considerable outcry in recent years about the dangers of using behaviour methods to shape the members of society into society's own image. Consider for example such works as *The Manchurian Candidate* or *A Clockwork Orange*. It must be admitted that some of the outcry has been promoted by intemperate and downright silly statements made by proponents of behavioural methods. Skinner himself has vastly exaggerated their potency in dealing with the problems of society, and at present psychologists are no better at designing methods of improving our educational system than are economists at devising means to prevent inflation. Another advocate of behavioural methods, J. V. McConnell, best known for his work on flatworms, wrote in an article entitled 'Criminals Can Be Brainwashed Now': 'We should reshape our society so that we would all be trained from birth to want to do what society wants us to do. We have the techniques now to do it.' In fact we do not have the techniques, even if it were desirable. A great stir was made about the methods of brainwashing used by the Chinese against American prisoners taken in the Korean War. Despite the fact that the Chinese had complete control over every aspect of these men's lives, at the end of the war only twenty-two American prisoners out of a total of four thousand four hundred and fifty elected to remain in China.

There are of course genuine ethical issues involved in the practice of behaviour therapy. Autistic children have been prevented from savagely mutilating their own bodies, but only by giving them strong electric shock for any attempt at such behaviour. How dangerous to himself does a child have to be before we punish his behaviour in this way? Are we justified in asking homosexual patients to accept high levels of shock even with their consent? One psychologist voluntarily exposed himself to the level of shock used: he was amazed by the degree of pain and observed 'how strongly motivated towards change a male homosexual would have to be to subject himself to a series of such shocks, visit after visit ... if other forms of psychotherapy were limited to such a select group of exceptionally motivated homosexuals the result would be better than average.' Except to save someone from death, it is doubtful if such punishing treatments are ever justified: it is known that strong punishment can lead to unexpected and rigid patterns of behaviour that are difficult to eradicate.

Again, are we justified in offering criminals remission of sentence in return for undertaking a course of behaviour treatment? Where the offence has the quality of a compulsion, as in many child rapists, and where the treatment has a reasonable chance of working, it would seem justifiable, provided that the nature of the treatment is explained in detail to the offender and his consent is obtained. It has to be remembered that it is virtually impossible to change people if they do not want to be changed: indeed it often turns out to be impossible with present techniques even where they do desire change. Subjecting prisoners to mutilating brain lesions is another matter to which I shall turn in the next chapter, but first I shall describe the most recent development in behaviour therapy.

Over the last few years a new approach to phobias and other forms of neurosis has been developed called 'stress inoculation'. It has long been known that what a person tells himself about an anxiety-producing situation may have considerable effects on the amount of anxiety felt. Severe pain that is not seen as a portent of death or disabling disease is more readily borne than pain that is thought to presage death or serious illness. In one experiment, subjects were given an inert drug which they were told was a pain-killer. They were then exposed to electric shocks which were increased to the highest level they could tolerate. Some patients were informed that the drug was in fact inert and had had no effect on the pain they felt, others were not so informed. After an interval long enough for any supposed effects of the drug to have worn off, both sets of subjects were retested to discover the threshold of shock which they could now tolerate. The subjects who had been told that the drug was inert and who had therefore gained confidence in their own ability to withstand shock without the drug were able to tolerate more severe shocks at this final stage than were those who thought they had previously been helped by the drug.

In stress inoculation, patients are taught a completely general method for controlling anxiety. They learn how to withstand moderately strong electric shocks delivered at unpredictable intervals, and they are given practice in muscular relaxation and in slow breathing, both of which are antithetical to the arousal of anxiety. They also practise giving instructions to themselves to help in coping with stressful situations: for example, they may be taught to say to themselves: 'Relax, I am in control of the situation, I can handle it; in the long run there is nothing to fear.' These techniques are practised whilst the patients experience the unpredictable shocks until they reach a point where they can endure the expectation of shock without anxiety. They then practise the same anxiety-reducing procedures in the real-life situations of which they have developed phobias, or whenever they feel anxiety. A recent study found that this procedure was considerably more effective than desensitization in helping patients to overcome phobias, and although the method has been developed too recently to be in widespread use or to have been subjected to thorough validation, it looks promising.

Allied to the methods of stress inoculation is the use of a new technique known as Biofeedback. The autonomic nervous system is heavily implicated in emotion. In Biofeedback, the patient sits before a screen that displays measures of his autonomic activity – heart rate, blood pressure and the electrical resistance of the skin, all of which alter during anxiety. The patient concentrates on attempting to change the indications on the screen in a way that corresponds to reducing the activity of the autonomic system – a change which would normally accompany the onset of a calmer mood. The rationale behind this procedure is that by seeing the physiological indications of his anxiety displayed, the patient is given immediate feedback for success.

Although a few normal people seem to be able to learn to reduce their autonomic activity in this way, and may even learn to produce patterns of brain-waves that normally only appear in tranquil states, there are no sound studies as yet showing that these methods can directly assist neurotic patients. The use of Biofeedback has become a popular craze in America and the equipment needed is now marketed by many firms and sold to the general public. It is too early to say whether the method is just another fad or whether it will prove helpful in giving people a measure of self-control: the best-conducted studies are somewhat discouraging. Its most promising use may lie in the alleviation of tension headaches caused by contracting the muscles of the neck and head.

What is particularly interesting about these methods is that the patient can employ them quite generally in any stressful situation in which he finds himself. We have in fact come full circle. In Victorian times neurotics were told to pull themselves together and exert some will-power. Freud's first ventures into psychiatry involved the use of hypnosis – he tried to cure patients by hypnotic suggestion. Today, behaviour therapists are trying to teach their patients self-control by methods making extensive use of suggestion. The techniques of stress inoculation were in fact used in Ancient Greece in the upbringing of Spartan children. They are also practised in many boarding schools in Britain (so called 'public schools'), many of whose alumni say that they suffered so much at school that they could never be seriously worried by anything in later life.

It will be interesting to see whether the key to helping the mentally ill lies after all in an old-fashioned remedy: the strengthening of the will by practice and auto-suggestion. If this turns out to be the case, psychotherapy will have travelled a long and circuitous route only to find itself back where it started. At least the experience gained on the way should be of some help. We now realize the dangers of accepting methods of treatment that have not been objectively validated and the importance of testing the components of each method carefully and developing it step by step. We may be in danger of adopting our grandmothers' methods, but before doing so, they will be scientifically validated.

In summary, then, behaviour therapy is markedly successful in the treatment of two kinds of neurotic disorders – phobias and compulsions. For such cases, the results of objective comparison suggest that it is markedly more effective than other forms of psychotherapy. Its success in the treatment of addictions is only partial, and there is little secure evidence that it is effective in the treatment of most neurotic disorders.

A recent study attempted to compare the efficacy of behaviour therapy and analytically oriented therapy for mild forms of neuroses: patients whom it was thought would benefit from drugs were excluded from the study. Patients given either form of treatment did improve slightly but significantly more than a control group which received no specific therapy. The differences in outcome between patients treated by behaviour therapy and by psychotherapy were small, and for the most part not significant, though behaviour therapy tended to have a slight edge, especially for the more severe cases. As usual, it is difficult to draw any very definite conclusions from the study. The improvements shown may have been due merely to a placebo effect brought about by having regular sessions with a sympathetic listener; since there were only three behaviour therapists and three psychotherapists, any differences in outcome between the two treated groups could have been due to differences in the characteristics of the individual therapists rather than to differences in the methods they used.

Behaviour therapy is currently the most promising psychological approach to mental illness, if only because its practitioners attempt to formulate and test precise hypotheses about human behaviour and are able to draw on the increasing corpus of knowledge provided by academic psychologists. We now know that in evaluating a treatment intuition is not enough: there is no substitute for careful and objective testing of its effects, and only those trained in the pitfalls of such testing can devise adequate methods. Most – but not all – behaviour therapists tend to be less dogmatic and to rely less on authority than do analysts, and this opens the way to replacing unsuccessful methods with methods that have more objective validity.

A few behaviour therapists have made wildly exaggerated claims. Especially in North America, clinical psychology in general and behaviour therapy in particular are in danger of being oversold. Needless to say, behaviour therapy has attracted its share of rogue practitioners: membership of the American Psychological Association is some guarantee of authenticity. There are nowadays a few clinics offering to treat all members of the family including the pets: in one room the mother may be under treatment for frigidity, whilst in the next father is being helped to reduce his alcoholic intake. Elsewhere in the same building the son may be having his stammer corrected and the daughter is being treated for temper tantrums: meanwhile the dog is being trained not to chase cats and an attempt is being made to improve the family parrot's bad language.

Many analysts continue to be highly critical of behaviour therapy. In the face of all the evidence, they allege that relieving a symptom does not cure the underlying disease. They also, in common with some members of the general public, regard behaviour therapy as involving treating human beings as machines. Such fears are groundless. No reputable behaviour therapist will embark on a course of treatment without the full consent of the patient, and although he may influence the patient towards adopting his own outlook, this applies equally to any other kind of psychotherapist. Moreover, there is no reason why behaviour therapists should treat people as machines. Their methods rely almost as much on rapport between patient and therapist ('transference' in analytic terminology) as do those of more traditional treatments. To most people rewards and punishments such as relaxation, sweets, tokens, and even electric shocks are probably of less consequence than the esteem or disapproval of the therapist, and praise and blame are of course meted out to patients by all analysts and psychotherapists, though perhaps in a less systematic way than by behaviour therapists. The problem was investigated in the study already mentioned and it was found that patients actually saw the behaviour therapist as being more empathic and making deeper personal contact than the analytically orientated psychotherapists. It may be that behaviour therapy is criticized precisely because it works. All cure depends on changing the patient in some way: behaviour therapy, at least in some instances, can produce the changes the patient desires.

Nor can I subscribe to the idea that because behaviour therapists attempt to manipulate (with his consent) the patient's behaviour, they thereby detract from the dignity of man. In so far as dynamic therapy has any effect at all, behaviour therapists would argue that it is mediated by the same mechanisms of reward and punishment – approval or disapproval by the analyst – and that the behaviour therapist is making explicit use of methods that the analyst is using implicitly. Many behaviour therapists believe that feelings follow actions, and if someone can be brought to act in a consistent manner they will eventually come to have the feelings appropriate to that manner of behaving. As far as the dignity of man is concerned, most people would probably prefer to believe that they had some control over their own feelings and could themselves try to modify them than to accept the Freudian doctrine that man is forever plunged in a cauldron of disreputable and unconscious drives, formed in infancy, and over which he has little or no control.

We have seen that behaviour therapy contains many paradoxes. It is based on scientific work and yet its methods are curiously akin to common sense; it uses techniques like progressive relaxation and the power of auto-suggestion that resemble the mystical techniques of Indian gurus and fakirs; stress inoculation is reminiscent of methods of child-rearing practised by the Ancient Spartans and the British upper classes. If it is so near to common sense, one may ask why it has taken so long to develop. Many of the scientific ideas on which it is based were current in the Thirties and Forties. Part of the answer almost certainly lies in the power that psychoanalysis had over men's minds in the second quarter of this century. As one behaviour therapist puts it:

'At least some of the blame must fall on Freud and his followers. He must be given credit for his enormous contribution in suggesting that disorders such as phobias were of psychological rather than neurological origin. However, he also emphasized that the symptoms of which the patient complained, such as phobias, were merely manifestations of an "underlying problem", towards which treatment should be direct by psychoanalysis. In this way he deflected therapeutic efforts and interest away from the problems for which the patients were actually seeking help, their symptoms. It has taken some time to get back on target.'

19

Manipulating the Brain

An alternative – or more often a supplement – to psychotherapy is the use of physical methods of treatment, based on drugs or direct manipulation of the brain itself. Both in Britain and in North America there is great variation amongst psychiatrists in the extent to which they rely on physical methods of treatment as opposed to some form of psychotherapy. Psychoanalytically oriented psychiatrists often abhor physical methods, since they believe that patients are most receptive to psychoanalysis if the edge of their worries is not blunted by drugs, and the scorn of my own analysts for drug treatment is a typical reaction.

Perhaps the most dramatic physical method of treating mental disorders is electroconvulsive therapy (ECT). It is dramatic both because it is a drastic procedure that is much feared and because it sometimes produces an almost instantaneous improvement in the patient's condition. Several patients on my ward were in fact transformed by ECT whilst I was there. For example, half-way through my stay someone was brought in with severe paranoid delusions. He thought that money was the root of all evil and refused to use it; in addition he thought that there was a vast conspiracy against him. One night, when I was telephoning, he hung round interrupting my every word. He heard me saying: 'I'll see you tomorrow,' and was convinced I was in a plot against him. 'I know you're in it with all the others. You're going to attack me tomorrow – don't deny it, you're plotting on the telephone –

I heard you plainly. Who are the others? Who's that you're phoning?' Three weeks later, after six electroconvulsive treatments, he was outwardly composed and cheerful and could talk interestingly and rationally. Four weeks after admission, he became an out-patient spending most of the day at the hospital but returning home each evening; within three months he was back at work.

ECT involves passing a large but carefully controlled electric current through the head by means of electrodes applied to the scalp. The procedure is much less drastic than it used to be: when first introduced, it was thought that to be effective it had to be given without an anaesthetic and with a current strength high enough to produce convulsions and subsequent coma. Nowadays the patient is always given a short-lasting anaesthetic, and he also receives a drug that produces muscular relaxation and hence decreases the strength of the convulsions. Any severe trauma to the brain produces a loss of memory for immediately preceding events: hence we can never know whether its administration to conscious patients was accompanied by pain, since they had no memory for the event. For whatever reason, its use was widely dreaded, and there are many reports from patients likening the atmosphere in hospital on days when ECT was to be administered to that of a prison on the day of an execution.

Although the administration of ECT is now a painless procedure, it is still feared, perhaps in part because the tradition of how unpleasant it used to be has been handed down from one generation of patients to another. On my ward, there was usually an unnatural silence when preparations were being made to give ECT, and although one rarely knew beforehand who was to be the recipient, he or she could always be identified afterwards by the small strip of sticking plaster covering the vein on the back of the hand where the anaesthetist had inserted the hypodermic. Patients wearing such sticking plaster were treated with great solicitude by the others.

The fear of ECT is also illustrated by the following incident. Jimmy, the Glaswegian alcoholic who had adopted a protective attitude towards me, was taken one day to a different hospital to have his brain-waves (electroencephelogram) recorded. A helmet containing several electrodes was strapped to his scalp and the recording duly taken. He returned to the ward convinced that he had undergone a particularly unpleasant form of ECT: he complained that current had been passed through his head to the accompaniment of terrible tingling sensations. For the rest of the day he felt dizzy and had a severe headache. No amount of reassurance from me would convince him that no current is passed when brain waves are recorded and that the procedure is completely painless. He insisted: 'Och, it was terrible, Stuarrt, just terrible: I got sich a prickling and tingling: it was like being in the electric chairr.' The agony he underwent could have been avoided if a doctor had taken the pains to explain the procedure before taking his electroencephalogram.

The method of giving ECT is in fact now so refined that it is administered in some hospitals to out-patients. They attend once or twice a week for about two hours, most of which time is spent recovering from the confusional state temporarily induced. When they come round from the anaesthetic, they may not realize where they are or what has happened; but this condition usually passes off within an hour or two, leaving a slight headache. A course of treatment by ECT normally involves about half a dozen applications. It is possible that there is some long-term impairment of memory, but the issue is difficult to decide: patients whose emotional state is helped by ECT usually do not complain of memory problems, and it is hard to establish whether complaints of memory-loss in patients not so helped are a symptom of their illness rather than a reflection of the direct effects of ECT on the brain. Today ECT is often administered to one half of the brain only. In most people, language is largely controlled by one hemisphere, called the dominant hemisphere and usually located on the left side of the brain, and trauma to the other hemisphere has less severe effects on mental function. Hence, giving ECT only to the non-dominant hemisphere should – and in practice does – minimize any adverse effects. The question of whether unilateral ECT is clinically as effective as when given bilaterally is still unresolved, since research findings on this issue are contradictory. With present procedures, it is unlikely that there is much long-term impairment of mental faculties, and its dangers are probably far less than those attending the prolonged use of alcohol.

ECT is used in the treatment of severe depression usually only after other forms of treatment have failed. I must admit that I would have resisted having ECT had it been offered to me, but my depression was neither as severe nor as long-lasting as many. In the case of a suicidal patient, giving ECT can save a life, and despite its drastic nature and our ignorance of its mode of operation its use in severe cases appears to be justified. Most surgical procedures and many drugs used in the treatment of physical illness carry dangers.

Since I shall consider several psychiatric treatments that have proved to be both dangerous and useless, it is worth emphasizing that such treatments abound in other forms of medicine. Tonsillectomy is a case in point. It is a more dangerous procedure than ECT both in terms of mortality rate and in its long-term effects. Removing the tonsils quadruples the risk of catching bulbar polio and triples the risk of Hodgkins disease, a form of cancer that is usually fatal. Out of every thousand children who have their tonsils removed one is killed by the operation and sixteen are made seriously ill. This compares with a one in fifty thousand risk of death due to a single administration of ECT.

Moreover, there is much better agreement on the indications for administration of ECT than for removing the tonsils. The American Child Health Association carried out an interesting study on the criteria used by doctors in recommending tonsillectomy. Of one thousand eleven-year-old children surveyed in New York schools, sixty-one per cent had already had their tonsils removed. When the remaining thirty-nine per cent were referred to physicians, it was recommended that forty-five per cent of them should have their tonsils out. The fifty-five per cent who had been passed as not requiring tonsillectomy by the first set of doctors were sent to other doctors who duly recommended that forty-six per cent of them should have their tonsils removed. This study suggests that many tonsils are removed more or less at random. It is of course true that one cannot justify the use of drastic procedures in psychiatry by comparing them with mistakes made in other branches of medicine, but in the case of ECT there is compelling evidence that it helps some people more than other procedures, and it is much less dangerous than many common surgical operations that are known to do little or no good.

Unfortunately it is not possible to be certain in advance who will and who will not respond favourably to ECT. In some cases, its administration appears to result in a complete alleviation of depression; in others the depression remits but may return later and be treated again by ECT; in yet others, it has little or no benefit.

The use of ECT has an interesting history. It has been held since the eighteenth century that traumatic events like ducking in icy water or exposure to snakes could alleviate or cure mental illness, and in the nineteenth century some physicians attempted to cure the mentally sick by deliberately infecting them with malaria, smallpox and typhoid, and by giving seizures induced by camphor. In the 1930s, insulin injections were first used to produce coma and convulsions in the insane. Insulin-induced coma is accompanied by writhing and moaning, and until recently it was quite common to bring on such comas in schizophrenics every day for periods of up to eight weeks. It was not until the mid-Fifties that a careful appraisal of the effects of insulin on schizophrenics was made: it was discovered that it had no beneficial effects whatever. Although still occasionally used, I shall not discuss this treatment further.

Partly as a result of the belief that convulsions helped schizophrenics, investigations were undertaken to discover what proportion of schizophrenics had epilepsy: it was found to be much more common in the general population than in schizophrenics, and this encouraged the belief that giving convulsions to schizophrenics might help them. At about the time that insulin treatment was introduced, a psychiatrist in Budapest began to induce convulsions in schizophrenics using injections of camphor, a drug used in the treatment of the insane in the late eighteenth century. He subsequently found that another drug – metrazol – was more reliable in bringing about convulsions, and switched to that. His work in turn prompted an Italian psychiatrist to experiment with convulsions induced by electro-shock, and this method completely supplanted the use of metrazol. Although the treatment has proved to be helpful, it was discovered as a result of a series of false assumptions. It turned out to be of little use for schizophrenia but proved helpful in the treatment of depression; more recently it was discovered that it works just as well when given under an anaesthetic and a muscular relaxant to reduce the strength of the convulsions. We still do not know why it works, though there are indications that it may stimulate the brain to increase the synthesis of an important set of complex molecules, known as the 'biogenic amines', which are thought to be implicated in determining mood.

It is in fact just possible that ECT works only through a 'placebo' effect. It has been known for many years that both physical and mental illnesses may be ameliorated by giving the patient tablets made of substances like sugar that have no direct curative effect. Such tablets are termed placebos, and the word has been extended to refer to any treatment that works only because of the patient's faith in it and not through any direct physiological or chemical effects. Because ECT is such a drastic and widely feared procedure, it seems possible that it has a particularly strong placebo action: I have already pointed out that the more suffering someone voluntarily undertakes in order to obtain something, the more faith they have in the procedure.

Carefully conducted clinical research has repeatedly shown that, at least for some patients, ECT has a large beneficial effect: none of the best studies has included the right control group to prove that this effect is due to the direct action of the shock on the brain rather than to its placebo action. Such a group would comprise people who thought they were receiving ECT but who were in fact not receiving it: it would be unethical to tell patients that they were going to be given ECT and then to anaesthetize them and withhold the ECT treatment, because of the slight risks due to the anaesthetic.

There is in fact one instance where this condition was achieved by an odd chance. A new ECT machine was installed in a British hospital and after it had been in use for about six months it was discovered that it was faulty and was not delivering any current. Not only did the doctors not notice that it was not functioning, they did not notice any difference in the effects of the treatment on their patients from that of proper ECT. It would be unwise to place too much reliance on this unintended and unsystematic substitution of a placebo for ECT, but the possibility should be borne in mind that the benefits of ECT may be due as much to patients' expectations as to its direct action on the brain. It should be noted that even if this were true, the case for continuing to use it would still be strong – at least until doctors and patients came to realize its placebo action, when it would of course become useless.

A second drastic physical treatment was also introduced in the late Thirties. It is usually called prefrontal leucotomy in England and prefrontal lobotomy in America. The procedure involves severing many of the fibres connecting the front part of the cerebral cortex to the remainder of the brain. It is now commonly thought that the harmful effects of this operation far outweigh any benefits. One of the saddest cases on my ward was a gently-spoken, slightly portly, middle-aged man who had been an accountant in a good post. He had had a breakdown in his twenties and had submitted to a prefrontal leucotomy (in a different hospital). He bitterly regretted having had the operation: he had been in and out of mental hospitals ever since, and was unable to hold down any job. He suffered from obsessive thoughts and complained that the leucotomy had made it impossible to follow any coherent train of thought – the only mode of thinking it had not removed from him were the agonizing obsessions for which the operation was performed in the first place.

Prefrontal leucotomy was introduced by a Portuguese psychiatrist named Moniz. He attended a talk given by two neurophysiologists, who reported the results of extirpating the prefrontal lobes of two chimpanzees: one animal that had previously been rather fractious was rendered tame and friendly by the operation. When Moniz told John Fulton, one of the neurophysiologists, that he was thinking of using the procedure on psychotics, Fulton was horrified. Although many now execrate the name of Moniz, he actually received a Nobel prize for introducing this operation on humans. He considered himself the best judge of whether the operation helped his patients, and reported that of the first twenty operated, seven were completely recovered, seven much improved, and the rest unchanged. In investigating the effects of any method of treatment, perhaps the most basic principle is that the evaluation must be carried out by independent investigators using systematic methods of assessment, not by the doctor who gives the treatment. Unconscious bias may lead him to see improvement where none exists. Moniz's career was terminated in 1944 when a leucotomized patient shot him in the spine, rendering him hemiplegic.

The history of leucotomy does little credit to the medical profession. It was introduced in the USA in 1936, and it is estimated that some forty thousand operations were carried out there in the next twenty-five years. British neurosurgeons were just as avid to use this new and unproven method of treatment and severed the frontal lobes of some ten thousand patients. Few adequate studies of the effects of the operation were carried out: it should be remembered that many mental patients improve spontaneously, and the fact that some people recover after leucotomy is meaningless unless it can be shown that a significantly higher percentage recovers than after no treatment or after less drastic forms of treatment. The two most carefully conducted studies involving large numbers of operated patients and unoperated control patients matched for severity of illness have shown no benefit from leucotomy.

It was known that removal of the frontal lobes in monkeys led to marked deficits in many tasks requiring intelligence, but no loss could be detected in leucotomized patients on standard intelligence tests; the operation may have rendered patients more tractable, and hence they may have cooperated on the tests more readily than preoperatively. There were many indications that the operation did lead to more subtle deficits: in particular, many leucotomized patients are incapable of forming and executing long-range plans, they are easily distractable, and if they are interrupted in the performance of some task they do not resume it. Their emotions are often shallow and short-lived, with a tendency to euphoria, tactlessness and sudden changes of mood. Although a few patients appear to be improved by the operation, it is unclear how far the semblance of improvement is produced merely because they become easier for others to manage, how far they are genuinely more at ease with themselves. It has been said that the operation turns people into cabbages, and although this may not be completely true in all cases it is the general impression gained by many of the close relatives and friends of leucotomized patients.

It should not be assumed that the surgeons who undertook this sensational operation did so merely to further their own careers or out of indifference to their patients' welfare: they were often presented with cases of people in dire misery, and at the time the operation was most popular other methods of treatment, such as psychotropic drugs, were not available. The real criticism that can be made of many of the doctors who performed the operation is that they did so without adequately exploring alternative methods of treatment and that they failed to undertake careful follow-up studies to determine its precise effects – a failure probably due less to arrogance than to ignorance of how to conduct the necessary research. Moreover, the operation came to be performed not just on desperate cases but on less severe cases. Leucotomy was also used for the relief of chronic pain: after the operation, patients would say their pain felt the same as ever, but it was more bearable because they did not pay so much attention to it. The wife of a patient who received a leucotomy for the relief of chronic back-ache told an investigating psychologist:

'That operation was performed on my husband in September 1949 and it has also been a very sad affair, and if the doctor had of spoke of it as you do we would never of had it done, but he said it would slow him up but he would be able to do the things he always did and even be able to get at his place of business, but he cannot do anything and do it right, he can't even take care of himself in the bathroom, and does not take any interest in anything. When he went into it mentally he was fine, kept in contact with his business, even done some of the book work, but he had suffered pain for years from back trouble . . . I some days think I will lose my mind going through this with him.'

The growing evidence that leucotomy led to intellectual deterioration coincided with the discovery of a series of drugs that could be used in the alleviation of mental disorder. Full-scale leucotomy was largely abandoned in the early Sixties. One would have supposed that the tragic history of its use would have made neurosurgeons more cautious about introducing irreversible damage to the brain without careful study of the consequences. For the most part it has had this effect, and indeed in the United States the National Institute of Mental Health has withdrawn all supporting funds for the investigation of psychosurgery. Nevertheless, the number of brain operations for mental disorder is still running at about six hundred a year in the US; some hospitals in Britain (for example, the Brook Hospital) also still resort to brain operations. With advances in the techniques of neurosurgery, it is now possible to destroy selectively and accurately small areas of brain tissue, and modern psychosurgery seeks to destroy much more restricted areas of the brain than those damaged by the massive cuts made in leucotomy. The areas destroyed, however, are still of crucial importance to normal brain functioning, and are invariably parts of the brain thought to be implicated in emotion and in the deepest aspects of personality. It is important to distinguish between psychosurgery and neurosurgery. In the operations so far discussed, the tissue removed is not, as far as we know, diseased or damaged. Where there is damaged tissue in the brain, as with a cerebral tumour or an epileptic focus, it is often essential to remove it, and such operations are called neurosurgery. Both tumours and epileptic foci may produce psychiatric symptoms, but the fact that their removal may benefit the patient does not justify the destruction of parts of the brain not known to be damaged.

In the absence of clear-cut signs of brain pathology, brain surgery for the mentally ill is today normally given only to patients with a long history of severe anxiety or of serious and uncontrollable violence, and then only after all other forms of treatment have been tried and found wanting. Unfortunately, these conditions are not always met. I recently came across a case of a twenty-one-year-old girl who received psychosurgery for a severe phobia. She had been seen by a clinical psychologist who was of the opinion that she could be helped by behaviour therapy, but his judgement was overruled by the psychiatrist in charge of the case and she was referred for leucotomy. In America some brain operations for violence have recently been performed on children and prisoners, and it is hard to see how they can give 'informed consent'.

A recent case has aroused considerable controversy. In 1967, Mark and Ervin of the Massachusetts General Hospital in Boston operated on 'Thomas R.', a thirty-four-year-old engineer who, according to them, was highly successful in his work but was given to outbursts of uncontrollable rage and violence, suffered from paranoia and occasionally had epileptic seizures. They destroyed the amygdala, a region of the brain known to be implicated in the control of aggression in animals. Before the operation they had implanted electrodes in the patient's brain and had repeatedly stimulated parts of it with electric current. Their own description of how they obtained his consent to the operation is as follows: 'We suggested to him that we make a destructive lesion . . . He agreed to this suggestion while he was relaxed from lateral stimulation of the amygdala. However, twelve hours later, when this effect had worn off, Thomas turned wild and unmanageable . . . it took many weeks of patient explanation before he accepted the idea of bilateral lesions being made in his medial amygdala.' In reporting the outcome, they state: 'Four years have passed since the operation, during which time Thomas has not had a single episode of rage. He continues, however, to have an occasional epileptic seizure with periods of confusion and disordered thinking.'

At the request of the patient's family, a further follow-up was under-taken by an independent psychiatrist. He reported that before the operation the patient 'had never been in any trouble at work or other-wise for aggressive behaviour'. Furthermore the hospital records prior to the operation revealed that he had no psychotic symptoms, no hallucinations, delusions, or paranoid ideas, and no signs of difficulty in thinking. His wife was having an affair with another man whom she subsequently married: it was this man about whom Mark and Ervin had alleged the patient was paranoid. The investigating psychiatrist dis-covered that after the operation the patient had become socially confused and was unable to cope with normal life. He moved to the West Coast, and was admitted to hospital there: that hospital placed him under sedation and they regarded his reports of what Mark and Ervin had done to him as evidence of a delusional state of mind. The patient was unable to care for himself and had to be hospitalized periodically for violent and psychotic behaviour. Eight years after the operation, another neurologist stated that 'the patient would never be able to function in society'.

I once travelled to a conference with a young neurosurgeon who has since become well known. He explained to me that he hoped to win a Nobel prize by opening up the skulls of patients with terminal cancers and observing the results of electrical stimulation of different parts of the brain. The excuse for using patients as guinea-pigs in this way was that he might find an area of the brain which on stimulation would reduce pain and cause pleasurable sensations – such areas do in fact exist. However, much of the work he described involved stimulating parts of the brain, such as the visual centres, that are known to have nothing to do with pleasure and pain. These operations were subsequently performed under a local anaesthetic on fully conscious patients, as indeed is most brain surgery, since it is necessary to obtain patients' subjective reports on the stimulation of various parts of the brain in order to discover whereabouts in the brain one is operating. The neurosurgeon in question, unlike Moniz, has not so far been awarded a Nobel prize, but he has achieved a certain degree of notoriety. Such cases of brain surgery are extreme, though there are similar ones on record. Moreover, the way in which cases of psychosurgery are followed up and reported by psychiatrists and neurosurgeons often continues to fall short of acceptable standards of scientific objectivity.

In summary then, where all else fails, ECT appears to be useful in the treatment of severe depression and may save patients from suicide. It seems doubtful whether destruction of brain tissue for psychiatric patients is ever justifiable, at least in our present stage of knowledge. The effects are irreversible, the efficacy uncertain, an1 we know almost nothing about the long-term outcome. At the very least, it should be restricted to chronic cases for whom every other form of treatment has been tried without success.

20

Psychotropic Drugs

Drugs that affect mental state are known as 'psychotropic': most can nowadays only be legally obtained on a doctor's prescription. They are used to induce sleep, to relieve anxiety (tranquillizers) or to produce an elevation of mood (stimulants and antidepressants).

Chloral and paraldehyde were employed in Victorian times to sedate patients: the first modern group of tranquillizing drugs that came into general use were the barbiturates. They are effective, at least at first, in reducing anxiety, but as the brain becomes habituated to them, larger and larger doses are needed to produce the same effect; like many psychotropic drugs, they are also highly addictive. Prolonged use leads to chronic intoxication accompanied by total deterioration of the personality: addicts cannot function in society and cannot hold down their job or keep friends. They become maudlin, moody and childish. In addition they tend to take overdoses that can readily lead to death whether by accident or design. In 1960 three hundred and fifty patients suffering from barbiturate poisoning were admitted to one hospital alone in Scotland. In the United States ten thousand people a year are killed by barbiturates, and they are still the favoured method of committing suicide amongst film stars and the jet-set. Withdrawal produces delirium tremens, insomnia and anxiety. Dr William Sargant has called attention to a more curious but equally real danger. He reports cases of

patients with chronic anxiety states who were given prefrontal leuco-
tomies: only after the operation was it discovered that the anxiety states
were themselves caused by barbiturate poisoning.

In 1967 there were an estimated one hundred thousand people in the
United Kingdom with chronic dependence on barbiturates as compared
to about seventy thousand chronic alcoholics. Although, when administered under strict medical supervision, the barbiturates helped in the
control of anxiety, their dangers were not appreciated early enough:
they are still quite widely prescribed by general practitioners both in
England and in North America.

The barbiturates have been largely superseded by a new range of
tranquillizers thought to be less addictive. How far this is true is, in
some instances, still an open question: there can, however, be no doubt
that they are much more expensive to manufacture and are therefore
correspondingly more lucrative to the drug companies who produce
them.

The first of the new tranquillizers, meprobamate, was put on the
market in 1955. Studies published in 1964 and 1966 suggested that like
the barbiturates it can produce dependence and withdrawal symptoms;
if large doses are taken over long periods of time, it may cause side-
effects that are equally unpleasant. The British National Formulary for
1971, published by the Department of Health and Social Security,
states: 'Clinical trials have shown that meprobamate, once widely used
as a tranquillizer, has no more effect than a placebo.' Despite the risk of
dependence and despite the doubts about its efficacy, the drug is still
marketed for the relief of anxiety, and many general practitioners
continue to prescribe it.

Its use has, however, declined and it has largely been replaced by a
new family of drugs known as the benzodiazepines, of which Valium
and Librium are examples. These drugs reduce anxiety at dosages well
below lethal levels, and the danger of taking overdoses is accordingly
much less than in the case of the barbiturates. They also appear to be
less addictive, though to quote from a recent textbook on psychopharmacology: 'Dependence can result from heavy, continuous and
uncontrolled benzodiazepine administration over several years and it
can degenerate into paradoxical reactions such as hallucinations, restlessness, and hostile-aggressive tendencies.' Administered judiciously,
they are undoubtedly useful in the control of anxiety, though they
palliate rather than cure. Moreover, there are reports that they can
cause an increase in aggression even at moderate dosages.

In the early Fifties more potent tranquillizing drugs, now known as the major tranquillizers, were discovered. They are known as the phenothiazines; the parent drug from which they were developed was first used as an insecticide. They are widely used in the control of schizophrenia and for neurotic patients exhibiting marked agitation. They are powerful and bring about a pronounced reduction in levels of anxiety, excitement and aggression. I have already described their rapid mode of action on myself. Their efficacy is well attested by the results of clinical trials and also by carefully collected data on their effects in reducing the incidence of broken windows, the extent to which patients have to be restrained and the number of assaults on staff. Amongst their undesirable side-effects are dryness of the mouth, impotence, lack of motor coordination and constipation.

Chronic schizophrenics are frequently maintained on one or other of the phenothiazines, and their introduction has been followed by a sharp fall in the number of beds occupied by chronic patients in psychiatric hospitals both in Britain and in North America: in Britain there are about one hundred thousand patients in mental hospitals today as against one hundred and forty thousand twenty years ago. Although these drugs slow down thought-processes, they have enabled many schizophrenics to function well enough to hold down jobs and to lead a semblance of normal life outside hospital. It is true that some authorities have questioned the direct role of the phenothiazines. It may be at least in part the psychiatrists' own faith in the drugs that enables them to discharge patients. Moreover, the psychiatrist will communicate his faith to the patients, thus helping them to cope with a more normal life.

Once again, the drugs do not cure, but they alleviate symptoms, and for someone in a desperate state of tension and anxiety this is no mean matter. Little is known about their mode of action, and prolonged usage can lead to the development of continual grimacing and writhing movements of the mouth and jaws: these grimaces persist after the drug is withdrawn. It has been suggested that the state of apathy to which the drugs reduce patients may prevent them from recovering of their own accord. They should be administered only in severe cases, and there would appear to be little justification for their use in rebellious children or delinquent adolescents as recommended by some of the manufacturers.

Tranquillizers calm the patient, but they do not elevate his mood: various stimulants are available for this purpose. The first were the amphetamines, discovered in the mid-Thirties and widely used in the Fifties and early Sixties. They are highly addictive and almost certainly do more harm than good, since withdrawal is accompanied by a rebound effect leading to even worse depression. In 1966, two hundred million amphetamine tablets were prescribed by general practitioners alone working within the National Health Service in Britain. When first taken, they reduce appetite, and they have been widely prescribed (and still are) for people wanting to slim. Despite the claims of the drug companies, they are useless for this purpose: if taken for any period of time their effect on appetite wanes, and in any case appetite returns to its previous level as soon as the would-be slimmer abandons the drug.

When given intravenously, amphetamine and its derivatives lead to pleasurable 'highs', and following their introduction into medicine they began to be taken for this purpose: there are now a large number of 'speed' addicts. Many members of the medical profession were blind to this danger. Amphetamines may even be as dangerous as heroin: chronic use can lead to psychosis and may cause permanent brain damage. In 1954 there were about half a million amphetamine addicts in Japan: in the same year the then chief medical officer of the British Ministry of Health wrote complacently: '[Amphetamines] have the advantage of being relatively non-toxic, addiction to them is rare and there are no serious ill effects.' Although he may have been unaware of what was going on in Japan, it is hard to believe that the international companies manufacturing the drugs and advertising them to doctors were not by then familiar with the dangers. In a book published in 1973, one of the world's leading psychopharmacologists sums up the present situation: 'Regardless of their very limited psychiatric indications, amphetamines have been and to some extent still are prescribed in many countries with an excessive confidence shown by the general practitioner in these agents as general anti-fatigue compounds and as anorexiants in the course of weight control therapy.'

The prescription of amphetamine compounds and barbiturates, particularly by general practitioners, has almost certainly done more harm than good. Many of the alcoholics and several of the other patients on my ward were dependent not merely on alcohol but on a variety of sedatives, sleeping tablets, and stimulants with exotic-sounding names like Mandrax, Moggies, Purple Hearts and Black Bombs. They were often taken off all drugs on admission and sometimes experienced withdrawal symptoms including sleeplessness, terrifying and persistent nightmares and extreme levels of tension and anxiety. Many alcoholics complained that they suffered more from having such drugs withdrawn than from alcohol withdrawal. Like alcohol, most of these drugs poison the centrel nervous system, and they have the added disadvantage of producing nastier side-effects and of being more expensive to manufacture.

In recent years a new use has been discovered for the amphetamines: particularly in the USA, they are frequently employed in the control of badly behaved children. According to Dr Wender, a well-known American child psychiatrist, between five and ten per cent of American children: 'Manifest dysfunction in the following areas: motor activity and coordination; attention and cognitive function; impulse control; interpersonal relations, particularly dependence-independence and responsiveness to social influence; and emotionality.' In other words, some children are clumsy, inattentive at school, impulsive, fractious, and disobedient. American paediatricians have invented a new illness from which such children are said to suffer. They call it 'Minimal Brain Dysfunction' or 'Minimal Brain Damage' (MBD): the damage is certainly minimal, since in most cases of children so diagnosed there is no evidence whatsoever of any organic damage to the brain – they are diagnosed as having brain dysfunction solely because they are fractious. It so happens that large doses of amphetamines and related compounds (the most common of which has the trade name 'Ritalin') have a paradoxical effect on some excitable people: instead of speeding them up, it slows them down.

It is now common, particularly in the USA but to a lesser extent in Britain, to diagnose MBD on the basis purely of the child's behaviour and to place him on continuous large doses of amphetamine. Such treatment frequently quietens the child down and makes him more tractable both at home and at school. Although we know that the long-term use of amphetamine may produce intellectual deterioration and permanent psychotic states, Wender advocates that more naughty children should have the benefit of such treatment: 'Minimal brain dysfunction is probably the single most common disorder seen by child psychiatrists. Despite this fact, its existence is often unrecognized and its prevalence is almost always underrated.'

Although he believes the 'illness' should be more widely recognized and the treatment more widely prescribed, Wender is sufficiently cautious to add that prolonged treatment can have untoward side-effects 'in an appreciable fraction of cases', while the long-term 'fate of the MBD child is uncertain and his clinical picture cannot be drawn'. Putting this another way, we already know that the bad child may grow up to be a good citizen if not treated with amphetamine: we do not at present know what sort of adult he will make if subjected to prolonged doses, though our knowledge of the ill effects of this drug is sufficient to cause concern. The diagnosis and treatment of MBD in cases where there is no direct evidence of brain damage appears to be ethically questionable.

Steve Chorover has pointed out that the ascription of childhood naughtiness to an illness given the pretentious name 'Minimal Brain Dysfunction' has interesting historical precedents. In 1851 an eminent American physician, Samuel A. Cartwright, published a paper in the *New Orleans Medical and Surgical Journal* setting out some of the diseases that were peculiar to negroes. Two of the commonest negro illnesses he named 'drapetomania' and 'dysesthesia aethiopsis': since few modern doctors have the benefit of a classical education, modern illnesses are given less impressive-sounding names, but the principles are sometimes the same. 'Drapetomania' is derived from two Ancient Greek words meaning 'runaway' and 'madness': its only symptom, according to Dr Cartwright, is absconding from plantations, and after regretting that this illness had previously been unrecognized by the medical authorities he states: 'It is as much a disease of the mind as any other species of mental alienation, and much more curable, as a general rule.'

Cartwright describes 'dysesthesia aethiopsis' (poor sensation in the Ethiop) as 'one of the most prevalent maladies of the negro race'. Its symptoms are 'a tendency to do much mischief, to slight the work, and to generally raise disturbance'; sufferers from this malady exhibit a 'pathological' change in their nervous system which produces 'an apparent insensibility to pain when being punished'. Fortunately, 'the complaint is easily curable': the treatment Dr Cartwright prescribes includes 'anointing the body with oil and slapping the oil in with a broad leather strap' and then putting the patient 'to some hard kind of work in the open air and sunshine'. The rationale for this therapy is spelled out in detail, with extensive discussion and lengthy citations of 'unalterable physiological evidence' to show that the cause of the disorder is an underlying defect in respiratory body function.

One of the reasons why amphetamine is no longer much used for depression is that a new group of drugs known as antidepressants was discovered in the late Fifties. The first of these was originally employed in the treatment of tuberculosis, and it was noticed that some of the patients taking it became very cheerful. The most commonly used of these drugs today are known as the tri-cyclic antidepressants, and are manufactured and sold in Britain and America under a variety of trade names: the generic names of the two most widely used are amitriptyline, which I was given, and imipramine. It is virtually certain that they are less addictive than amphetamine: one reason may be that they take much longer to have any effect (several weeks rather than a few minutes). There is no evidence that the elevation of mood produced is followed by deep depression as a rebound effect when they are withdrawn. They do not work in all cases of depression but there is unequivocal evidence that they help some people. Few psychiatrists would claim that they effect a cure, but they may give the patient a breathing space during which the natural processes of recovery from depression can operate.

As I have described in my own case, the side-effects of these drugs can be very unpleasant: they include extreme dryness of the mouth, constipation (or sometimes diarrhoea), disorders of vision, impotence in man and loss of sexual drive in women, disorders in the functioning of the heart and vascular system, muscular weakness and tremor, and difficulty in urinating. With so many undesirable side-effects it is perhaps not surprising that no cases of addiction have been reported. These drugs are little used in the treatment of schizophrenia, and indeed they sometimes reactivate schizophrenic episodes in patients prone to this illness. As far as I know, no patients are maintained indefinitely on the tri-cyclic antidepressants.

Over the last few years, yet another substance – lithium – has leapt into the top ten of drugs in psychiatric use. It was originally employed in the treatment of mania, but well-controlled studies have shown that when manic-depressive patients are permanently maintained on lithium it reduces the severity and incidence of both mania and depression. The use of lithium has an interesting history. It occurs naturally in many mineral springs, and the drinking of such waters was advocated by an ancient Greek physician from Ephesus for the reduction of manic excitement. Its beneficial effects on mania were rediscovered by an Australian medical research worker, Cade, in 1949: as so often happens, the discovery was made by chance on the basis of following up an incorrect hypothesis. Cade found that injecting the urine of manic-depressives into guinea-pigs often proved fatal to the animals, and he thought that this was caused by the presence of uric acid. To test this suggestion, he injected with the urine a salt of uric acid based on lithium, expecting to increase the toxicity, but found to his surprise that the mixture was less toxic than plain urea. Moreover, guinea-pigs given the lithium salt lost much of their natural timidity and became more tranquil. When he administered a lithium salt to manic patients, the mania was much reduced.

Many years passed before lithium became widely used in the treatment of manic-depressive psychoses. Its toxic effects may have been partly responsible for this delay, but J. O. Cole writing in the *American Journal of Psychiatry* has suggested that the delay may have in part been caused by the fact that lithium is remarkably cheap to produce and hence the drug companies saw little profit in marketing and promoting it: moreover, since it is a naturally-occurring substance, its use for therapeutic purposes could not be patented. It did not in fact become commercially available in the United States until 1970, and one authority believes that since then 'the drug companies have probably proceeded to lose money consistently on the product'.

Once introduced, it became the new wonder drug: it has been administered to control aggression, particularly in fractious children and adolescents, and has also been used in the treatment of schizophrenics, psychopaths, mental defectives, alcoholics and women with premenstrual tension. There is little or no evidence that it helps in any of these conditions, but its value in the treatment of mania and in the long-term treatment of manic-depressive psychosis is well attested. Within the last few years, it has come to be increasingly used with patients suffering from recurrent depression. First indications are that it reduces both the frequency and severity of depressive episodes, and as I write the Medical Research Council of Great Britain has just announced the inception of large-scale and properly controlled clinical trials to validate this use of lithium.

Properly administered, the risks of lithium therapy are probably no greater than those of any other psychotropic drug. There is, however, a rather small margin between the dosage needed to produce therapeutic effects and a highly toxic or even lethal dose. For this reason, the amount of lithium in the body needs to be monitored by taking blood samples, and the dosage is adjusted according to the level of lithium found in the blood. When patients are first placed on lithium, blood samples are taken several times a week, but once the body settles down to the presence of the drug and the right dosage for the individual has been established, it is only necessary to monitor its level about once every two months.

Manic-depressives given lithium on a long-term basis often become outwardly more normal, but the patients sometimes pay a price for the ensuing tranquillity. Some complain that lithium therapy makes their life flat and less colourful and prevents them going as fast as they would like: some businessmen claim that a degree of manic energy is necessary for their work, and artists assert that lithium reduces their creative power. Many who at first make such complaints find to their surprise that once they become used to living without manic episodes and adjust to a more stable pattern of life, their productivity and creativity become as good or better than before.

I have stressed that our basic knowledge is at present insufficient for us systematically to synthesize psychotropic drugs aimed at correcting this or that mental disorder. Most existing drugs have been discovered by chance, not design. Once a new psychotropic drug is discovered the drug firms attempt to produce variants of the basic molecular configuration in the hope of discovering a related compound that has less undesirable side-effects or is more potent or that circumvents a rival's patent. In this way a whole range of phenothiazines and tri-cyclic anti-depressants has been produced, and many of those in current use are more effective than the original substances from which they were developed.

The fact that we do not understand the basic mode of action of such drugs is no excuse for not undertaking careful empirical tests of their efficacy: in fact, it makes it even more necessary. Although the situation is improving, such tests have often been conducted only long after the introduction of the drug and have not been sufficiently careful or thorough. There are many reasons why this is so.

First, the drug companies, the communication media, the public and the medical profession are all motivated to accept uncritically the beneficial effects of a new drug. The drug companies' main goal is profit, and they are interested in selling as much of a new drug as they can. Hence their advertising claims are often exaggerated and insufficient warnings are given of the dangers attendant on the use of a new drug. Many advertisements suggest by implication that powerful psychotropic drugs should be prescribed by general practitioners for comparatively trivial complaints. For example, one new tranquillizer was advertised with four pictures of endearing children suffering from such 'complaints' as being picky eaters or troublemakers. Another was recommended as suitable for the anxious housewife with the caption: 'She welcomed marriage, children, domesticity. But sometimes the change seems too much, too sudden. She is frustrated and lonely. To lighten her load for worries comes' ... a new tranquillizer.

These advertisements were withdrawn several years ago and there has been a tendency for the advertising of psychotropic drugs to be toned down, but it has not changed that much. The reader who wishes to find out how drug companies rate the intelligence of doctors has only to pick up a copy of any magazine aimed at them. Taking an issue of *World Medicine* at random, I discovered an advertisement for a tranquillizer showing an attractive young mother who is able to combine playing hockey with looking after two young children, presumably thanks to the action of the drug which is advertised as 'the tranquillizer for active patients'. The same issue carried an advertisement for an anti-depressant: a picture of a happy if somewhat chaotic child's birthday party is accompanied by the slogan 'for the treatment of depression in general practice'.

The public is of course almost as anxious as the drug companies to believe in new and wonder cures, and in this they are abetted by the press, which often sensationalizes the effects of new drugs even more than the drug companies themselves. Finally, doctors do not like to admit either to themselves or their patients that for many complaints there is little they can do to help. They therefore tend to seize eagerly on new treatments, and of course they are besieged by the public to hand out drugs. Osler remarked in the nineteenth century that 'a desire to take medicine is perhaps the great feature that distinguishes man from the animals.'

A second factor contributing to an insufficiently critical evaluation of new drugs is the archaic fashion in which medicine has been taught, at least in Britain: the teaching methods have furthered a tendency to rely on authority rather than to question and evalute research results. In many medical schools, students are still taught to learn things off parrot-fashion, and they are rarely encouraged to query the judgement of the consultants who teach them. Many consultants regard diagnosis and treatment as an art rather than a science and, although in some cases this belief may be correct, it can serve as an excuse for not carrying out properly controlled empirical research.

Moreover, medical schools in Great Britain make little attempt to give a training in research methods. Intending doctors are taught little about how to prescribe and virtually nothing about how to evaluate the literature with which drug companies smother them. The general practitioner's main source of information about new drugs comes from the drug companies themselves: each family doctor in Britain receives free between twenty-five and forty different journals or newsletters published by the drug companies and promoting their wares. The advertising of drugs available only on prescription can only be directed to doctors. Until recently much of it was accompanied by female nudes, and it still appeals more to the doctor's emotions than to his reason. As a senior advertising copy writer put it: 'Razzle-dazzle promotion has come to play a more decisive role than scientific evaluation of drugs in determining the career of a pharmaceutical product.' The drug companies also offer more direct bribes to general practitioners: one doctor has estimated he could have one expensive meal a week at their expense if he wished. It is small wonder that many family doctors remain gullible targets for the mass of advertising directed at them by the drug companies.

A third and related reason for the inadequate investigation of new drugs is that standards of research in medicine are often poor. Many medical journals accept and publish research studies that are ill-designed and badly conducted. Such studies would get short shrift from most journals of physiology, agriculture or experimental psychology. Out of about a dozen papers recently presented at a meeting of the Royal Society of Medicine, only one produced statistical calculations to show that the results being presented were significant and not merely due to chance: this paper was given not by a doctor but by a psychologist. In a report published by the Council for International Organizations of Medical Sciences, it is alleged that the standards of most published work on clinical trials of new drugs are abysmal, partly through lack of good research facilities and partly through a dearth of first-class investigators.

The acceptance of woefully low research standards in medicine may arise from historical causes. There has always been a mystique attached to the practice of medicine, and the medical profession is encouraged by the general public to preserve this mystique: the public desperately want to have faith in their doctors, while they remain properly suspicious of the activities of many other applied scientists like engineers and architects. In addition, many medical journals are financed by advertisements placed by drug companies, and this is scarcely the best way of securing independence.

A concrete instance of the backwardness of medical research is the belated introduction of the 'Randomized Control Trial'. This method consists of assigning patients suffering from a given complaint at random to different treatments: one group might be given either a traditionl treatment or no treatment, whilst a second group receives the new treatment whose effects are to be evaluated. All patients are assessed before and after treatment by doctors who do not know to which group a given patient was assigned. Corresponding techniques were introduced into agriculture and psychology around the turn of the century: in medicine the first randomized control trial was conducted in 1952. It met with considerable resistance from many doctors. The first such test of the effectiveness of coronary care units was undertaken in 1971, against considerable medical opposition. The results were negative – heart patients treated at home did slightly better than those treated in coronary care units. When the outcome was reported to one of the leading opponents of the test, it was inadvertently given the wrong way round, that is to say, as validating the efficacy of coronary care units. He immediately pointed out that it fully confirmed his opinion that such tests were unethical, since they were unfair to the control group who did not get the treatment. When he subsequently learned the correct results of the trial, he failed to draw the inference that it was coronary care units themselves that were unethical.

This story brings us to a fourth reason for the lack of sufficient good research into new drugs. There are considerable practical difficulties. If a doctor has great faith in a new method of treatment, he may feel it unethical to withhold it from a random group of patients for the sake of a clinical trial. This is often a rather spurious reason for not conducting adequately controlled tests, since, as in the case of the coronary care units, there is a good chance that it will be the patients not given the new treatment who are the lucky ones. Further difficulties arise in persuading a sufficient number of hospitals or doctors to take part in clinical tests, in ensuring that the groups given the new drug and those given the placebo are properly matched for the severity of the illness, and in securing objective evaluation of their progress. Finally in the case of some drugs, any ill effects may take many years to show.

A fifth and final reason for the uncritical use and apparent success of many new drug treatments is that when a new drug is launched it has one great advantage – its placebo effect. The more faith the drug companies, the press, the public and the doctors have in a new drug, the more likely it is to be efficacious, at least for a time. At the University of California three genuine tranquillizers and an inert placebo tablet were administered to four different groups of patients complaining of anxiety. The group given the placebo showed exactly the same amount of improvement as the three groups given the tranquillizers. Several studies have found that the doctor's faith in a drug directly affects the extent to which it helps the patient. Placebo drugs administered by a psychiatrist who believed in their efficacy had a larger beneficial effect than when they were prescribed by a psychiatrist sceptical of their usefulness. For these reasons, a new drug may have a genuinely helpful effect on patients that depends purely on faith and has nothing to do with its direct action. The more doctors and patients believe in the drug, the more it helps, and hence the doctors' faith in it is yet further confirmed.

This situation is of course not confined to psychiatry. The history of medicine is full of examples of the enthusiastic adoption of useless and dangerous treatments. Our ancestors were bled to death by leeches and poisoned by the mercury present in calomel. Indeed, calomel was an ingredient in many teething powders until 1948, when it was discovered that 'pink disease' from which so many babies suffered was in fact the early stages of mercury poisoning caused by swallowing calomel.

There are several reasons, then, why research on new psychotropic drugs is not carried out as quickly and efficiently as it should be; none of them excuse the ease of introduction of new drugs of unknown efficacy and carrying unknown dangers. Although the prescription of amphetamines and barbiturates has probably caused more human misery, the most dramatic disaster caused by a psychotropic drug was the thalidomide tragedy. Introduced as a sedative in Germany in 1957, it was in wide use there and in Britain, Canada and Japan in 1960. In December 1960 a letter appeared in the *British Medical Journal* claiming that it caused irritation of the nerves, and by May 1961 no less than one thousand three hundred cases of this dangerous side-effect had been reported. Although no adequate testing on pregnant animals had been undertaken, one drug company stated in a leaflet that the drug 'can be given with complete safety to pregnant women ... without adverse effects on mother and child.' It was still being advertised as a completely safe drug in late 1961. It continued to be prescribed, and was not removed from the market in Europe until November 1961; it was on sale in Canada until April 1962 and in Japan for a further six months. It is estimated that thalidomide caused the birth of about ten thousand horribly crippled children, as well as directly harming some of those taking the drug.

Thalidomide was never marketed in the USA, where existing legislation prevented the use of any drug until it had been shown to be both efficacious and safe to the satisfaction of the Food and Drug Administration. A member of their staff, Dr Kelsey, pointed out that thalidomide had a similar chemical formula to a drug known to produce monster births in rats. Legislation controlling the introduction of new drugs was introduced in Britain only in 1968, partly as a result of the thalidomide tragedy: amazingly, the legislation provided only that new drugs must be shown to be reasonably safe, not that they should also be shown to be effective. The fact that there is some legislative control over drugs is no cause for complacency. The drug companies continue to advertise and the doctors to prescribe barbiturates to help sleep, amphetamine for obesity and potent antidepressants like amitriptyline for bedwetting in children – a condition that usually passes of its own accord and should not normally be regarded as meriting clinical intervention.

In view of their addictive properties, the tragic consequences of long-term use, and the availability of alternative drugs that appear to be less dangerous, it is doubtful if barbiturates and amphetamines should ever be employed clinically. Their administration to fractious children with no physical sign of brain damage is hard to justify. The minor tranquillizers and some antidepressant drugs appear to be helpful in cases of anxiety and depression respectively, though with the minor tranquillizers there is a risk of dependence. In the absence of any other effective treatment for schizophrenia and manic-depressive psychosis, the use of phenothiazines and lithium appears to be beneficial, despite their adverse effects on some aspects of the personality and of intellectual functioning.

All the drugs mentioned poison the central nervous system, but then so does alcohol, which is freely taken by most of the adult population. The ignorance of general practitioners about the effects and optimal mode of use of most of these drugs is such that with the exception of the minor tranquillizers they should probably not be allowed to prescribe them. They are no less gullible than the general population, and are usually much busier; their main source of information about drugs comes from literature put out by the drug companies, which are not noted for their objectivity about their own products.

The reader will have noticed one curious fact about the psychotropic drugs in use: most were discovered by accident. There is now a vast volume of work on the chemistry of the brain, but the subject is so complicated that the knowledge we are acquiring can still not be put to direct use in the alleviation of mental distress. We do not in fact know the precise mode of action of any of the drugs currently in use, any more than we know why aspirin reduces pain. It seems likely that with advancing knowledge we shall discover over the next decade more psychotropic drugs that will have a useful part to play in the alleviation of the misery of nervous illness.

Nevertheless, it is unlikely that Freud's belief that we will one day be able to cure all mental illness with drugs will ever be borne out. In chapter 9, I argued that most neurosis probably arises as are sult of experiences that are unfortunate in the context of the individual's genetic make-up. In all probability, neurotics are people who have learned habits and ways of thought that do not fit them to cope with the particular stresses to which they are exposed. The faulty learning is doubtless reflected in connections made between nerve cells in the brain, but the changes in brain circuitry that underlie learning are almost inconceivably complex: the alterations in neural conductivity that mediate the memory of a single experience are widely scattered throughout the brain. In consequence, it is most unlikely that we shall ever be able to cure neurosis by physical methods of treatment, anymore than we can cure a fault in a computer program by tinkering with the computer's hardware.

The outlook for psychotics may be somewhat different. There is a considerable hereditary component in both schizophrenia and manic-depressive psychosis. If what is inherited is a deficiency in some aspect of brain chemistry then it might be possible one day to cure these illnesses by chemotherapy rather than, as at present, merely to alleviate some of their symptoms. Even this hope is a remote possibility: the form that psychoses take is certainly determined by experience, and even if a chemical defect is involved the defect itself may result in faulty learning from childhood. Although chemotherapy given in later life might cure the underlying chemical deficit, it would not alter the maladaptive circuitry already set up.

21

Ethics and Mental Illness

I have now described the major methods currently available for helping the mentally ill, and have tried to assess their efficacy. The picture I have drawn is dark but, I believe, realistic. If we are ever to improve treatment it is important to understand how little we know about mental illness. No school of thought has a monopoly of the truth, though some may have caught fragmentary aspects of it. Drugs can palliate some conditions, they do not cure; behaviour therapy can help phobics and obsessives, but is still only a promising method for other conditions; psychoanalysis appears to be unhelpful, and most other forms of psychotherapy also meet with indifferent success; the personality of the therapist may be more important than the theories he espouses. We know that mental breakdown can be triggered by a wide variety of crises – marital problems, failure in business, battle shock and even an all-pervading discontent with one's lot. We know little of ultimate causes. Genetic endowment can undoubtedly predispose to schizophrenia and manic-depressive psychosis and is implicated in some neuroses. Early learning and parental upbringing may play a part in determining some of the details of how a breakdown is expressed, but how far such factors are actually responsible for causing mental disorder we do not know.

In the final chapters, I consider both what society can do about the problem and also what action should be taken by the individual confronted by a neurosis of his own or of someone close to him. I shall start with broad problems often of an ethical nature and move successively towards more specific issues.

The very concept of mental illness is complex and treacherous. If someone complains of an incapacitating paralysis, there are three possibilities. He may have an organic disease of the nervous system – a physical illness; or he may have developed this symptomatology through psychological causes of which he is unaware and be unable voluntarily to control it; or he may simply be malingering – to obtain discharge from the army, to absent himself from work or to seek refuge in a hospital, he may quite consciously decide to simulate illness. It was Charcot, working in Paris towards the close of the last century, who first clearly recognized the second possibility, and he regarded it as hysteria: he also labelled it as an illness.

Now it is clearly important both for society and for the individual presenting the symptoms to distinguish between these three categories. If someone has a neurological disease, they should not be blamed for their condition, and the appropriate treatment is usually physical intervention with their bodies. If we are certain that someone is deliberately malingering, we may feel entitled to blame him and on occasion to punish him in an effort to make him return to his duties. If, however, someone is unable to carry out the duties they owe to society because they are, without consciously willing it, in a psychological state that precludes their effective functioning, it is useless and inhumanitarian to blame or to punish. We must seek whatever means we can to help. By labelling hysteria and other neuroses as mental illness, Charcot and subsequently Freud, who initially worked under him, undoubtedly helped the lot of those who were incapacitated or in misery for psychological rather than physical reasons.

Szasz and others have argued that it is wrong to extend the term illness to people who are incapacitated through psychological causes. The arguments are complex, and although some of them have some substance others appear to be muddled. Moreover there is such a wide spectrum of disorders nowadays referred to as mental illness that it is necessary to make many distinctions: perhaps some mental disorders should be classified as mental illness and others should not be so designated. I shall start by asking the question how far, given the accepted meaning of the term illness, mental disorder falls within its scope, and will then consider the consequences both desirable and undesirable of regarding mental disorders as illnesses.

Everyone would surely agree that if an organ of the body is malfunctioning for physical reasons the use of the term illness is appropriate. There is considerable evidence that abnormalities in the biochemistry of the brain are involved in schizophrenia and manic-depressive psychosis: if we knew for certain that such psychoses were directly caused by abnormalities in brain biochemistry, then we would not hesitate to classify them as illnesses. Moreover, both conditions, in common with many other illnesses, respond to drugs: the drugs in question are known to affect the biochemical systems thought to be implicated in each disorder. Cases of poisoning are invariably described as illness and there is no question but that psychoses can be produced by direct poisoning of the central nervous system due to taking alcohol, opiates and other drugs over long periods of time. It would appear then to be reasonable to ascribe most cases of psychoses to illness. Szasz has argued that if physical causes were fully established, they should be called 'neurological illness' not 'mental illness', but this seems a mere quibble: the primary effects are on the mind, not on the body.

In the case of the neuroses, it is more difficult to reach a definite decision. Most people would consider the severe neurotic to be incapacitated for psychological reasons: I can best illustrate what this involves by drawing an analogy with computers. A computer may produce output that is distorted or unintelligible either because there is a fault in the hardware (physical illness) or because there is a fault in the way it has been programmed (faulty learning). The former kind of fault can be corrected by engineers (doctors), the latter by programmers (psychologists) who may know little or nothing of the details of the construction of the computer but who understand the relationship between its input (environment) and output (behaviour).

The analogy is of course too simplistic. Even though neurotic disorder may be triggered by unfortunate experiences, the connections set up in the nervous system affect the remainder of the body and some genuine physical pathology may develop. The autonomic nervous system may be overactive and produce physical symptoms such as fluctuations in heart rate, sweating, and high blood pressure; indeed actual tissue damage like the formation of stomach ulcers may result. Moreover, the delicate biochemical balance of the brain may be affected, and for this reason it becomes possible sometimes to alleviate the neurotic's condition by means of engineering – administering drugs or giving ECT.

The involvement of physical symptoms in severe neurosis and the fact that it can be alleviated by physical methods of treatment once again suggest that it is reasonable to regard it at least in part as an illness. Moreover, it cannot be argued that because neurotic disorder may be largely of psychogenic origin it should not be classified as an illness. Severe headaches are often the direct result of constricting muscles because the sufferer feels tense or anxious, and there are considerable psychogenic predisposing factors in the development of many organic diseases including tuberculosis. Although it is not a conclusive argument, my own breakdown felt to me very much like an illness: during my spells of elation I did not admit that I was still unwell, but in retrospect I can see that I was not myself. Moreover, as I have explained, I now think that I could not voluntarily have done anything to help myself, and this was brought home to me during my last bout of depression when I fought hard to keep going. An inability to restore oneself to effective functioning by a conscious effort of will does have some bearing on whether a condition should be classified as an illness. Although the course of a physical illness may certainly be affected by one's attitude it cannot be willed away, nor can some forms of mental disorder.

For all these reasons then, it seems reasonable to regard anyone severely incapacitated by a neurotic disorder as mentally ill. One of the arguments adduced by the antipsychiatry movement against the use of the term 'mental illness' is the difficulty of deciding who should be so labelled. The argument can be highlighted by some research undertaken by Professor Rosenhan of Stanford University. He and seven collaborators set out to gain admission to psychiatric wards. They presented themselves at eight different hospitals complaining that they had been hearing voices. When asked what the voices said, they replied that they were often unclear but they seemed to be saying 'empty', 'hollow' and 'thud'. They assumed that the interviewing psychiatrist would interpret this to mean that their lives were empty and hollow. Throughout the remainder of their initial psychiatric interview and during the whole of the rest of their stay in hospital they behaved completely normally. They gave the psychiatrist detailed and accurate accounts of their life histories, including their relationships with their parents, their immediate family and their friends. All eight were admitted to psychiatric wards, and all but one were given the diagnosis 'schizophrenia'.

Whilst in hospital, they behaved normally except that they took detailed notes on everything that happened: at first they did so in secret, in order not to arouse suspicion, but when they found that their 'compulsive writing behaviour' (to quote from the case notes) was accepted as part of their illness, they wrote out their observations in public. Each pseudo-patient remained in hospital until the psychiatrist agreed to his discharge: their average stay was nineteen days, with a range of seven to fifty-two days. None of the hospital staff saw through the deception, though about one third of their fellow-patients did. In fact, on discharge their case notes were marked not 'recovered' but 'schizophrenia in remission'.

Their experiences show that it is difficult for psychiatrists and other hospital staff to distinguish between the mentally ill and the malingerer. This is scarcely surprising: if you went to a hospital simulating the symptoms of acute appendicitis, you would probably find yourself on the operating table within a matter of hours. In the case of voluntary admissions, it is understandable that psychiatrists should err on the side of admitting people who do not need to be admitted: the risk of suicide must be for ever present in their minds, and with the exception of a few malingerers, and the occasional research worker, it is inconceivable that anyone should voluntarily seek admission to a psychiatric ward unless he were in a dire mental condition. What is perhaps more surprising is that in the course of up to fifty-two days in hospital, no psychiatrist changed his initial diagnosis, despite the fact that throughout their stay the pseudo-patients presented no symptoms whatever and claimed that they felt fine and no longer heard voices. This result is all the more alarming when it is remembered that the agreement between different psychiatrists on diagnostic category is often poor. When two psychiatrists independently interview genuine patients on admission, they only place five or six out of every ten patients in the same diagnostic category, for example schizophrenia, obsessive-compulsive neurosis, anxiety neurosis.

Rosenhan's results suggest that psychiatric labels should be used with caution and that psychiatrists, like everyone else, should remember that they are fallible and should be prepared to revise their judgements in the light of new evidence. Some psychiatrists apparently find it difficult to distinguish even between schizophrenia and malingering. If this is true, how much more difficult must it be to distinguish between the different shades of neuroticism and to decide how severe a neurosis must be before it is labelled as a mental illness. Neuroticism is of course a continuous variable. Even the sanest amongst us usually exhibit some neurotic traits at one time or another: we do things that rational reflection would show to be self-destructive, we suffer unreasonable fears and anxieties, and without thinking about it we may fall into innocuous forms of obsessive behaviour: the distinction between normal grief and neurotic depression is hard to draw.

Although some have used this as an argument for discontinuing the use of the term mental illness, it is a poor one. Many physical illnesses also lie on a continuum with physical health. Whether we are examining respiratory function or blood pressure, there is no cut-off point at which we can say everyone on one side is healthy and everyone on the other side is ill. Nor can we lay down that everyone having fewer than a specified number of hairs is bald, and everyone with more is not. There are nonetheless clear-cut cases of baldness and of clinically high blood pressure, and it appears to me that there are also clear-cut cases of people who are mentally ill and of people who are not. In our present state of ignorance, it is perhaps not worth attempting to specify too closely where to draw the boundary. It may well be that current fashion has swung too far and that many of those who attend psychiatric clinics or are given psychotropic drugs by their general practitioners have no organic malfunction and would be better off in the long run if they were made to take responsibility for their own behaviour. Moreover, there are instances where psychiatrists themselves have changed their mind about what should and should not be called mental illness: it was only recently that the American Psychiatric Association decided that homosexuality should not be regarded as a classifiable mental illness, and this is a warning that we should be on our guard against applying the label mental illness to all forms of behaviour that either differ from the norm or are disapproved of by society.

As a rough guideline it seems logical to conclude that anyone exhibiting self-destructive or maladaptive behaviour as a direct result of damage to nervous tissue or disordered brain biochemistry should be regarded as having an illness whether the physical abnormalities are caused by genetic or psychogenic factors or are due to poisoning by drugs and other agents or to infection. Until we know a great deal more than we do at the moment, there are bound to be large differences of opinion about who comes under this definition and who does not. It would be nice to think that those suffering from the above conditions can no longer voluntarily control aspects of their behaviour whereas those without such physical pathology could and should take responsibility for their actions, but the whole concept of the will and of what can and cannot be done voluntarily is one of the most obscure issues in psychology and philosophy. In practice, we are predisposed to think of people as being mentally ill where they perform deviant actions under a compulsion.

Compulsive pederasts and exhibitionists would often like to have better control of their desires, and describe themselves as acting in the grip of some external force.

I now examine some of the remaining arguments of Szasz and others against the use of the term 'mental illness'. These arguments turn not so much upon the definition of illness and the nature of mental disorder as on the consequences of using the term.

First, Szasz argues that labelling anyone as mentally ill has deleterious effects on the person so labelled. Others may fear and despise anyone thought to be mentally ill, depersonify him by failing to take him seriously ('fail to treat him as a person' in current jargon) and strip him of his legal rights. Such is the prejudice against mental illness that once a person has been so labelled he may be penalized in many ways, for example when he comes to seek a job, as I have already illustrated.

Although Szasz is undoubtedly right in thinking that there is considerable prejudice against those suffering from mental illness and even against those who have recovered from it, he is surely wrong in supposing that this prejudice arises from the name we give the condition. All known societies appear to have a word for 'insanity', and in Western civilization there was more prejudice against and more inhumane treatment of the insane before the label 'illness' was applied. Mental illness is a distressing condition not merely for the sufferer but for those around him. Neurotics tend to be extremely selfish and to be unintentionally destructive to others, as indeed I was myself. Dealing with a neurotic is a frustrating experience for family and friends: some of his behaviour and many of his feelings will be irrational and inappropriate to the circumstances and, with the best will in the world, it is often difficult or impossible to help him. Moreover, many of those in contact with him may at some level fear that they might one day lose control of themselves and may disguise their own fears by despising or blaming the neurotic. None of these problems would be overcome be ceasing to regard extreme forms of mental disorder as an illness: indeed they might well be exacerbated, since it is easier to forgive someone for behaving badly if we think of him as ill.

Laing has developed one form of this argument in relation to schizophrenia. Much of what the schizophrenic says can be regarded as an attempt at communication, albeit using language in an oblique way that is difficult to understand. By adopting an attitude of superiority, the psychotherapist fails to understand what the schizophrenic is trying to communicate – he puts everything the patient says down to madness. It is doubtful, *pace* Laing, if schizophrenics can be helped towards recovery by any form of psychotherapy. Nevertheless, adopting superior attitudes and failing to take patients seriously can certainly make them feel very unhappy, as I have stressed in my account of my own breakdown, and could well help to perpetuate the illness. Whilst, therefore, Laing's point has some validity, it cannot be met by a change in terminology: we must seek rather to change our attitudes to the mentally incapacitated.

The second argument is that, by labelling people as mentally ill and segregating severe cases from society, we are concealing from ourselves the alleged fact that society is to blame for the creation of mental illness. Different writers have blamed different aspects of society. Laing attributes schizophrenia to the hypocrisy practised in the nuclear family: parents say one thing whilst meaning another and the growing child does not know where or who he is. Laing is, however, unable to explain why some children survive such treatment whilst others become psychotic. Some authorities have blamed society at large for imposing 'false' values on its members. As we have seen, the false values vary with the theorist, and include sexual taboos, sanctions against the expression of strong feelings, the cult of success, a materialistic outlook, too authoritarian an upbringing, an insufficiently authoritarian upbringing, and so on and so on. It may be true that some mental illness is produced by the way society is organized, and maybe we should attempt to change society, but this is no reason for not recognizing the existence of psychological casualties and doing what we can to help them.

The argument that by treating the mentally ill we merely postpone the problem of dealing with the underlying causes in society seems both repulsively callous and curiously illogical. They do need help, and it would be absurd to withhold it from them on the grounds that society is to blame for their condition. Moreover, there is no reason at all why helping those in distress should prevent us from trying to improve society. The real problem in changing society is that we cannot agree on what changes to make.

A third argument against treating people as mentally ill is that by caring for them as sick people we make them dependent on such help and prevent them taking responsibility for their own actions. Again, this may be an argument for restricting medical care for mental disorder to those who would benefit from it, but it is not an argument for ceasing to use the term 'mentally ill'. One proof of this is that Illich has recently applied a parallel set of arguments to attack the increasing use of medical care for the physically ill. He suggests that it is pointless, cruel and insulting to the dignity of man to prolong the life of those incapacitated by terminal illness by resorting to the long-term use of machinery to sustain the action of the heart, lungs and kidneys; that the overuse of medicine produces as much illness as it cures; and that it prevents patients taking responsibility for their own condition. Although he advocates restricting the institutionalized treatment and care of the ill, he does not of course wish to abandon the use of the term 'physical illness'.

The question of how much and what kind of care society provides for the mentally disordered remains an important issue, and the anti-psychiatry movement has been helpful in drawing attention to it. Both in Britain and North America the use of psychiatric and counselling service has enormously increased over the last twenty years. The number of attendances at out-patient departments of psychiatric hospitals in Britain increased threefold between 1964 and 1970. Such increases do not reflect a change in the prevalence of mental illness or neurotic disorder. As I have already pointed out, mental disorder is as common in under-developed countries as in the West. Neurotic unhappiness is perhaps a permanent part of the human condition. The increase in the extent to which society cares for the mentally disordered is part of a general tendency for the state to assume responsibility for its weaker or more unfortunate members, whether they be the unemployed, the old, children in need of education, the physically ill or the mentally disabled.

It may be that many of those currently attending psychiatric clinics would be bettered cared for within a family, but the extended and closely knit family is becoming increasingly rare in the Western world. In Italy, the old have a traditional and useful role to occupy within the family, and they appear to be happier than in America and Britain, where they often depend largely on facilities organized for them by the state. We cannot, however, legislate to recreate the extended family, and in its absence some of the roles it formerly performed must be taken over by professionals who are paid to do so.

A further reason for the increase in psychiatric and counselling services may lie in a redistribution of professional duties. In particular, the Church is coming to play a smaller part in society and presumably fewer of the mentally distressed are receiving guidance and comfort from the clergy. A national survey conducted in the late Fifties showed that at that time forty-two per cent of Americans seeking help for personal problems turned in the first instance to the clergy.

Moreover it is likely that modern society does present its members with more psychological problems than many previous civilizations, if only because of the accelerated rate of change. Within the span of a lifetime, we now have to accustom ourselves to radically new ways of living. Much of this is due to technological innovations – the motor car, the aeroplane, television, the birth-control pill and the computer which is only just beginning to make its presence felt. Sudden and radical changes in our artefacts have been accompanied by and have in part produced equally drastic changes in mores and attitudes. Whether or not they are realized, the expectations of women, the poor, and the under-privileged are completely different today from twenty years ago. Few people are content, as during most of history, merely to accept their lot in life, and all notions of social justice are in the melting pot. If the underprivileged have raised expectations to which it may be difficult to adapt, the privileged have the equally difficult problem of accepting new ways of thought that threaten their way of life.

The rate of change in our artefacts means that the slow process of trial and error, by which in the past houses, spoons, or chairs evolved, is no longer satisfactory: millions of copies of a new artefact may be produced before its use has stood up to the test of time. It was many years after high-rise flats began to be built that research revealed the psychological problems they created. We have therefore had to sub-stitute self-conscious design criteria based on psychological research for the gradual evolution of new articles, though we clearly have a long way to go in this respect. Just as we need professionals to help in the design of manufactured goods, so we need professionals to help us to face the changes in life-style. The changes affect not merely individual localities or sects as heretofore, but, through the influence of the mass media and the ease of transportation, the whole of the Western world. The role of the psychologist, therefore, is likely to become more rather than less important both in helping individuals to adjust to change and in under-taking research on the likely consequences of change and advising on its probable effects.

For the first time in history we have the technology to control fire, pestilence, flood and starvation. We have yet to learn how to control ourselves, and until we do so we are likely to put our technological knowledge to ill use. If we are to improve man's lot – and perhaps if we are to survive as a species – we need a greater understanding of man himself, and it is hard to see where this is to come from except from the systematic investigation of man. Although the danger of making people dependent on professional help and therefore less able to help themselves is a very real one, I believe there is no alternative. We cannot, as Illich would have us do, put aside the knowledge and power that we have gained and revert to the mythical simplicity of the Golden Age.

The antipsychiatry movement in general and Szasz in particular believe that nobody should be detained in hospital for psychiatric reasons against their will. The ethical problem is a difficult one to which there is no clear solution, although most of Szasz's own arguments are based on rhetoric and on a misleading comparison between the condition of the detained mental patient and slavery. The comparison is misleading, since the purpose of slavery is the exploitation of the labour of the slave or of his or her body for sexual purposes. The reasons for compulsory psychiatric detention are quite different: they are either to protect the patient or to protect society from him. The extent to which society should protect the individual from his own self-destruction is a debatable issue, and is at the centre of the question of how noxious a drug has to be before its sale is banned by law. On humanitarian grounds, most of us would favour the hospitalization of the mentally incapacitated where there was a serious risk of suicide or self-mutilation. Similarly, if we knew for certain that someone, if left at large, would commit a murder we would surely feel justified in detaining him. In practice the problem is to know whether someone whose mind is deranged really is a danger either to himself or to others, but the difficulty of taking a decision in some instances is not a good reason for shirking it in all.

If the principle of compulsory detention in psychiatric wards is accepted, a further problem arises: to what extent should the patient be compelled against his will to submit to treatment? In the case of talking psychotherapy, the issue hardly arises: mere talk is unlikely to change anyone against their will. Irreversible brain operations, ECT, drug treatment and severe electric shocks as delivered by some behaviour therapists present a different problem. In practice the line between giving such treatments with and without a patient's consent is a thin one. Many psychiatric patients who admit themselves to hospital voluntarily are in such a state of misery that they will clutch at any treatment offered. Moreover, they are often dependent on the psychiatrist and readily suggestible; few of them have the knowledge to assess realistically the wisdom of accepting a given form of treatment. It is surely impossible to draw up any hard and fast guidelines on ethical grounds. In view of the irreversibility of brain lesions and our lack of knowledge of their long-term effects, I believe they should never be offered to psychiatric patients whether or not the treatment is accepted voluntarily. On the other hand ECT may on occasion save someone from suicide, and as a temporary measure drugs may help to control homicidal impulses.

Freedom is not the only goal of human existence, and it seems reasonable to take the decision about certain kinds of treatment out of the hands of the patient where there is a real risk of suicide or where, by giving drugs, homicidal impulses are reduced and the patient is able to live in a less constrained way. It is in fact comparatively rare for the mentally deranged to be a danger to others. It is not at present possible to change people's outlook by making them sick with apomorphine or giving them severe electric shocks whilst watching scenes of violence. If we ever were in a position to control others' behaviour in these ways, it would be a difficult ethical question to decide when society should exercise such control. Few people challenge society's right to lock up violent and dangerous criminals in order to protect the innocent, and if we were sure of the effectiveness of our methods, it would again seem more humanitarian to offer the dangerous criminal treatment as an alternative to more or less permanent incarceration.

Most of the issues are of course not as clear-cut as saving someone from suicide or homicide. How unbalanced does someone have to be before we save him from giving away all his worldly possessions? It is easy for Szasz to talk about stripping people of their legal rights, but as someone who has been mentally ill though not certifiably so, I think that had I been saved by compulsory detention from acts highly damaging to myself I would on recovery have been grateful to society. Despite the many borderline cases between madness and sanity, there are people who are so clearly deranged that it is unfair to them to allow them to take responsibility for their own actions. I have no sympathy whatever for Laing's view that madness is a state to be admired, in which the sufferer has transcendent and valuable experiences: it is usually a state of abject suffering and degradation.

Nor does it seem true, as Laing and Szasz have suggested, that it is common in Western society to label people as mentally ill simply because they deviate from society's norms: the severe schizophrenic is not incapacitated merely because society provides him with the wrong milieu in which to live. He is out of touch with reality, is unable to formulate his own ends or to govern his actions in such a way as to achieve those ends, he makes little or no contribution to society, and cannot maintain himself. If he is to survive at all, he must be nurtured and nursed by society. There is a clear distinction between those who dislike the way in which society is organized and who seek to change it in well thought out ways such as forming political parties, writing pamphlets or planting bombs, and the inconsequential behaviour of a schizophrenic, which serves no conscious goals.

Although in arguing that by labelling people as mentally ill, society is merely protecting itself from those who deviate from its norms, Szasz may have overstated his case, this does not mean that no problems arise. The Russian government's use of detention and compulsory treatment in psychiatric wards for political dissidents is a clear case in point. In the West a large measure of political dissidence is tolerated, and where it oversteps the mark, as in incitement to violence or acts of terrorism, it is usually dealt with by a process of law rather than by psychiatric detention. There are, however, once again bound to be borderline cases where we are in doubt whether fanatics should be restrained from committing criminal acts by imprisonment or whether their actions should be regarded as the symptoms of a mental illness and they should be dealt with as psychiatric cases. It is, moreover, necessary to exercise vigilance lest the sedation of psychiatric patients or the administration of amphetamines to children diagnosed as minimally brain damaged is carried out not for their own good but to make life easier for those around them.

Such difficulties can only be ameliorated by obtaining greater understanding into the nature of mental disorders than we have at present. In the meantime, for both practical and humane reasons, it seems essential to recognize the existence of mental illness and to take steps to protect the insane from themselves and society from them. Present arrangements are not always satisfactory, and they can be abused. In Britain, people can be committed to a psychiatric ward for up to twenty-eight days on the signed statement of two physicians, one of them a psychiatrist, who testify that the interests of the patient's health and safety or the protection of other persons cannot be secured otherwise than by such detention. Application for committal has to be made either by the nearest relative or by a social worker after consultation with the nearest relative. Under an emergency procedure, a patient can be committed for up to seventy-two hours on the statement of a single doctor: this procedure can also be used to detain for three days voluntary patients already in hospital who wish to discharge themselves but who in the opinion of the psychiatrist are a danger to themselves or others.

After a patient has been admitted on a twenty-eight-day order, the social worker or nearest relative supported by two doctors may seek committal for further periods of up to one year. The nearest relative has the right to challenge in the courts a committal order of this kind. The patient and nearest relative may appeal for release any time within six months of initial committal and thereafter at yearly (or two-yearly) intervals when committal orders are due for renewal. The appeal is made to a Mental Health Review Tribunal which is composed of doctors, lawyers and other senior citizens. Similar provisions exist in most parts of America, though committal usually requires an order from a judge, or in some states, a jury.

Although most psychiatrists presumably act in the best interests of their patients, they are put in an unfortunate position in having also to consider the interests of society in discharging patients: as the results of the Rosenhan study show, they may be unwilling or unable to recognize having made a mistake. Nor will the patient's nearest relative necessarily act in the patient's interest when it comes to securing release. It might be safer to allocate to each patient a counsel whose duty would be to secure his release at the earliest moment consistent with his own health and safety, so that the onus of proof for continued detention would fall on the psychiatrist. Putting one person or group of people in sole charge of others is a procedure always liable to abuse, and it is particularly dangerous in the case of the mentally ill, who are not able to fend for themselves.

It has frequently been pointed out that the wholesale discharge of large numbers of mental patients from hospitals is in itself no solution to the problem of mental illness – either for the patients themselves or for the community. In Bayshore, Long Island, discharged patients were 'frequently found wandering across neighbours' lawns in the middle of the night. Several appeared on the main thoroughfare directing traffic.' Many former mental patients 'are walking the streets of Manhattan: many of the derelicts and alcoholics in New York City who sleep in the doorways at night and panhandle in the daytime were formerly patients at Central Islip Hospital.' The presence of a schizophrenic in a family can be a severe burden and may render all the other members of the family wretched. Even the provision of aftercare facilities does not entirely meet such problems, since the majority of discharged patients fail to keep the appointments made for them.

Szasz has pointed out that conditions inside many psychiatric hospitals may actually promote insanity, so that a committal order can constitute a self-fulfilling prophecy. It is clear that psychiatrists should not be the judge of their own case, and since the medical profession is notorious for rarely being prepared to give evidence against fellow-members, it is essential that conditions inside psychiatric hospitals should be subject to independent scrutiny from outside the profession. There have been several cases in England recently of long-term patients being abused and even beaten to death by nurses. At a hospital in Lancashire a senior nurse was convicted of the manslaughter of a patient. A Committee of Inquiry into conditions in the hospital was set up and in its report, published in 1972, concluded that nurses had been systematically defrauding and stealing from patients; the inquiry also accepted some allegations of cruelty to patients, including setting alight the slippers of one and the dressing-gown of another; the standards of catering were condemned, and it was alleged that some patients were kept in dank rooms at temperatures of 46°F with insufficient clothing. In 1974, two members of the staff of a hospital in Kent submitted to the British National Health Authorities a document alleging cruelty to long-stay patients: the document was signed by forty further members of the nursing staff. They alleged that they had witnessed physical assualts on patients by other members of staff, cruel and unnecessary regimentation of patients, and the deliberate taunting of patients by staff. In fairness to the hospital authorities it should be pointed out that such troubles are largely caused by the difficulty of obtaining suitable nurses and by woefully inadequate budgets.

There is a need for closer inspection of psychiatric wards. If all committed patients were provided with agents who could act in their interests, the agents could also be charged with this duty. The size of the problem of involuntary commitment may be gauged by the numbers so committed at any one time: in England and Wales only six per cent of psychiatric in-patients are compulsorily detained in hospital: this means that the total number is about seven thousand, as compared to some thirty thousand detained in prisons.

The problem appears to be of a different order of magnitude in the USA. In 1972 over half the admissions to public mental hospitals there were involuntary: nearly 200,000 patients were committed against their will. In America, even voluntarily committed patients can have their rights as citizens seriously infringed. On admission, patients may be asked to sign an agreement with the director of the hospital that they will agree to remain in hospital for a minimum specified period of time. Such agreements are not legally binding, but many patients presumably do not appreciate this. Even voluntary patients may be restricted to closed wards, or allowed access to the hospital grounds but not allowed outside the institution (grounds parole). Some hospitals censor patients' mail, a practice of doubtful legality. It is of course necessary to have some discipline in any institution and patients' freedom (to have visitors, get out of bed and so on) is limited even in ordinary hospitals. Nevertheless it is questionable whether the restrictions imposed on voluntary patients by many psychiatric hospitals, particularly in America, are justifiable as being in the patient's own interest. Again, it is hard to see any solution to these problems other than setting up inspectors not themselves medically qualified but with the power to take legal action on patients' behalf where maltreatment or unnecessary infringement of liberty occurs.

In the United States the courts have recently been increasingly concerned with the rights of mental patients. In one of the most important cases (*Wyatt* v. *Stickney*), an action was brought against the state of Alabama for depriving a patient of his legal rights. The court found against the state, and the judgement was recently upheld by the Fifth Circuit Court of Appeals in New Orleans. The court's ruling is likely to be influential. It decided that psychiatric patients have a constitutional right to a comfortable bed with screens or curtains to ensure privacy, a locker for personal belongings, nutritionally adequate meals, visitors, regular physical exercise and access to the outdoors, interaction with the opposite sex and (a nice touch) a television set in the day room. In addition, committed patients have a right to receive treatment.

The action was a class action in which several bodies including the American Psychological Association were involved in an attempt to make the state of Alabama improve the standards of its mental hospitals. The court ruled that an individualized course of treatment must be drawn up for each patient, and its execution be supervised by a qualified mental health worker. There should be a minimum of two psychiatrists and four other doctors in addition to four clinical psychologists to every two hundred and fifty patients. At the time the suit was brought, the ratios obtaining in two Alabama psychiatric hospitals were one doctor with some psychiatric training for five thousand patients and one psychologist for every one thousand six hundred and seventy. In his appeal, Governor Wallace argued that mental hospitals served the function of custodial care, not treatment. He claimed that the state of Alabama could not afford the cost of effecting the improvements in care directed by the court. One effect of the case is that in Alabama the population of state mental hospitals has been halved and the mental health budget increased by a factor of four.

In another case (*O'Connor* v. *Donaldson*), a Tallahassee court awarded compensatory and punitive damages of $23,000 against a psychiatrist: the patient had brought an action claiming that the psychiatrist had maliciously detained him in hospital against his will for fourteen years without giving him any treatment. The court also ordered the release of the patient. On appeal, the Supreme Court affirmed that non-dangerous patients could not be held in confinement if they were able to live safely outside an institution. It took no decision on the issue of whether committed patients have a right to treatment, and referred the question of damages back to the lower court.

There was a further facet to the Wyatt case. In the original ruling by the District Court, made in 1972, it was explicitly stated that: 'Patients have a right not to be subjected to . . . electroconvulsive treatment . . . without their express and informed consent after consultation with counsel or interested party of the patient's choice.' In *Wyatt* v. *Alderholt*, charges of contempt of court were brought against the director of Bryce Hospital, Alabama, for violating this injunction. It was alleged that seven patients had been given ECT without adequate consent being obtained. Six of the seven patients were diagnosed as having schizophrenia, a condition for which ECT is usually not thought to be indicated. The doctors claimed that in most cases ECT had only been given as an emergency measure, but even here the original court ruling was that the consent of a relative or 'interested party' is required. Although the original charges of contempt of court stand, the court has now revised its ruling on ECT and has ruled that it can be given as an emergency measure but only under a set of carefully prescribed circumstances.

The practice of committing criminals to institutions that attempt reform through behaviour modification is also being queried in the United States. There are two problems. First, some criminals, classified as being defective, have been committed to such institutions and then held there for terms long in excess of the prison sentence they would have received for the crime committed. In 1971, the US Supreme Court ordered the release of one such person who had spent six years in a reform institute in Maryland called Patuxent: had he gone to an ordinary prison he would have been eligible for parole after fifteen months. Second, since anyone committed to such an institute can only obtain release by cooperating with the authorities, there may be unreasonable pressure brought to bear to submit to forms of treatment in conditions that virtually preclude voluntary assent. Much of the treatment may be punitive in nature. In 1971, a court ruled that some of the punishments (described by psychologists as 'negative reinforcements') meted out at Patuxent were 'contrary to the rehabilitation of the inmates and serve no therapeutic value of any kind'. The Maryland legislature is at present reviewing the future of Patuxent and is considering closing it down.

It would be a pity if abuses of this nature resulted in abandoning all efforts to reform criminals by the application of behaviour-modification techniques. Such reform programmes should, however, probably only be available to volunteers, if only because they are most unlikely to work unless the criminal himself wishes to change; as one inmate of Patuxent said: 'Look, man, most of us are good at shamming . . . You spill your guts out in a nice kind of way and act as if you're gaining all these insights . . . Hell, everything I've told 'em is a lie. One big sham.'

The instances given above show the need for vigilance against the infraction of the rights of mental patients. The problems appear to be worse in the USA than in Britain, possibly because state mental hospitals are often run on wholly inadequate funds. A psychiatrist who finds himself in charge of five thousand patients must know that his task is hopeless. Abuses should of course be corrected: the fact that they occur does not mean that there is not a need to recognize that mental illness exists and, as a last resort, to commit some patients against their will.

It will be remembered that throughout the book I have stressed how difficult it is to give any form of psychotherapy without the therapist imposing his own view of life on the patient. This is the final ethical dilemma that I would like to discuss, and since I have said little about sex therapy I will illustrate the dilemma in that context.

Most psychotherapists are currently united in their insistence that everyone should have a rip-roaring sex life. It is of course true that many forms of mental illness, particularly those involving extreme depression or anxiety, are accompanied by a lack of sexual drive. Sexual appetite is normally governed more by psychological than by physiological factors. Although many neurotics have sexual worries, such problems were rated third on the list drawn up by Yalom's patients, as described in a previous chapter. Many patients and many normal people are surprisingly ignorant of sexual techniques and because of the still existing taboo on open discussion of the subject do not know how to give either themselves or their partners the maximum sexual pleasure. The psychotherapeutic profession can clearly play a useful role in imparting such knowledge.

Provided the client wants to know, it can only do good to teach him where the clitoris is located and that most women benefit from clitoral stimulation. The problem is that not everyone does want to know, and that in imparting such knowledge it is often difficult for the therapist to refrain from imposing his own views about what is normal or desirable. For example, Masters and Johnson, on the basis of physiological measurements, have come to the conclusion that the vaginal orgasm is a myth, and partly thanks to them, many therapists teach that there is no benefit to be derived from simultaneous orgasm based on penetration. This view ignores the psychological implications of achieving simultaneous orgasm, and I have known patients become very upset because they could never really come to enjoy the techniques of mutual masturbation as advocated by some therapists. I have forgotten who made the splendid comment on sexual therapy: 'After all, sexual intercourse is no substitute for masturbation.'

Again, the vibrator is probably a useful device for some women, but if others find it distasteful or aesthetically unpleasing, preaching its benefits is likely to make them more rather than less worried. I know one woman who attended a clinic for marital therapy. She had a normal sex life but was undergoing a stormy emotional passage with her husband. She revealed in an aside that she never masturbated. The therapist seized on this remark and advised her to buy a vibrator and practise. She duly did so, and proved to her satisfaction that using this device she was sufficiently normal to obtain three or four orgasms in thirty minutes: she then proceeded to throw the vibrator away, having decided that she preferred sexual intercourse.

Sexual activity varies greatly from person to person, but the myth that it is necessary for well-being is now widely spread in the Western world, partly as a result of the activities of sexual therapists; there is as little evidence for it as for the Victorian idea that women should not seek sexual pleasure or that masturbation leads to insanity. It is of course hard to say how far therapists fall in with the myths of their day and how far they create them, but we have moved from a situation in which people felt ashamed of liking sex too much to one where people are made to be ashamed if their sexual performance does not match that of the sexual athletes who report their real or imaginary sexual triumphs in *Forum* – a magazine to which almost every psychotherapist I have encountered appears to subscribe.

I recall one patient in the hospital who was in a truly sorry state. He was about forty-five and shy but friendly. He was upset by the efforts of therapists to persuade him to masturbate: he lived alone and was desperately shy of women. Although he was provided with a liberal supply of dirty pictures, his puritanical conscience was revolted, and so far from turning him on I suspect they gave him an even deeper aversion to sexual activities. Attempts to increase sexual activity in the mentally ill are often more likely to distress than to help them.

The great variation in sexual tastes presents obvious difficulties to the sexual therapist who has the delicate task of imparting information without imposing his or her predilections on patients who may be quite otherwise inclined. It is amusing that in his book *The Joy of Sex* Alex Comfort puts the Good Sex Guide's seal of approval on bondage but not on flagellation or buggery. The same considerations apply more generally to any form of psychotherapy, and the extent to which therapists are justified in persuading patients to adopt their views poses a difficult ethical problem. In normal life, one may try to persuade others to change their beliefs knowing that they will not necessarily accept one's arguments but that, if they do, the responsibility is theirs. In the case of severely neurotic or psychotic patients, it is a different story: I have given many instances of their dependence on their therapists, and they are not in a position to take responsible decisions themselves. It is all too easy for the therapist to persuade them of the correctness of his own viewpoint, even when it is diametrically opposed to their own and when acceptance of it may be accompanied by great anxiety because the patient may be being asked to follow a line of action that goes completely against his inclinations.

On the other hand, one may ask: how is the therapist to help the patient without changing him? There is no solution to this dilemma: all one can hope for is that therapists should be aware that there are many different ways to live and that no one way is necessarily better than some other. The therapist should be constantly on his guard against forcing patients to adopt values or life-styles that are not for them. Persuading a patient to adopt a particular view might be justifiable if it were known that some forms of psychotherapy actually helped recovery: unfortunately, existing forms of psychotherapy have little effect on recovery, and it therefore behoves the psychotherapist to practise his profession with humility and to remember that it is likely that the only good he can do is to alleviate present distress. In these circumstances, it is difficult to justify the use of methods that cause patients additional alarm by trying to persuade them that they should be something other than they are.

On this score, the analysts have perhaps been the most guilty, since they base their therapy on a particular view of the nature of man. Existential therapists, humanistic psychologists and Gestalt therapists emphasizing self-actualization and the overriding importance of immediate experience come not far behind. Behaviour therapy relies less on beliefs about what man ought to be and is freer of the taint of influencing people to accept goals imposed by the therapist. It relies on techniques rather than a dogmatic view of the nature of man and his goals. Its techniques are geared to helping the individual achieve his own ends, and although behaviour therapists would rightly not assist a patient to pursue aims they thought wrong – like summoning up the courage to commit a murder – the techniques can be adapted to help the patient pursue those goals that *he* thinks are worthwhile. Of all therapists, therefore, the behaviour therapist is least likely to impose his own views on the patient. Particularly in North America, it is becoming increasingly common for behaviour therapists to draw up a written contract with the patient setting out the detailed aims and methods of therapy before any attempt at treatment is made. Nevertheless, many neurotics are confused about their own aims, and even the behaviour therapist may exert undue influence in trying to reach agreement on what the aims of the therapy should be.

I must admit to a feeling of dissatisfaction with parts of this chapter. When I told a psychiatrist friend that I was not happy about my attempt to sort out the use of the term 'mental illness', he said: 'Anyone who wrote on that topic and felt happy with it would need his head examined.' Part of the problem may be that as we discover more about the origins of human conduct, our view of human nature changes. If it is established that someone is acting strangely because he has a brain tumour or has received an unfortunate genetic inheritance or has undergone a deprived childhood, we cease to hold him responsible for his actions. We operate with two distinct models of human behaviour – the first, that it has direct causes in happenings within the central nervous system, and the second that it results from more or less rational processes of thought, and depends upon intentions rather than causes. Although the two models are not necessarily in conflict, we do not understand how to put them together, and we are often uncertain when it is appropriate to use one and when to use the other. To the extent to which we use the causal model, we tend to think of mental disorder as an illness and to absolve the sufferer of responsibility.

22

Improving Methods of Treatment

Perhaps the most undesirable feature of the term 'mental illness' is that it suggests that doctors are the right people to treat neurotics and psychotics. In practice, there are aspects of the training and background of doctors that may make them unsuited to give psychotherapy.

Particularly in Britain, doctors are drawn predominantly from an upper-middle-class background. According to the Report of the Royal Commission on Medical Education, in 1966 seventy-six per cent of entrants to medical school came from the upper two social classes, which make up about eighteen per cent of the population: only 2.5 per cent came from the two lowest classes constituting thirty-two per cent of the population. Those who entered from the lower social classes did considerably better in examinations than those from the upper through-out their medical course. At the prestige medical schools in London, Oxford and Cambridge only about thirty per cent of students came from state schools, although seventy-one per cent of school-leavers qualified to enter a medical course come from such schools. Only twenty-five per cent of entrants were women. It may be doubted how far a private school education in Britain, with its insistence on a stiff upper lip attitude to life, is an ideal background for the practice of psychiatry, which is said to require warmth and genuineness. One might also wonder how far the scions of the professional classes can show 'empathic understanding' to the poor.

Doctors in general, then, tend to have a rather limited background, but there is a further factor that affects the calibre of entrants into psychiatry. It is often claimed both in Britain and to a lesser extent in North America that psychiatry is held in poor repute by other members of the medical profession: there are therefore not enough recruits to the subject and the quality of some of those entering it is suspect. The point is forcibly made in the Brook Report published in 1973 by the Royal College of Psychiatrists. It concludes that psychiatry 'is not getting the best young doctors'. No less than sixty per cent of trainees in psychiatry in Britain are in fact foreign doctors, and two in every five 'have come into psychiatry as a second best and this figure may well be an underestimate'. A distinguished British psychiatrist, Aubrey Lewis, has referred to 'the withering effect upon students of prominent and admired teachers of other branches of medicine [who] adopt a frankly derisory attitude towards psychiatry'. One mark of the low status of psychiatry in Britain is that there are less than half as many professorships in the subject as in surgery, despite the fact that there are twice as many psychiatric as surgical beds, and psychiatrists have to deal with huge numbers of out-patients whereas many surgeons see out-patients only occasionally.

If recruitment to the subject is unsatisfactory, we may go on to ask whether the training doctors receive fits them to practise psychiatry efficiently. In general, the whole ethos of a traditional medical education would appear to be inimical to the production of the qualities needed in a psychiatrist. Particularly in Britain, the training methods used may well engender authoritarian attitudes. Medicine remains the most hierarchical of professions, and medical students are expected to defer to consultants and show them a degree of obedience and respect unknown in any other walk of life outside the armed services. Since people tend to model their own behaviour on figures they respect, it is scarcely surprising that many doctors themselves come to behave in authoritarian ways towards their patients, and also towards workers in ancillary services, such as clinical psychologists, social workers and nurses. Indeed considering the way doctors are trained, it is surprising that so many of them do practise their profession with kindness and humility. Arrogance and an unwillingness to admit mistakes are of course also fostered in doctors by the attitudes of their patients. Most people in trouble, whether physical or mental, want to feel there is someone on whom they can rely, and they encourage doctors in their feelings of omniscience.

One of the worst features of the British Health Service is that it has encouraged a few doctors to treat patients like cattle. I once attended a clinic with a minor bladder complaint. Thirty patients were assembled in a small room at two o'clock. When the urologist arrived two and a half hours late, none of the hospital staff either apologized for or explained his lack of punctuality. When, an hour later, my turn came, I lay on a bed with my behind uncovered. There were six beds in a row screened from one another each containing a patient in a similar posture. The urologist came along, thrust a finger up the behind of each patient in turn, and said: 'Get dressed.' He then saw each patient individually for about two minutes. I attended on another occasion to have a bladder X-ray, and on a third to obtain the results. The urologist said: 'Nothing showing on the X-ray: you should come back for a cytoscopy.' I knew this was an unpleasant procedure and asked whether it was necessary and what it might show. He said: 'I wouldn't advise you to have it if it weren't necessary,' and refused to provide any other information. In the event, I decided to forgo the cytoscopy and the complaint cleared up of its own accord.

There is a tendency for doctors to treat members of their own social class better than they treat the poor. The poor in Britain have little knowledge of their rights and often behave towards doctors in an almost servile fashion, being grateful for the tiniest mark of attention. I have witnessed doctors treating the sick poor with such contumely that I have with difficulty restrained myself from physical assault. There can be no justification for a paid servant of the state treating the public with contempt, and indeed it is known to be bad medical practice. Several studies show that the satisfaction a patient obtains from a consultation, the degree to which he follows the doctor's instructions, and the speed of recovery depend in part upon the extent to which the doctor is prepared to reassure him and talk to him on a personal level.

To all this, many doctors will reply that much of the problem lies not with the doctors themselves but with the organization of the Health Service. Doctors are expected to cope with too many patients and do not have enough time for each. Many consultants who undertake private practice claim to do so because they cannot otherwise practise medicine in the way they feel it should be practised, with sufficient time allowed to deal fully with the needs of the individual patient. Although it does not excuse some of the worst instances of discourtesy, there is certainly some justice in this argument. The solution may lie in having some of the doctor's traditional functions taken over by paramedical professions.

Nor do I suppose that the majority of psychiatrists are as insensitive as my urologist. The point at issue is whether medical education in Britain is calculated to produce good psychotherapists. In so far as many British psychiatrists do become proficient at psychotherapy, they do so despite their training rather than because of it.

The problem is by no means confined to Britain. One investigator interviewed graduate students of forty-one American medical schools and concluded: 'Psychiatry is regarded as one of the most poorly taught, poorly remembered, generally inadequate courses in medical school.' In the study discussed in the previous chapter, Rosenhan gives some interesting examples of the authoritarian behaviour of psychiatrists in the hospitals to which he and his colleagues were admitted. They found that they rarely saw a psychiatrist. The average amount of contact time between patients and all professional staff, including psychiatrists, other doctors, and psychologists, was 6.8 minutes per day. Moreover, he and his colleagues, who were completely sane, had worse experiences than I did in their contacts with doctors and nurses: they were for the most part not treated as people, their complaints were not taken seriously and they were humoured like children.

As part of the study the pseudo-patients made a point of approaching staff members in the hospitals and making a legitimate query: for example, they might ask when they would be eligible for grounds privileges, or when they might be presented at a case conference. The standard response was to evade answering the patient's question, and Rosenhan records as typical the following bizarre interchange. 'Pardon me doctor – can you tell me whether I am likely to be discharged soon?' To which the psychiatrist would reply: 'Oh good morning, Dave. How are you today?' and then walk away without waiting for any response. It is known that looking someone in the eye is an indication of sincerity and warmth. Rosenhan therefore recorded how often psychiatrists and nurses actually met the pseudo-patients' eyes when such questions were asked. On seventy-one per cent of occasions, psychiatrists responded by averting their head and gaze and moving on; this behaviour was elicited from nurses on eighty-eight per cent of the occasions on which they were questioned. On only six per cent of occasions did psychiatrists actually stop and chat, that is to say treat the patient as a fellow human being. Rosenhan argues that the discourtesy shown to patients is not merely the result of psychiatrists and nurses being too busy. University staff and general physicians are equally busy, but when one of the investigators approached professors and physicians on Stanford campus with a request for the whereabouts of a particular building all of them made eye contact and stopped to talk.

Striking though Rosenhan's findings are, they should be treated with some care. Neurotic patients become very dependent on their therapists, and psychiatrists doubtless believe that if they were to engage patients in casual conversation on the ward, the patients would come to make increasing and unreasonable demands upon their time. It is, however, difficult to absolve psychiatrists of all responsibility for the depersonifying atmosphere on psychiatric wards.

It will be remembered that as a genuine patient I was most touched when the woman registrar actually stopped her car to ask how I was. My hospital appears to have been highly enlightened compared to those encountered by Rosenhan's pseudo-patients. Rosenhan himself saw one patient beaten up because he had approached an attendant and said: 'I like you.' In another hospital patients were woken with the call: 'Come on you mother-fuckers, out of bed.'

If Rosenhan's experiences are anything to go by, then it would appear that either the training or the basic personality of many American psychiatrists unfits them for their profession. He points out that their authoritarian attitudes and refusal to spend time with patients set a poor example to nurses and attendants working on the wards.

Medical training in general, then, does not apparently foster those qualities needed to practise psychiatry well – empathy, genuineness, and warmth. In Britain there has been much criticism not merely of the spirit in which medical training is carried out but of the specific contents of courses in psychiatry. Although the dominant illness in fifteen out of every hundred patients seen by family doctors is psychiatric, and although neurotic symptoms are present in many others, the majority of medical schools in Britain give little training in psychology as part of their general medical course and give a wholly inadequate training in psychiatry. As the Report of the Royal Commission on Medical Education put it: 'Any doctor who remains ignorant of human psychology (both normal and abnormal) must be considered ill-educated, however thoroughly he may be trained in his own speciality, because this subject permeates the whole of medical practice. We have been dismayed to find how inadequate is the teaching of psychiatry in most medical schools.' These words were written seven years ago; unfortunately they apply with almost equal force today.

In 1973 the Royal College of Psychiatrists itself published a devastatingly critical report on the training of psychiatrists. The report states:

'Only two-fifths of trainee psychiatrists are getting adequate training in psychotherapy, either group or individual, and judging from the comments of consultants and tutors these figures are on the optimistic side.' It is also noted that the newly established Royal College of Psychiatrists was unable to introduce an original dissertation as a requirement for membership (now the primary qualification for becoming a consultant psychiatrist), at a time 'when psychiatric postgraduate education is so unsatisfactory and when teachers are in such short supply'. I have myself prepared candidates for parts of the diploma examination in psychiatry (D.P.M. – now supplanted as a qualification by M.R.C. Psych.), and I was appalled by the standards expected, and by the fact that the award-giving body recommended textbooks that were forty years out of date. The Report of the Royal College concludes that if the level of psychiatric training in Britain 'is not raised rapidly, there is a very real risk of an increasing number of doctors going to Canada and the USA for comprehensive, well organized, and well paid training.'

The evidence I have quoted suggests, then, that in Britain there is a desperate need to increase the number and improve the quality of entrants to psychiatry and that the training given in psychology and psychiatry both to ordinary doctors and to psychiatrists themselves is woefully inadequate. The respect in which the behaviour sciences are held in North America has produced a rather better situation, but Rosenhan's study and the recent outcrop of successful suits against psychiatrists demonstrate that in the United States some members of the profession are prone to authoritarian attitudes. Psychiatrists there appear to be more frequently placed in a custodial role than in Britain, and A. J. Mandell has found that many medical students in America feel psychiatrists are the policemen of society, victimizing persons who have been branded as having a mental disease.

Apart from improving methods of training, there are other steps that can be taken to ameliorate the situation. One possibility would be to recognize that a conventional medical education is not a suitable training for coping with psychiatric patients, and to place the prime responsibility for care and non-physical methods of treatment in the hands of workers with a training in psychology: as I have already noted, there is a move in this direction in both Canada and the United States.

The main resistance to allowing psychologists and psychiatric social workers more responsibility in caring for the mentally unwell has come from psychiatrists themselves. At the 1975 Annual General Meeting of the American Psychiatric Association, the president openly revealed some of the psychiatrists' fears: 'If we are not different from and superior to clinical psychologists, psychiatric social workers and nurses, who are being increasingly licensed for independent practice, is not our financial security and professional integrity going to be increasingly at risk?' Despite rearguard actions fought by psychiatrists to preserve their own interests, many insurance schemes in America, including Blue Cross, the Federal Employees Compensation Scheme and the Defence Department's scheme for its employees, have now recognized that qualified psychologists may treat mentally ill patients without referral by a doctor and that their fees will be payable under insurance.

Clinical psychologists are less valued in Britain than in America, and indeed even if the medical profession were willing to grant them more responsibility there are too few of them at present to make much difference. In Britain there is only about one clinical psychologist per hundred thousand of the population, whereas in North America there is over one to every eight thousand: there are thus over ten times as many clinical psychologists per head in America as in Britain.

Psychologists are of course as imperfect human beings as anyone else, but their training is less authoritarian than that of doctors. It has, moreover, more relevance to the task of helping neurotics, if it is accepted that neurosis is caused by faulty learning rather than by organic damage to bodily tissue. If further research demonstrates that only therapists displaying warmth, genuineness and empathy can help the mentally ill, then there is a case for screening clinical psychologists and psychiatrists for these qualities, though it must be admitted that present methods of assessment are not very satisfactory.

My plea for the involvement of psychologists in the treatment of mental disorder does not conflict with the notion that psychoses and severe neurotic breakdown should be regarded as illnesses. On the contrary, a strong case can be made out for psychologists playing a more active role even in the treatment and care of the physically ill, since psychological factors play a considerable role both in susceptibility to illness and in the course of recovery therefrom. For example, in one study patients admitted to hospital for abdominal surgery were randomly assigned to two groups: before the operation took place, the patients in one group were given full information about how long it would last, the circumstances under which they would regain consciousness, the nature of the pain they were likely to experience and so on. This information was not supplied to the second group, who went through the standard hospital procedures. The patients who were thoroughly briefed about the operation subsequently complained less about pain, needed fewer sedatives and recovered more quickly: on average they were discharged from hospital three days earlier than the other group.

Many doctors argue that psychologists should not have sole charge of the mentally unwell because it is necessary to monitor their physical condition and to administer drugs. It has, however, been pointed out that by taking a three-month course, psychologists could become just as expert in assessing the signs of neurological or hormonal dysfunction as most doctors, and could also acquire the knowledge needed to prescribe psychotropic drugs and monitor their effects. It does not of course really matter what name we give to the profession that treats the mentally ill – except in so far as it affects the prestige and pocket of the professions concerned. What matters is the kind of treatment given and the training and personality of those who give it. The substantive issue is that to the extent to which mental disorder is caused by psychogenic factors and can be ameliorated by psychotherapy or behaviour therapy, those responsible for helping the mentally disordered should receive a training in psychology.

One way in which psychiatric services could be better deployed is through community mental health care, a policy now officially espoused in both Britain and the USA. The idea is to have a large mental clinic located in a community serving about fifty thousand people. Such clinics have attached to them a full range of the different professions involved in mental health and provide facilities for out-patients, day care, and residential treatment. In addition, the clinics keep in touch with all other organizations in the community, including voluntary ones, that undertake responsibility for helping the mentally unwell. Some examples of such organizations are local churches, local branches of Alcoholics Anonymous and the Samaritans.

Under a federal law passed in John Kennedy's time, five hundred such centres have now been established in the United States. They appear to have met with some measure of success, but a recent bill allocating continuing federal funds was vetoed by President Ford and their future financing is in doubt. Although it is being implemented rather slowly, it is also official National Health policy in Britain to replace mental hospitals by psychiatric units in district general hospitals charged with developing 'a high-quality, locally based comprehensive psychiatric service'. Such units are likely to be understaffed. One psychiatrist would be responsible for a population of about sixty thousand. At any one time he would have about five hundred patients in his care, of whom one hundred would be long-stay patients in a mental hospital that might be located some way from the district hospital. He would also have about thirty beds for short-stay patients and a large number of out-patients, and patients spending the daytime in the clinic. His team would include ten health visitors and ten social workers, and he would be expected to keep in touch with and to help all the general practitioners operating in his area. It is clearly sensible for psychiatric services to be so organized that they cooperate with and receive help from local organizations helping the mentally unwell. Moreover, if they had closer collaboration with psychiatrists, family doctors might be less likely to overprescribe psychiatric drugs, and their ignorance of the problems of mental health might be alleviated.

Apart from improvements in training and organization, psychiatry would benefit from better research. I was tempted to write 'more' research, but there is already a formidable amount of work undertaken on mental illness and its alleviation. The real problem is that, even given the difficulties of conducting such research, most current investigations do not meet adequate standards of rigour. As already noted, few psychiatrists have a proper training in research methods, though some overcome this handicap and produce well-designed studies.

Although many psychologists are trained in research, those who enter clinical psychology tend not to be the brightest members of their profession. Just as the neurologist or the physician looks down his nose at the psychiatrist, so the experimental or social psychologist tends to undervalue his colleagues in clinical psychology. This is compounded by the fact that, at least in Britain, the career prospects in clinical psychology are worse than in other branches of the subject. As far as I know there is only one professorship in clinical psychology in the whole of Britain, and that is occupied by someone whom most psychologists would regard as an experimental rather than a clinical psychologist. The earnings of the clinical psychologist are very much less than those of psychiatrists, although he is doing similar work and, if he has taken a Ph.D., has invested just as many years in training. Some wag asked to define the difference between a psychiatrist and a psychologist answered: '$10 an hour.' Finally, particularly in Britain, the clinical psychologist has to accept a role that is subservient to the dictates of the psychiatrists with whom he works. In these circumstances, it is small wonder that the brightest students in psychology rarely choose to become clinical psychologists: academic intelligence is not necessarily a *sine qua non* for the successful psychotherapist, but it is a prerequisite for anyone who is going to perform useful research.

As we have seen, the whole area of mental illness is beset by ethical problems, and research on the subject is no exception. I have explained that much the most satisfactory way of investigating the efficacy of a method of treatment is to run random control studies in which some patients are assigned to the treatment under evaluation and others are randomly assigned to some other treatment method or to a no-treatment condition. Many psychiatrists believe that it is unethical to withhold a new method of treatment from patients. Such attitudes are typified by a recent article in *The Times* newspaper written by the British psychiatrist William Sargant. He attacks the British Medical Research Council for sponsoring trials of a new long-acting phenothiazine used in the treatment of schizophrenics. Some patients who were being maintained on this drug were taken off it unknown to themselves and given an inert placebo instead: a few of them relapsed, according to Sargant an outcome 'only too well known for many years already by all doctors treating their patients themselves'. Writing of proposed tests of a new drug for schizophrenia, known as Inderal, Sargant states: 'Already those who have actually used the drug know it helps.' Here we have the typical arrogance of the clinician: he knows.

The whole history of medicine in general and psychiatry in particular demonstrates that the clinician rarely knows how helpful a new method of treatment is, as I have already tried to document. The clinician's faith in his favourite new treatment biases his observations: moreover he communicates his own faith to the patient, and this in itself may assist recovery regardless of the direct effects of the treatment methods. It is perhaps for this reason that so many new treatments hailed at first as major breakthroughs appear to have become decreasingly effective and after the passage of several years have been recognized to be at best useless and at worst actively harmful. In practice, new treatments can rarely be made available at once to all patients who might benefit; selecting patients by lot for a new method of treatment might be more just than letting it depend upon how much influence or money the patient has. Nevertheless, there can be problems: some research workers are more concerned with furthering their careers by getting a paper into print than with making useful new discoveries. To protect the interests of the patient in medical research it is desirable to have all such research sanctioned by bodies containing a proportion of lay members. This procedure is admittedly cumbersome, but it is currently being implemented in various ways in hospitals and research institutes in both North America and Britain.

In the long run, of course, improvements in the care, treatment and prevention of mental illness must depend on how much of its resources society is prepared to devote to the problem. The money spent on treating the mentally ill does not at present match the funds spent on those who are physically ill. In American psychiatric hospitals there is one doctor per one hundred beds, as against one per ten beds on wards dealing with physical complaints. There is of course great variation from one hospital to another, and I have already mentioned one Alabama hospital with one psychiatrist to five thousand patients.

In Britain about half the hospital beds are occupied by the mentally ill or mentally handicapped, but of every £100 spent by the National Health Service, only £14 is spent on mental disorders. Per day passed in hospital, three times as much money is spent on patients suffering from physical illness as on those in psychiatric wards. In 1972, nearly one psychiatric patient in three was on a ward housing fifty or more patients. There are over three times as many consultants per patient on wards dealing with physical illness as on wards dealing with mental illness, and there are about twice as many nurses. Again, there is great variation from one hospital to another. In 1972, one psychiatric hospital had only one consultant for nearly two hundred in-patients; in contrast, the hospital with the highest ratio of staff to patients had one consultant for every twenty-five patients. It is apparent that, despite wide variation in the facilities for helping psychiatric patients, they are in general much worse than for physical illness. It is clear that at the very least funds are needed to improve the standards of care in the more poorly financed psychiatric hospitals.

In view of my reservations about the efficacy of many forms of psychotherapy, my plea for devoting more resources to psychiatry and for increasing, at least in Britain, the number of clinical psychologists may seem unjustified, but there are several reasons why it is important.

First, there is no question but that sympathetic psychotherapy can alleviate some of the distress of mental illness whether or not it shortens its term. Second, even where it is known that psychological methods can help there are not enough clinical psychologists to apply them: there are about twenty thousand people in Britain with seriously disabling phobias or compulsions who could be helped by behaviour therapy but who have no access to the treatment since they live in areas where it is not available. Third, more clinical psychologists are urgently needed to take part in the training of psychiatrists and ordinary doctors. Finally, improvements in methods of treatment depend on the employment of more clinical psychologists in Britain, and of psychologists with more aptitude for research in both Britain and America. In that it has been shown that the methods of behaviour therapy can speed recovery from some neurotic conditions, we have for the first time a non-physical method of treatment that is known to work, and it is important to explore its benefits and limitations for the whole range of neurotic and psychotic disorders.

I have now reviewed a number of steps that society could take to improve the treatment of the mentally ill. They include better training for psychiatrists and family doctors, more use of clinical psychologists, particularly in Britain, the integration of the different organizations offering help, better research, and the allocation of more resources. Many of these improvements will not come about and would in any case fail in their beneficial effects without one further change. It is essential that society alter its attitude to mental illness. I cannot subscribe to many of the ideas of the antipsychiatry movement: mental illness is not enviable; those suffering from it need to be treated – occasionally against their will; and it is probably an integral part of the human condition rather than being caused by damage inflicted by parents or by society at large. Nevertheless, the antipsychiatry movement has helped to produce some change in attitude towards mental illness, and to this extent it has been beneficial. One token of such change is that in 1974 the US Civil Service Commission removed from its standard application form for potential employees a question asking: 'Do you have or have you had . . . a nervous breakdown?'

It cannot be too much emphasized that the great majority of neurotics and many psychotics, particularly with the help of new drug treatments, do recover, and that those who do not often show remission. There should be no disgrace in suffering a mental breakdown: under sufficient stress of the kind that finds the chinks in our own armour, we are all liable to it. It is as likely to affect the great, like Newton or Van Gogh, as the lowly. Sargant, a well-known British psychiatrist, claims that more than one British prime minister has made suicide attempts before attaining that office. Many others have suffered attacks of depression, often described in the newspapers as 'nervous exhaustion' or 'fatigue'.

Asquith verged on alcoholism. In America, Lincoln suffered recurrent melancholia and Forrestal committed suicide during a depression; Eagleton was unable to stand for office when it emerged that he had had ECT.

Sargant writes: 'To eliminate all those in high public positions in Great Britain who have had ECT would deplete our ranks of some very competent people indeed, still more so if one extended the ban to all those with a history of depression.' Moreover, there are few, if any, psychiatric cases who are insane in everything they say and do. If they are to be helped to recover their self-esteem, it is important for doctors, nurses and the general public to take most of what they say seriously and not to assume that all their behaviour is merely the effect of madness.

23

The Choice of Treatment

My views on what one should do if confronted by a breakdown either in oneself or in someone close to one have probably been made obvious throughout the book. At the risk of repetition, I will summarize some of the lessons I learned as a result of my own experiences and through the reading I undertook in preparing this book.

(1) If you are desperately anxious or depressed, do not seek psychoanalysis: it is unlikely to help and may make you worse.

(2) If you wish to explore your personality through psychoanalysis and feel strong enough to do so, check the analyst's credentials through the institute at which he was trained. Before agreeing to treatment, discover what his own ideals are; if they are different from yours, seek another analyst. You are unlikely to change very much through analysis, and if the analyst tries to change you into the sort of person you are not, the treatment is particularly likely to be painful and useless.

(3) If you find your analyst or psychotherapist unsympathetic, he is most unlikely to help you: seek another. Never be talked into prolonged analysis against your will by the promise that only prolonged treatment can help.

(4) If you have a phobia or an obsessive-compulsive disorder, obtain treatment through behaviour therapy. Many normal people with minor but annoying phobias of such things as public speaking or flying can be helped by behaviour therapy.

(5) If you are anxious, sleepless, given to bouts of anger or very depressed without external cause, do not accept therapy from an analyst or psychotherapist without first having a physical examination. If a psychiatrist offers to treat you for any of these conditions without insisting on a physical examination, find another psychiatrist.

(6) If you are unable to function properly through anxiety or depression, try to find a psychiatrist who is eclectic in his approach. Mistrust anyone who is dogmatically in favour of one approach at the expense of others, whether that approach be drugs, behaviour therapy, client-centred therapy or analysis. It is likely that different people benefit from different approaches, and you need to be treated by someone who will try to find what is right for you.

(7) If you need voluntary hospitalization, try to find out what conditions are like in different hospitals in your area. In general, teaching hospitals are likely to have better facilities and to be better staffed than non-teaching hospitals.

(8) Before commencing any psychotherapy in earnest you should agree on its aims and methods with the therapist. If you cannot agree, seek another therapist.

(9) Never consent to a brain operation to relieve psychological distress unless there is evidence of organic brain damage.

(10) Except to help you through a short period of externally imposed stress, do not accept psychotropic drugs from general practitioners. They are often ignorant of the dangers of such drugs and also of the proper methods of use. If you are disturbed enough to need drug treatment, then you should be referred to a psychiatrist.

(11) If you live in Britain and run into difficulties over psychiatric treatment either for yourself or in the case of a friend or relative, then you should try contacting the National Association for Mental Health (addresses in the telephone directories for London, Cardiff and Leeds): this is a voluntary body which exists to protect and further the interests of the mentally unwell, and they will try to help with advice wherever possible.

(12) If you are British and using the National Health Service, remember that you are entitled to the opinion of a second consultant if you are dissatisfied with the first one you see. If you think you need psychiatric help and your doctor refuses to refer you, there are many psychiatric departments in hospitals that will see patients without a referral.

(13) Mistrust any therapist who tells you you must get worse in order to get better.

(14) If you are seriously ill, you would be well advised to avoid psychotherapists without formal qualifications.

(15) Unless you are reasonably robust psychologically, avoid encounter groups. Group therapy run by an experienced psychotherapist is a very different matter.

(16) In dealing with friends or relatives undergoing a breakdown, take what they say seriously. Unless they are severely psychotic, most of their remarks will be based on reality and should not be treated merely as a symptom of illness. Be sympathetic without being sentimental and try to restore their faith in themselves. Anything good you can point to in their past or present behaviour is likely to be helpful. Avoid recrimination or passing moral judgements. Try to give them hope for the future: the restoration of hope is often the most significant step towards ultimate recovery.

(17) Remember that it is no disgrace to be mentally ill and that it rarely incapacitates for life. Many depressives feel they will never recover, but that is a symptom of the illness. In Britain, fifty per cent of psychiatric patients admitted to hospital are discharged within a month and ninety per cent within a year. Moreover, the rate of production of new drugs and advances in psychotherapeutic methods of treatment provide some hope even for the chronically ill.

I am aware of course that in putting forward my own suggestions both in this chapter and elsewhere throughout the book, I will be accused of displaying personal bias: I am myself a psychologist and I have made a case for the importance of my own profession; most of my career has been devoted to research, and I am pleading that we can only develop more successful treatments for mental illness by undertaking more careful research; I have exhibited some scorn for psychoanalysis and I have myself suffered at the hands of analysts; I have also drawn attention to faults as I see them in the training and selection of psychiatrists and of the medical profession in general, and my own dealings with doctors have not always been completely amicable. I can only plead with the reader to consider the arguments I have deployed in their own right: their force – or lack of force – is independent of my own personal history.

I am conscious that by emphasizing the shortcomings of the psychiatric services, I may have said too little about the difficulties faced by mental health practitioners and about the devotion that many of them display in their attempts to help the mentally ill. Their difficulties stem from our ignorance of the subject and from insufficient resources: neither problem is easily overcome. Psychiatry is currently a much maligned profession. In another context, I wrote:

The psychiatrist is in danger of becoming a greater scapegoat than his patients. Pilloried by the press and on the screen and stage, he finds himself continually impaled on the horns of multiple dilemmas. If he commits a dangerous or suicidal patient, he is accused of being a jailer; if he discharges one, he is thought to be callous and incompetent. The public besiege him for drugs and then accuse him of treating them as machines. If he gives psychotherapy, he can be simultaneously charged with using techniques of doubtful therapeutic value and with imposing on the patient his own view of how to live. If he preserves an eclectic approach to treatment, he is indecisive or wishy-washy: if he opts firmly for one or other of the dozens of fashionable varieties of psychotherapy or physical treatment, he is a bigot. His patients often start by ascribing to him the wisdom of a God, and end up hating him for his failure to produce the magical solution to their problems. If he conducts careful trials of a new therapeutic method using a no-treatment control group, his colleagues write letters to *The Times* accusing him of unethically withholding a treatment intuitively known to be valuable; if he fails to conduct controlled trials, the remainder of his colleagues write to *The Times* pointing out that he is an unscientific quack.

The psychiatrist, then, is caught in a series of double-binds that make the nuclear family seem a refuge of sweetness and reason. Nevertheless, sympathy for his plight should not blind us to the need to improve the treatment and care of the mentally ill and with this need in mind, I may have concentrated too much on the failings of contemporary psychiatry and too little on its virtues and achievements.

In conclusion, I hope that I have provided enough information to enable those confronted with the problem of mental illness to avoid making some of the mistakes I made by being talked into unsuitable forms of treatment. Many, if not most or indeed all, of the arguments I have rehearsed will be familiar to experienced members of the mental health professions: they are, however, often ignored by those ensnared by the dogma of a particular method of treatment, and are not sufficiently pondered by those embarking on a career in mental health. There is no one method that is suitable for all patients, just as there is no one end that all men should pursue. Indeed whatever we choose to do precludes us from doing something else: we develop our emotional sensitivities only at the expense of using time and energy that someone else might wish to devote to academic or business pursuits. Nor do I believe in the concept of the well-rounded man who cultivates in equal parts his body, his feelings and his intellect. Great achievements in literature, art, science, medicine, politics or business are often attained by individuals who are driven by a single purpose to the detriment of other sides of their lives: without such people the world would be a poorer place. We should never presume to dictate ends to others: the most we are entitled to do is to ask that they should not tread on too many toes in pursuing their own goals. As my old aunt used to say, 'it takes all types to make a world' – a remark that psychiatrists, psychoanalysts and clinical psychologists would do well to note.

Glossary

All technical terms are explained in the text as they are introduced. The glossary is not intended to be comprehensive, but contains a few terms that occur in many different parts of the book and about which it is easy to become confused.

Behaviour Therapy A newly developed form of therapy, in which the therapist attempts to teach the patient new ways of behaving by applying the principles of learning theory. Concentrates on removing the patient's symptoms and distress, without probing into the dynamics of his mental life.

Clinical Psychologist Has a higher degree in psychology and specializes in its clinical applications. Most clinical psychologists give psychotherapy or behaviour therapy: they tend to be more eclectic than psychoanalysts and to have a more empirically based approach. They do not have a medical training and therefore cannot prescribe drugs or other physical methods of treatment.

Dynamic Psychotherapy Any psychotherapy that concentrates on giving the patient insight into his motives and conflicts: a slightly broader term than 'psychoanalysis' and would include, for example, Gestalt Therapy.

Functional Psychosis *See* psychosis.

Organic Psychosis *See* psychosis.

Placebo　An inert substance made up in the form of a pill and given to a patient under the pretence that it is an active drug. It is normally used to measure the psychological benefit due merely to taking a pill: the only way to prove that a particular drug directly helps the patient is to show that its effects are more beneficial than those of a placebo.

Psychiatrist　A medically trained doctor specializing in the care and treatment of mental illness and emotional disorders.

Psychoanalyst　A psychotherapist who treats the mentally ill by interpreting their thoughts and feelings and attempting to make them conscious of underlying motives and conflicts, often by tracing them back to childhood experiences; reputable analysts should have undergone analysis themselves and have been trained at a Psychoanalytic Institute.

Psychology　*See* clinical psychologist.

Psychosis　A severe mental illness in which the patient loses touch with aspects of reality. *Organic psychoses* are caused by known pathological functioning of bodily organs. The physical causes, if any, of *functional psychoses* have not yet been established with certainty: they include schizophrenia and the various affective psychoses in which the predominant symptom is an abnormally depressed or elated mood.

Psychotherapy　The attempt to help the mentally ill by talking with them.

Transference　The process whereby a patient responds to his therapist in the way in which he has previously responded to figures of importance in his early life, particularly his parents.

Notes

These notes are intended for the reader interested in following up arguments and evidence in more detail. Rather than list all the relevant publications, I have frequently referred only to review articles which provide detailed references for the reader to track down. Nor have I listed references where there is general agreement on a topic: the interested reader can consult an up-to-date textbook on psychiatry such as Freedman, A. M., Kaplan, H. I. & Sadock, B. J., *Comprehensive Textbook of Psychiatry* (Baltimore: Williams & Wilkins, 1975). Where possible, I have provided guidance to further books suitable for the general reader at the beginning of the notes to each chapter.

Chapter 8

General I do not know of any popular source that sets out the different kinds of mental illness and indicates their prevalence. On classification, I have relied largely on General Registry Office, *Studies on Medical and Population Subjects, No. 22: A Glossary of Mental Disorders* (London: HMSO, 1968), which is in turn based on the World Health Organization's eighth revision of *The International Statistical Classification of Diseases, Injuries and Causes of Death* (Geneva, 1965).

252   *Breakdown*

Page
79, line 8 On witches and drugs see Rothman, T., *Bulletin for the History of Medicine, 46,* 562–7 (1972).
80, line 25 For a summary of recent research on the classification of depressive illnesses see Akiskal, H. S. & McKinney, Jr. W. T., *Archives of General Psychiatry, 32,* 285–305 (1975).
82, line 13 Study reported in Abrams, R. *et al., Archives of General Psychiatry, 31,* 640–4 (1974).
86, line 14 Shepherd, M. *et al., Psychiatric Illness in General Practice* (London: Oxford University Press, 1966).
86, line 21 Figures on prevalence of various kinds of neuroses are from Cooper, B., *Proceedings of the Royal Society of Medicine, 65,* 509–12 (1972).
86, line 31 Agras, W. S. *et. al., Comprehensive Psychiatry, 10,* 151–6 (1969).
87, line 4 For references to these studies and for reviews of epidemiological research in psychiatry see Cooper, A. & Morgan, H. G., *Epidemiological Psychiatry* (Springfield, Ill: Charles C. Thomas, 1973) or Gruenberg, E. M. & Turns, D. M., in Freedman, A. M., Kaplan, H. I. & Sadock, B. J., *Comprehensive Textbook of Psychiatry,* vol. I, pp. 398–412 (Baltimore: Williams & Wilkins, 1975).

Chapter 9

General I know of no recent popular review of the causes of mental illness. Marks, I. M., *Psychological Medicine, 3,* 436–54 (1973) gives a readable and not too detailed survey of the problem.

Page
88, line 11 Recent evidence on the genetics of mental illness is set out in Fieve, R. *et al., Genetics and Psychopathology* (Baltimore: Johns Hopkins Press, 1974).
89, line 26 For a review of the effects of social and cultural factors on psychopathology, see Dohrenwend, B. P. & Dohrenwend, B. S., *Annual Review of Psychology, 25,* 417–52 (1974).
89, line 35 For a review of the studies on the prevalence of mental illness in African countries see German, G. A., *British Journal of Psychiatry, 121,* 461–79 (1972).
90, line 3 Eaton, J. W. & Weil, R., *Culture and Mental Disorders* (New York: The Free Press, 1955).
90, line 18 Goldhamer, H. & Marshall, A. W., *Psychosis and Civilization* (New York: The Free Press of Glencoe, 1949).
91, line 19 For a review of studies on interactions in families containing a schizophrenic see Jacob, T., *Psychological Bulletin, 82,* 33–65 (1975).

91, line 25 Seligman, R. *et al.*, *Archives of General Psychiatry*, *31*, 475–9 (1974).

91, line 32 Vaillant, G. E., in Ricks, D. *et al.* (eds.), *Life History Research in Psychopathology*, vol. 3, pp. 230–42 (Minneapolis: University of Minnesota Press, 1974).

92, line 10 For a review of the relationship between childhood and adult neurosis see Rutter, M. L., *Acta Psychiatrica Scandinavica*, *48*, 3–21 (1972).

92, line 26 For a review of the effects of stressful events see Dohrenwend, B. S. & Dohrenwend, B. P. (eds.), *Stressful Life Events: Their Nature and Effects* (New York: Wiley, 1974).

92, line 28 Brown G. W. & Birley, J. L. T., *Journal of Health and Social Behaviour*, *9*, 203–14 (1968).

92, line 32 Glass, A. J. & Bernucci, A. J. (eds.), *Neuropsychiatry in World War II* (Washington, D.C.: Office of the Surgeon General, Department of the Army, 1966).

93, line 19 For a brief review of biochemical factors implicated in the functional psychoses see Kety, S. S. in Freedman, A. M., Kaplan, H. I. & Sadock, B. J., *Comprehensive Textbook of Psychiatry*, vol. I, pp. 178–87 (Baltimore: Williams & Wilkins, 1975).

93, line 33 Seligman, M. E. P., *Helplessness* (San Francisco: Freeman, 1975).

94, line 3 Freedman, D. G. & Freedman, N. C., *Nature*, *224*, 1227 (1969).

Chapter 10

General Freud is much the best expositor of his own ideas. His *Introductory Lectures on Psychoanalysis* (delivered between 1915 and 1917) is an excellent starting point. *The Interpretation of Dreams* and *The Psychopathology of Everyday Life* are also highly readable. References to Freud given below are from the Standard Edition of the Complete Psychological Works of Sigmund Freud (London: Hogarth Press, 1953–64).

Page
97, line 33 Freud, S., op. cit., XVI, p. 248.

99, line 6 Freud's paper on Leonardo is reproduced in Freud, S., *Leonardo* (Harmondsworth, Middlesex: Penguin Books, 1963): the book includes an essay by Brian Farrell which presents a careful analysis of the ways in which Freud distorted historical evidence in an attempt to make it support his case.

99, line 14 On the history of parental practices, the following books are of interest: Ariès, P., *Centuries of Childhood: A Social History of*

Family Life (New York: Vintage Books, 1974); Hunt, D., *Parents and Children in History: the Psychology of Family Life in Early Modern France* (New York: Basic Books, 1970); DeMause, L., *The History of Childhood* (New York: Psychohistory Press, 1974).

Chapter 11

General For brief and revealingly arrogant account of the status of Freudian psychoanalysis written by a current practitioner, see Fine, R., in Corsini, R., *Current Psychotherapies*, pp. 1–33 (Itasca, Ill: Peacock, 1975); for a vitriolic but amusing attack see Salter, A., *The Case against Psychoanalysis* (New York: Citadel Press, 1973).

Page
104, line 27 Freud, S., op. cit., XV, p. 179.
105, line 3 Freud, S., op. cit., XVIII, p. 50.
105, line 24 Some of these studies are reproduced in Eysenck, H. J. & Wilson, G. D., *The Experimental Study of Freudian Theories* (London: Methuen, 1973).
105, line 31 Holmes, D. S., *Psychological Bulletin, 81,* 632–53 (1974).
106, line 8 On the normality of monkeys raised without parents but with other monkeys of the same age, see Harlow, H. F., in Abrams, A. *et al.* (eds.), *Unfinished Tasks in the Behavioral Sciences,* pp. 154–73 (Baltimore: Williams & Wilkins, 1964).
106, line 22 The efficacy of psychotherapy in general and psychoanalysis in particular is a much debated issue. For a recent review that comes to unfavourable conclusions see Rachman, S., *The Effects of Psychotherapy* (Oxford: Pergamon Press, 1973). It is instructive to consider some of the reviews of the subject that try to present a more favourable case. For example, Bergin, A. E., in Bergin, A. E. & Garfield, S. L., *Psychotherapy and Behaviour Change*, pp. 217–70 (New York: Wiley, 1971) challenges the conclusions of Eysenck (Eysenck, H. L., *Journal of Counselling Psychology, 16,* 319–24, 1952) that patients treated by psychoanalysis and other forms of psychotherapy do not have a better outcome than those not so treated. Bergin reviewed forty-eight studies involving fifty-two groups of treated patients: treatment was found to be beneficial for twenty-two groups, and had no effect or a deleterious effect on fifteen; in the remaining groups the results were inconclusive. Bergin's own conclusions are cautious: 'It now seems apparent that psychotherapy, as practised over the past forty years, has had an average effect that is modestly positive. It is clear, however, that the averaged group data ... obscure the existence of a multiplicity of processes occurring in therapy, some

of which are now known to be unproductive or actually harmful.'

107, line 20 The 'placebo' effect is discussed in more detail in Chapter 20, where references to the relevant studies will be found.

107, line 38 Hamburg, D. A. *et al.*, *Journal of the American Psychoanalytic Association*, *15*, 841 (1967).

108, line 5 Malan, D. H., *Archives of General Psychiatry*, *29*, 719–29 (1973).

108, line 18 Kernberg, O. F. *et al.*, *Psychotherapy and Psychoanalysis: Final Report of the Menninger Foundation's Psychotherapy Research Project* (Topeka, Kansas: Menninger Foundation, 1972). For a critical review see Rachman, S., *Bulletin of the British Psychological Society*, *26*, 343–6 (1973).

Chapter 12

Page

109, line 11 The importance of differences in the personality of the therapist is developed in more detail in Chapter 15.

109, line 22 Freud, S., op. cit., XII, p. 115.

110, line 10 Malan, D. H., op. cit.

110, line 19 Dewald, P. C., *Contemporary Psychology*, *20*, 492 (1975).

111, line 7 Quoted in Landis, C., *Journal of Abnormal and Social Psychology*, *35*, 17–28 (1940).

111, line 19 For evidence on the tendency to overvalue anything that has involved much effort to obtain, see for example Festinger, L. *A Theory of Cognitive Dissonance* (New York: Row Peterson, 1967).

111, line 40 Freud, S., op. cit., XI, p. 142.

112, line 5 Freud, S., op. cit., X, p. 104.

114, line 5 Eysenck, H. J., *Penthouse*, *6*, No. 9 (1971).

115, line 10 Freud, S., op. cit., XVI, p. 452.

116, line 4 Freud, S., op. cit., XV, p. 50.

116, line 38 Greenbank, R. K., *Pennsylvania Medical Journal*, *64*, 989 (1961).

117, line 24 The chairman was M. K. Stein: his remarks are reported in Lussier, A., *International Journal of Psychoanalysis*, *53*, 13–19 (1972).

117, line 33 Cooper, I. S., *The Victim Is Always the Same* (New York: Harper & Row, 1974).

Chapter 13

General None of Freud's successors wrote with his clarity and elan. I have dipped into Jung, Adler, Reich and others, but have never been able to read them extensively. For more information on Jung and Reich, the general reader can consult Storr, A., *Jung* (London: Collier, 1973) and Rycroft, C., *Reich* (London: Collier, 1973). They are fair and eminently readable exegeses. Kiernan, T., *Shrinks, etc: A Consumer's Guide to Psychotherapies* (New York: The Dial Press, 1974) also gives helpful synoptic accounts of the different schools of analysis.

Page

120, line 22 Jung's remark about the penis is reported in Storr, A., op. cit., p. 113.

121, line 4 The interchange between Jung and Freud is set out in Jung, C. G., *Memories, Dreams and Reflections* (ed. Jaffe, A.), pp. 146–169 (New York: Vintage Books, 1965) and is reported in Cohen, E. D., *C. G. Jung and the Scientific Attitude* (New York: Philosophical Library, 1975): although more difficult than Storr's book, it is also a useful account of Jung.

121, line 34 Quotations on extroversion-introversion are from Jung, C. G., *Collected Works*, vol. VII, p. 43 (London: Routledge & Kegan Paul, 1959); see also, Storr, A., op. cit., p. 64.

122, line 20 The incident of the patient who thought he could see the sun's penis is taken from Jung's works and is quoted in Cohen, E. D., op. cit., p. 30.

123, line 7 Quotation from Storr, A., op. cit., p. 88.

123, line 31 Storr, A., op. cit.

124, line 15 The story about Adler and the psychiatrist is taken from Mosak, H. H. & Dreikurs, R., in Corsini, R., *Current Psychotherapies*, pp. 35–84 (Itasca, Ill: Peacock, 1973).

126, line 11 Information on applications to Karen Horney clinic from Kiernan, T., op. cit., p. 154.

127, line 23 Quotation from Rycroft, C., op. cit., p. 66.

127, line 31 Quotation from Rycroft, C., op. sit., p. 93.

128, line 29 Rycroft, C., op. cit., p. 11.

130, line 37 Binswanger, L., *Being in the World*, p. 291 (London: Souvenir Press, 1975).

Chapter 14

General Rogow, A., *The Psychiatrists* (London: Allen & Unwin, 1971) reports the results of a questionnaire he administered to psychoanalysts and psychiatrists: he also reports much other interesting data, mainly of a sociological kind, on these two professions. The book is useful for both the general reader and the specialist and I have drawn on it heavily in the preparation of this chapter.

Page
136, line 9 Rogow, A. A., op. cit., p. 101.
138, line 9 Rogow, A. A., op. cit., p. 84.
138, line 22 Quotation from Rogow, A. A., op. cit., p. 99.
138, line 25 For the report on what makes a good analyst, see Rogow, A. A., op. cit., p. 50.
138, line 43 Estimate of number of analysts from Fine, R., in Corsini R., *Current Psychotherapies*, p. 5 (Itasca, Ill: Peacock, 1973).
138, line 17 Rogow, A. A., op. cit., p. 41.
138, line 35 Rogow, A. A., op. cit., p. 83.

Chapter 15

General Reading the works of Rogers and of Perls requires little or no previous knowledge but in my experience makes considerable demands on one's patience. Rogers, C., *Client-Centred Therapy* (Boston: Houghton Mifflin, 1954) is as good an introduction to his ideas as any. For an account of Gestalt therapy with do-it-yourself exercises, try Perls, F. S. et al., *Gestalt Therapy: Excitement and Growth in the Human Personality* (New York: Julian Press, 1951); a more up to date treatment is given in Fagan, J. & Shepherd, I. L. (eds.), *Gestalt Therapy Now* (New York: Science and Behaviour Books, 1970). The relevant chapters in Corsini, R. (ed.), *Current Psychotherapies* (Itasca, Ill: Peacock, 1973) give useful accounts.

Page
145, line 22 References to this study and most of those quoted on the following pages will be found in Truax, C. B. & Mitchell, K. M., in Bergin, A. E. & Garfield, S. L. (eds.), *Handbook of Psychotherapy and Behavior Change*, pp. 299–344 (New York: Wiley, 1971).
145, line 37 Ricks, D. R., in Ricks, D. R., et. al., *Life History Research in Psychopathology*, vol. 3, pp. 275–97 (Minneapolis: University of Minnesota Press, 1974).
146, line 30 Quotation from Truax, C. B. & Mitchell, K. M., op. cit., p. 340.
147, line 34 Mindess, H., *American Psychologist, 30*, 598–600 (1975).
149, line 21 The quotation is from Perls, F. S., in Fagan, J. & Shepherd, I. L., op. cit., p. 19.
150, line 29 Quotations are from Perls, F. S. et al., op. cit.
151, line 4 Berne has written a popular account of transactional analysis: Berne, E., *Games People Play* (New York: Grove Press, 1964).

258   *Breakdown*

Chapter 16

General   Yalom, I. D., *The Theory and Practice of Group Psychotherapy* (New York: Basic Books, 1970) reports a careful investigation of group therapy: it is clearly written and can be read by the general reader. There are many popular books on encounter groups. Maliver, B., *The Encounter Game* (New York: Stein & Day, 1973) gives their history in the USA and was written primarily for the general reader. Lieberman, M. A. *et al.*, *Encounter Groups: First Facts* (New York; Basic Books, 1973) reports the most systematic investigation yet conducted on the effects of encounter groups. I have drawn extensively on all three sources.

Page
155, line 6 Yalom, I. D., op. cit., pp. 70–1.
155, line 33 Information on T-groups from Maliver, B., op. cit.
156, line 10 Maliver, B., op. cit., p. 179.
156, line 37 The quotation from Perls appears in Maliver, B., op. cit., p. 179.
157, line 26 American Psychiatric Association, Task Force Report. *Encounter Groups and Psychiatry* (Washington, D.C.: American Psychiatric Association, 1970).
158, line 7 Maliver, B., op. cit., p. 130.
158, line 22 The Stanford University study is reported in Lieberman, M.A. *et al.*, op. cit.
159, line 9 Braginsky, B. M. & Braginsky, D. D., *Mainstream Psychology: a Critique*, p. 85 (New York: Holt, Rinehart and Winston, 1974).

Chapter 17

Page
161, line 5 See Lowen, A., *The Language of the Body* (New York: Collier, 1971).
161, line 18 Information from Braginsky, B. M. & Braginsky, D. D., op. cit.
162, line 24 Quotations are from Maslow, A. H., *Journal of Humanistic Psychology*, 7, 93–127 (1967).
162, line 32 Braginsky, B. M. & Braginsky, D. D., op. cit., pp. 79–80.
162, line 45 The account of the Woods' case is taken from Kiernan, T., *Shrinks, etc: a Consumer's Guide to Psychotherapies*, pp. 1–5 (New York: Dial Press, 1974).

Chapter 18

General   I have not come across a popular account of behaviour therapy. There are many textbooks on the subject, e.g. Rimm, D. C. & Masters,

J. C., *Behavior Therapy: Technique and Empirical Findings* (New York: Academic Press, 1974).

Page

166, line 11 Skinner has written several popular books. Perhaps the best known is Skinner, B. F., *Beyond Freedom and Dignity* (New York: Knopf, 1971). Despite the claims he makes for the usefulness of behavioural methods, he nowhere attempts to give an all-round picture of behaviour therapy as currently practised.

167, line 1 Wolpe, J., *Psychotherapy by Reciprocal Inhibition* (Stanford, Cal.: Stanford University Press, 1958).

167, line 9 Hoon, P. W. & Lindsley, O. R., *American Psychologist, 29,* 694–5 (1974).

167, line 24 For a critical appraisal of Freud's use of evidence in the case of Little Hands, see Wolpe, J. & Rachman, S., *Journal of Nervous and Mental Disease, 130,* 135–48 (1960).

169, line 2 For the effectiveness of flooding under tranquillizers, see Marks, I. M. *et al.*, *British Journal of Psychiatry, 121,* 493–505 (1972).

169, line 3 On modelling as a technique, see Bandura, A., *Principles of Behaviour Modification* (New York: Holt Rinehart and Winston, 1969).

170, line 18 This investigation is reported in Paul, G. L., *Insight vs Desensitization in Psychotherapy: an Experiment in Anxiety Reduction* (Stanford, Cal.: Stanford University Press, 1966).

170, line 36 The psychiatrist was Isaac Marks and his findings are reported in Hand, I., Lamontagne, Y. & Marks, I. M., *British Journal of Psychiatry, 124,* 588–602 (1974).

171, line 11 Paul, G. L., op. cit.

171, line 30 See Marks, I. M., *Journal of Nervous and Mental Disorders, 156,* 420–6 (1973).

172, line 1 Compare Seligman, M. E. P., *Helplessness* (San Francisco: Freeman, 1975).

173, line 37 Schachter, S., *Emotion, Obesity and Crime* (New York: Academic Press, 1971).

174, line 20 Compare Bray, G. R. (ed.), *Obesity: a National Symposium* (Washington D.C.: National Institute of Health, 1976).

176, line 7 Purcell, L. P. & Berwick, P. T., *Archives of General Psychiatry, 31,* 502–4 (1974).

177, line 22 For a discussion of these studies, see Notz, W. W., *American Psychologist, 30,* 884–91 (1975).

178, line 8 McConnell, J. V., *Psychology Today* (April 1970), p. 14.

178, line 14 Facts on prisoners of war in Korea taken from Russell, A. W.,

260 Breakdown

Journal of Clinical Psychology, *30*, Special Monograph Supplement, 111–36 (1974).
178, line 27 Russell, A. W., op. cit.
179, line 9 The experiment on the effect of a placebo on tolerance to pain is reported in Davison, G. C. & Vallins, S., *Journal of Personality and Social Psychology*, *11*, 25–33 (1969).
179, line 40 For a critical review of Biofeedback, see Birk, L., *Biofeedback: Behavioral Medicine* (New York: Grune & Stratton, 1974).
181, line 10 Sloan, R. B. *et al.*, *Psychotherapy versus Behaviour Therapy* (Cambridge, Mass: Harvard University Press, 1975).
183, line 31 Quotation from Teasdale, J. D., in Sutherland, N. S. (ed.), *Tutorial Essays in Psychology* (Hillsdale, N.J.: Erlbaum Associates, 1976).

Chapter 19

General A good account of the techniques involved in manipulating the brain is Valenstein, E. S., *Brain Control* (New York: Wiley, 1973): it is scholarly and clear and requires no previous knowledge. An excellent popular book giving many examples of useless and dangerous treatments that have been or are widely used in medicine without adequate evidence on their efficacy is Malleson, A., *Need Your Doctor Be So Useless?* (London: Allen & Unwin, 1973).

Page
186, line 21 For a review of unilateral ECT, see D'Elia, G. & Raotma, H., *British Journal of Psychiatry*, *126*, 83–9 (1975).
187, line 8 For the mortality rate in tonsillectomy, see Ministry of Health *Report on In-patient Enquiry for the Year 1961* (London: HMSO, 1962) and Wolman, I. J., *Quarterly Review of Paediatrics*, *2*, p. 109 (1956).
187, line 11 Bakwin, H., *New England Journal of Medicine*, *232*, 691 (1955). This and other studies on tonsillectomy are reviewed in Malleson, A., op. cit.
187, line 33 For the history of convulsive therapy through administration of insulin or metrazol and the way in which it led to ECT, see Valenstein, E. S., op. cit.
188, line 4 The study that finally disproved the use of insulin was Ackner, B. *et al.*, *Lancet*, *1*, p. 607 (1957), but it had been anticipated by several smaller scale studies, e.g. Bourne, H., *Lancet*, *2*, p. 964 (1953).
189, line 10 The story of the faulty ECT machine is reported in Jones, J. E., *World Medicine*, *9*, No. 25, 24 (1974).

189, line 22 For a history of leucotomy and further references, see Valenstein, E. S., op. cit.

190, line 27 These two studies were Robin, A. A., *Journal of Neurology, Neurosurgery and Psychiatry*, *21*, 262–9 (1958) and McKenzie, K. G. & Kaczanowski, G., *Canadian Medical Association Journal*, *91*, 1193–6. Valenstein, who takes a slightly less pessimistic view of psychosurgery, does not mention either of them.

191, line 26 Quoted in Valenstein, E. S., op. cit., pp. 310–11.

192, 15 line The restricted forms of leucotomy currently practised appear to have less harmful side-effects: some careful studies have indicated that there may be some clinical benefits, particularly in cases where anxiety is a prominent symptom. See, for example, Tan, E. *et al.*, *British Journal of Psychiatry*, *118*, 155–64 (1971) and Marks, I. M. *et al.*, *British Journal of Psychiatry*, *112*, 757–69 (1966) who report some slight benefit of restricted leucotomy for severe obsessive-compulsive and agoraphobics at five-year follow-up with matched control groups.

192, line 36 The account of the activities of Mark (not to be confused with Marks) and Ervin is drawn partly from their book Mark, V. & Ervin, F., *Violence and the Brain* (New York: Harper & Row, 1970) and partly from reports privately circulated by Peter Breggin, who undertook a follow-up of the case. For a fuller discussion of the cases referred to here and of the dangers of psychosurgery, see Chorover, S., in Boston University Law Review, and Center for Health Sciences Boston University School of Law, *Psychosurgery: A Multidisciplinary Symposium*, pp. 15–32 (Lexington, Mass: Lexington Books, 1974).

Chapter 20

General Coleman, V., *The Medicine Men* (London: Temple Smith, 1975) gives a revealing account of the activities of the drug companies and their relations with doctors; Malleson, A., *Need Your Doctor Be So Useless?* (London: Allen & Unwin, 1973) gives a well-documented and highly readable account of some of the uses to which drugs should not be put. Except where otherwise indicated, I have relied mainly on a recent textbook, Valzelli, L., *Psychopharmacology: an Introduction to Experimental and Clinical Principles* (New York: Spectrum, 1973).

Page

195, line 15 Data on admissions for barbiturate poisoning to Royal Infirmary, Edinburgh, reported in Malleson, A., op. cit., p. 76.

195, line 17 For deaths from barbiturate poisoning in the USA, see

Proceedings, White House Conference on Narcotic and Drug Abuse (Washington, D.C.: Government Printing Office, 1962).

195, line 20 Sargant, W., *Proceedings of the Royal Society of Medicine, 51,* p. 353 (1958).

196, line 3 Bewley, T., *Bulletin of Narcotics, 13* (1967).

196, line 18 Essig, C. F., *Clinical Pharmacology and Therapeutics, 5,* p. 334 (1964) and Essig, C. F., *Journal of the American Medical Association, 196,* p. 714 (1966).

196, line 33 Valzelli, L., op. cit., p. 173.

196, line 40 Greenblatt, D. J. & Schacter, R. I., *Benzodiazepines in Clinical Practice* (New York: Raven Press, 1974).

198, line 4 Number of amphetamine tablets prescribed in Britain is reported in Malleson, A., op. cit., p. 63 and is derived from the Statistical Office of the Ministry of Health.

198, line 11 On the use of amphetamines in weight control, see Modell, S., *Journal of the American Medical Association, 173,* 1131 (1960).

198, line 25 Facts from Malleson, A., op. cit., pp. 63–4.

198, line 31 Valzelli, L., op. cit., p. 218.

199, line 12 Wender, P., *Minimal Brain Dysfunction in Children,* p. 12 (New York: Wiley, 1971).

199, line 34 Wender, P., op. cit.

200, line 7 Chorover, S., *Psychology Today* (October 1973), p. 43. I am indebted to Chorover for having read a longer unpublished article of his on 'The politics of psychobiology'.

201, line 8 There have now been many well-controlled trials of the clinical effects of the tri-cyclic antidepressants reporting beneficial results. One of the largest was undertaken by the Medical Research Council in Britain and is reported in *British Medical Journal, 1,* 881–6 (1965). For other references, see Valzelli, L., op. cit., p. 197.

201, line 23 On lithium, see Johnson, F. N. (ed.), *Lithium Research and Therapy* (London: Academic Press, 1975), from which most of my information on it is derived.

202, line 5 Cole, J. O., *American Journal of Psychiatry, 125,* 556–7 (1968).

205, line 22 On the CIOMS report, see Coleman, V., op. cit., p. 66.

206, line 17 For a history of random control trials in medicine including this story, see Cochrane, A. L., *Effectiveness and Efficiency: Random Reflections on the Health Service* (London: The Nuffield Provincial Hospitals Trust, 1972).

206, line 39 Brill, N. Q. et al., *Archives of General Psychiatry, 10,* 581–95 (1964).

207, line 8 For references to further studies and for an excellent account of placebo effects, see Shapiro, A. K., in Bergin, A. E. & Garfield, S. L., *Handbook of Psychotherapy and Behavior Change* (New York: Wiley, 1971).

207, line 15 See Malleson, A., op. cit., p. 25 for references on calomel.
207, line 22 For a resumé of the thalidomide tragedy, see Coleman, V., op. cit.

Chapter 21

General The writings of the antipsychiatry movement, as represented by Thomas Szasz and R. D. Laing, have reached a wide readership. Laing's case histories are interesting, e.g. Laing, R. D., *The Divided Self* (London: Tavistock, 1960) and Laing, R. D. & Esterson, A., *Sanity, Madness and the Family* (London: Tavistock, 1964), but his more recent works are obscure and his arguments hard to follow. Szasz writes with vigour and clarity, but he is very repetitive and appears to believe in the Bellman's principle that: 'What I have said three times is true': Szasz, T. S., *The Myth of Mental Illness* (New York: Hoeber-Harper, 1961) and Szasz, T. S., *The Manufacture of Madness* (New York: Harper & Row, 1970) are representative.

Page
213, line 24 Rosenhan, D. L., *Science*, *179*, 250–8 (1973).
217, line 39 Illich, I., *Medical Nemesis* (London: Calder & Boyars, 1975).
218, line 15 Statistics from Department of Health & Social Security, *Statistical and Report Series No. 10: Census of Mentally Ill Patients* (London: HMSO, 1975).
218, line 39 On the role of the clergy, see Gurin, G., Veroff, J. & Field, S., *Americans View their Mental Health* (New York: Basic Books, 1960).
219, line 21 On the effects of high-rise flats, see, for example, Fanning, P., *British Medical Journal*, *1*, 382–6 (1967).
222, line 34 Bellak, L. (ed.), *A Concise Handbook of Community Psychiatry and Community Mental Health*, p. 9 (New York: Grune & Stratton, 1974).
224, line 9 Cmnd. 4861, *Report of the Committee of Enquiry into Whittingham Hospital* (London: HMSO, 1972).
224, line 31 For number of patients committed in England and Wales, see Department of Health and Social Security, op. cit.
224, line 33 National Institute of Mental Health Statistical Note 105: *Legal Status of In-patient Admissions to State and County Hospitals United States 1972* (Washington, D.C: D.H.E.W., 1974).
225, line 12 For the account of recent court cases in the USA affecting the rights of the mentally ill, I have relied on reports appearing in the *American Psychological Association Monitor* for the years 1974 and 1975.

228, line 5 Masters, W. H. & Johnson, V., *Human Sexual Inadequacy* (Boston: Little Brown, 1970).

229, line 8 Comfort, A., *The Joy of Sex* (London: Modsets Securities, 1972).

Chapter 22

General A good popular book on the potential role of the psychologist in helping the mentally unwell and in medicine in general is Rachman, S. J. & Phillips, C., *Psychology and Medicine* (London: Temple Smith, 1975). *The Report of the Royal Commission on Medical Education* (London: HMSO, 1968) is remarkably well written and is of interest to the general reader. For a ferocious onslaught on modern medicine, those who can stand his style can consult Illich, I., *Medical Nemesis* (London: Calder & Boyars, 1975).

Page

232, line 6 Brook, P., *Psychiatrists in Training. British Journal of Psychiatry, Special Publication No. 7* (Ashford, Kent: Headley Brothers, 1973).

232, line 14 Lewis, A., in *Psychiatrie der Gegenwart* (Berlin: Springer, 1961).

232, line 19 Figures on professorships calculated from *Commonwealth Universities Yearbook* (London: The Association of Commonwealth Universities, 1973).

234, line 9 Castelnuovo-Tedesco, P., *Archives of General Psychiatry, 16,* 668–75 (1967).

236, line 3 Brook, P., op. cit., pp. 38–9.

236, line 16 Brook, P., op. cit., p. 58.

236, line 27 Mandell, A. J., *American Journal of Psychiatry, 130,* 529–31 (1973).

237, line 6 Quoted in *American Psychological Association Monitor, 6,* No. 7, p. 4 (1975), from an address given by J. Spiegal entitled 'Psychiatry: A High-Risk Profession'.

237, line 18 Figures for Britain from the British Psychological Society's report on *Training Needs in Clinical Psychology* (unpublished) and for America from National Institute of Mental Health data reported in Kramer, M., *Milbank Memorial Fund Quarterly, Health and Society* (Summer, 1975), pp. 279–336.

237, line 35 Egbert, L. *et al.*, *New England Journal of Medicine, 270,* 825 (1964).

239, line 9 Description of official British policy on psychiatric units in

general hospitals taken from Cawley, R. & McLachlan, G. (eds.), *Policy for Action* (Oxford: Oxford University Press, 1973).
241, line 26 Statistical facts from Ennals, D., *Out of Mind* (London: Arrow Books, 1973).
242, line 37 Sargant, W., *British Journal of Psychiatry*, Notes and News, 9–10 (December, 1972).

Chapter 23

247, line 4 Quotation from Sutherland, N. S., *Psychology Today*, 1975 (in press).

Author Index

Abrams, A. 254
Abrams, R. 252
Ackner, B. 260
Adler, A. 112, 124–5, 132, 135, 255–6
Agras, W. S. 252
Akiskal, H. S. 252
Alexander, F. 135, 138
Ariès, P. 253

Bakwin, H. 260
Balint, N. 137
Bandura, A. 259
Bellak, L. 263
Bergin, A. E. 254, 257, 262
Berne, E. 151, 257
Bernucci, A. J. 253
Berwick, P. T. 259
Bewley, T. 262
Bindrim, P. 161
Binswanger, L. 130, 256
Birk, L. 260
Birley, J. L. T. 253
Bourne, H. 260
Braginsky, B. M. & D. D. 159, 162, 258
Bray, G. R. 259
Brill, N. Q. 262
Brook, P. 232, 264
Brown, G. W. 253

Cade, J. F. J. 201
Cartwright, S. A. 200
Castelnuovo-Tedesco, P. 264
Cawley, R. 265
Charcot, J. M. 211
Chorover, S. 200, 261, 262
Cochrane, A. L. 262
Cohen, E. D. 256
Cole, J. O. 202, 262
Coleman, V. 261, 262, 263
Comfort, A. 264
Cooper, A. 252
Cooper, B. 252
Cooper, I. S. 117, 255
Corsini, R. 254, 256, 257

Davison, G. R. 260
D'Elia, G. 260
DeMause, L. 254
De Vries, Peter 58, 66
Dewald, P. C. 255
Dohrenwend, B. P. & B. S. 252, 253
Dreikurs, R. 256

Eaton, J. W. 252
Egbert, L. 264
Ellis, Havelock 117
Ennals, D. 265
Eriksen, Erik 131

Ervin, F. 192, 261
Essig, C. F. 262
Esterson, A. 263
Eysenck, H. J. 113, 167, 254, 255

Fagan, J. 257
Fanning, P. 263
Farrell, B. 253
Festinger, L. 255
Field, S. 263
Fieve, R. 252
Fine, R. 254, 257
Freedman, A. M. 252, 253
Freedman, D. G. 253
Freedman, N. C. 253
Freud, Anna 125
Freud, Sigmund 83, 95–119, 120–1, 123, 124, 125, 130, 131, 132, 134, 135, 149, 153, 167, 180, 209, 211, 253, 254, 255, 256, 259
Fromm, Erich 131
Fulton, J. F. 190

Garfield, S. L. 254, 257, 262
German, G. A. 252
Gilbert, W. S. 130
Glass, A. J. 253
Goldhamer, H. 252
Greenbank, R. K. 255
Greenblatt, D. J. 262
Grinker, R. R. 135
Gruenberg, E. M. 252
Gurin, G. 263

Hamburg, D. A. 255
Hand, I. 259
Harlow, H. F. 254
Heidegger, Martin 130
Holmes, D. S. 254
Hoon, P. W. 259
Horney, Karen 125–6, 135, 136, 144, 256
Hunt, D. 254

Illich, I. 217–18, 220, 263, 264

Jacob, T. 252
Jacques, E. 14
Jaffe, A. 256
James, William 95
Janet, P. 95
Janov, A. 127
Johnson, F. N. 262

Johnson, Samuel 13
Johnson, V. 228, 264
Jones, J. E. 260
Jung, C. G. 112, 120–4, 125, 130, 135, 144, 255, 256

Kaczanowski, G. 261
Kaplan, H. I. 252, 253
Kelsey, F. 207
Kernberg, O. F. 255
Kety, S. S. 89, 253
Kiernan, T. 256, 258
Kline, M. 125
Koch, S. 159
Kramer, M. 264

Laing, R. D. 91, 216–17, 221, 263
Lamontagne, Y. 259
Landis, C. 255
Lewis, Aubrey 264
Lieberman, M. A. 258
Lindsley, O. R. 259
Lomas, Peter 131
Lowen, A. 161, 258

Malan, D. H. 108, 137, 253
Maliver, Bruce 158, 257
Malleson, A. 260, 261, 262, 263
Mandell, A. J. 236, 264
Mark, V. 192, 261
Marks, I. M. 252, 259, 261
Marshall, A. W. 252
Maslow, A. H. 131, 162, 258
Masters, J. C. 258
Masters, W. H. 228, 264
May, Rollo 131
McConnell, J. V. 177, 259
McKenzie, K. G. 261
McKinney, Jr., W. T. 252
McLachlan, G. 265
Mindess, H. 257
Mitchell, K. M. 257
Modell, S. 262
Moniz, E. 189–90, 194
Moreno, J. L. 151
Morgan, H. G. 252
Mosak, H. H. 256

Notz, W. W. 259

Paul, G. L. 259
Perls, Frederick 147–51, 156, 158, 257
Phillips, C. 264
Purcell, L. P. 259

Rachman, S. 254, 255, 259, 264
Rank, Otto 126, 135
Raotma, H. 260
Reich, Wilhelm 127–30, 135, 149, 161, 255, 256
Reik, T. 125, 135, 144
Ricks, D. R. 145–6, 253, 257
Rimm, D. C. 258
Robin, A. A. 260
Rogers, Carl 144–7, 151, 156, 257
Rogow, A. 133, 136, 138, 139, 256, 257
Rosenhan, D. L. 213–14, 223, 234–5, 236, 263
Rothman, T. 252
Russell, A. W. 259, 260
Rutter, M. L. 253
Rycroft, C. 256

Sadock, B. J. 252, 253
Salter, A. 254
Sargant, William 195, 240, 242–3, 262, 265
Sartre, J. P. 130
Schachter, Stanley 173–4, 259
Schacter, R. I. 262
Schutz, W. R. 156
Seligman, M. E. P. 253, 259
Seligman, R. 253
Shapiro, A. K. 262
Shephard, M. 158
Shepherd, I. L. 257

Shepherd, M. 252
Skinner, B. F. 166, 177, 259
Sloan, R. B. 260
Smith, Sidney 9
Spiegal, J. 264
Stein, R. K. 255
Storr, A. 123, 256
Sullivan, H. S. 131, 149
Szasz, T. 211, 216, 220–2, 223, 263

Tan, E. 261
Teasdale, J. D. 260
Thorndike, E. L. 166
Truax, C. B. 146, 257
Turns, D. M. 252

Vaillant, G. E. 91, 252
Valenstein, E. S. 260, 261
Valling, S. 260
Valzelli, L. 261, 262
Veroff, I. 263

Weil, R. 252
Wender, P. 199, 262
Wilson, G. D. 254
Wolman, I. J. 260
Wolpe, J. 167, 259
Wood, Albert & Maya 162–3

Yalom, I. D. 152–5, 227, 258

Subject Index

addiction, *see* alcoholism, drugs, smoking
affective psychoses, 79, 80–3
See also depressive illness
aggression, control of, 193, 202, 221, 222
agoraphobia, 84, 167, 169
Alcoholics Anonymous, 153, 173, 238
alcoholism, 41, 51–2, 78, 173, 196, 198–9
alienation, 126, 130
American Academy of Psychoanalysis, 135, 139
American army, casualties and neurosis, 92
American Psychiatric Association, 86, 134, 157, 215
American Psychoanalytic Association, 134–5, 138
American Psychological Association, 182, 225
amitriptyline, 81, 201
See also antidepressants
amphetamines, 78, 198–200, 208
'anal' characteristics, 99, 100, 105
'anima' & 'animus', 122, 123
anorexia nervosa, 85, 174–5
antidepressants, 27, 49, 50, 60, 81, 82, 94, 200–1, 204

'anti-psychiatry' movement, 211–13, 216–18, 220–2, 242
anxiety neurosis, 82, 86
appetite, 80, 104
See also obesity
'archetypes', 122
'ASCID', 161
assertion training, 124, 176
assessment, *see* diagnosis
autism, 178
autosuggestion, 179–80

barbiturates, 78, 195–6, 203
'behaviour therapy', 45–8, 124, 166–183, 226–7, 230, 242
comparison with psychoanalysis, 181–3
for addictions, 173–6
for control of bad habits, 176–9
for neuroses, 171–2
for phobias and compulsions, 167–71
origins, 166–7
research on, 169–71, 181
stress inoculation, and, 179–81
benzodiazipines, 196
biochemistry, *see* brain, biochemistry of
'bio-energetics', 161
'bio energy', 127 8

'biofeedback', 179–80
bipolar illness, 80–2
  See also manic-depressive illness
birth, premature, 89
birth-trauma, 126
brain,
  biochemistry of, 80–1, 93, 94, 188,
    204, 212, 215
  damage to, 78–9, 117–19, 165, 192,
    198, 199–200, 215
  electrical stimulation of, 193–4
  See also psychosurgery
brainwashing, 178
British Psychoanalytic Society, 138

calomel, 207
'CARE', 144–7
  See also psychotherapists, desirable
    qualities in
case-meetings, 49–50, 61
castration complex, 98
'censor', 102
certification of psychotherapists etc,
  136, 140–1, 165
childhood and mental illness, 91–2, 94,
  98–9, 105–6, 124, 125, 217
children, therapy of, 117–19, 125
chlorpromazine, 82
  See also tranquillizers, major
classification of mental disorders,
  77–87
clergymen, 143, 218
'client-centred' therapy, 144–7
cultural factors, role of in mental
  illness, 89–91, 125–6, 217, 218–19
clinical psychologists
  role of, 140–2, 236–42
  status of, 141, 239
  training of, 140–1
'community mental health care', 238–9
complexes, 121, 124
compulsory hospitalization, 220–7
computers, 147, 209
'corrective emotional experience', 154
coronary care units, 206
couch, role of in analysis, 101–2
criminals, 178, 221, 222, 226–7
'crotch-eyeballing', 161–2

da Vinci, Leonardo, 99, 116
defence mechanisms, 68–9, 96, 149
delinquency, 92, 145
'delirium tremens', 78, 195

depersonalization, 30, 216, 235
  See also institutionalization, *and*
    mental illness, stigma of
depressive illness, 79–83, 86, 143,
  171–2, 186, 198, 200–3, 206
  author's, 1–2, 75
  causes of, 89, 91–4
'desensitization, systematic,' 47, 167–
  171, 179
diagnosis, 77–87, 213–14
'displacement', 98
doctors,
  authoritarianism of, 232–5
  selection of, 231
  training of, 204, 231–2, 234–6
  See also general practitioners,
    psychiatrists
dreams, 96, 97, 102, 104, 121, 122,
  124, 150
drugs, psychotropic, 28, 31, 32–3, 61,
  134, 143, 194–209, 238
  addiction to, 86, 195–6, 198–9
  research on, 203–9
drug companies, 197, 198, 202, 203–9
'dystonia musculorum deformans',
  117–18

ego, 98, 102, 113
'ego-strength', 101, 108
elation, 80, 63–9, 80
  See also mania
electric shock, *see* punishment
electro-convulsive therapy, 81, 134,
  143, 165, 184–9, 226, 243
emotion, expression of, 6, 18–19, 26,
  148–50, 153–5, 156, 159
encounter groups, 35, 150, 156–60,
  161–2
Equanil, 146
ergot, 78
Eros, 103, 104–15, 114
Esalen, 156, 158
existential analysis, 123, 130–1, 134
existential neurosis, 85
extraversion, 121

family relationships,
  as cause of mental illness, 91–2, 94,
    98–100, 105–6, 125, 172, 216, 217,
    218, 223
  effect of mental illness on, 117–19,
    139
  See also marital therapy

feminism, 134
  See also Women's Liberation movement
'flooding', 168–71
Forum, 228

'galvanic skin response', 121, 180
'game playing', 148–9
Gay Liberation movement, 86
general practitioners, 204, 205, 208, 239
genetics of mental illness, 80, 88–9, 94
'genital' stage, 99
Gestalt therapy, 123, 143, 147–51
group therapy, 51–4, 151, 152–5, 173

hallucinations, 79
headaches, 213
'helplessness, learned', 93
homosexuality, 85–6, 98, 104, 127, 175, 178, 215
  repression of, 20, 104
hospitals, *see* mental hospitals
humanistic psychology, 150, 162
Hutterites, 90
hypomania,
  author's, 63–9, 80
  See also mania
hypnotism, 101, 151, 180
hysteria, 81, 83, 118–19, 211

id, 98, 102, 104, 113
Imipramine, 81, 201,
  See also antidepressants
individualization, *see* self-actualization
institutionalization, 30–1, 176–7, 223–4
insulin therapy, 187–8
International Psychoanalytical Association, 127
introversion, 121

Korsakov psychosis, 78

leucotomy, 189–96
libido, 95, 97–102, 103–5, 113, 120–1, 174, 227–8
Librium, 196
lie detector, 121
life events, 81, 92–3
lithium, 80, 82, 201–3
Little Hans, 167
lobotomy, 189–96

Long Island Institute for Emotional Disorders, 162–3
'LSD', 80

malingering, 211, 213–14
mania, 80, 201–3
  See also hypomania
manic-depressive illness, 79–82, 201–203, 209
masturbation, 99, 113, 116, 127, 228
marital therapy,
  author's experiences of, 72–4
  See also sex therapy
Maudsley Hospital, 167, 170
medical research, 205–6
  See also mental illness, research on etc
memory defects, 78, 185–6
Menninger Foundation, 108, 255
Mental Health Review Tribunal, 223
mental hospitals,
  admission procedures, 27, 214
  author's sojourn in, 26–62
  conditions in, 223–6
  number of patients at, 197, 218
  See also compulsory hospitalization, psychiatric services
mental illness, 88–94
  causes of, 88–94
  concept of, 211–22, 230
  prevalence of, 8, 86–7, 89–91, 218
  research into, 80–2, 239–40
  stigma of, 34–6, 70, 216, 221–2, 242–3
mental patients,
  attitudes of to hospital, 30, 34, 37, 40, 42–3
  behaviour of in hospital, 26–43
  dependence of on therapists and doctors, 29, 40, 48, 49, 137, 182, 206, 217–18, 220, 229
  drop out rates, 106, 137
  exaggerated sensitivities of, 29–31, 35, 41
  rights of, 220–1, 224–7
  selection of by analysts, 101, 106, 110
  self-esteem of, 54, 153, 176, 177
  See also compulsory hospitalization
meprobamate, 196
metrazol, 188
Miltown, 196
minimal brain damage, 199–200

misfortune, personal,
  role of in triggering mental illlness,
    81, 92–3
Mithraism, 122
'modelling', 169, 171
monkeys, 106, 190
muscle tension, 128, 150, 180
  See also relaxation, progressive
myth, 121–3

National Training Laboratory, 158
neurasthenia, 83–4
neurosis,
  causes of, 88–94, 126, 209
  nature of, 78, 212–13, 214–16
  prevalence of, 8, 86–7
  types of, 82–6
  See also anxiety neurosis, hysteria,
    phobias, etc
Nightingale, Florence, 172
non-directive therapy, 144–7
nurses, 27, 28, 30–4, 51, 54, 143, 234

obesity, 85, 173–4, 198
obsessive-compulsive disorders, 81,
  84, 86, 171, 181, 242
obsessive ruminations, 47
O'Connor v. *Donaldson*, 226
occupational therapy, 28, 29, 32, 37–9,
  48
'Oepidal complex', 98–9, 104, 114,
  125, 167
'oral' characteristics, 99, 100, 105, 174
orgasm, 127–8, 130, 228
orgones, 127–8

pain, 126, 179, 191, 237–8
'paradoxical intention', 74, 172
paranoia, 79, 184–5
parents,
  loss of, 91
  See also family relationships
patients, *see* mental patients
Patuxent, 226–7
'penis-envy', 98, 125
perception, 96, 142, 148
'persona', 122, 123
personal growth, *see* self-actualization
personality disorders, 85
phenothiazines, *see* tranquillizers,
  major
phobias, 84, 86, 130, 167–71, 179, 181,
  183, 242

physical illness,
  contrasted with mental, 111, 211–12,
    215, 217–18, 241
  psychological factors in, 237–8
placebo effect, 107, 181, 188–9, 206–7
poverty,
  association with mental illness, 90–1
primal therapy, 126–7, 161
projection, 98, 112, 122
pseudo-patients, 213–14, 234–5
psychiatric services, 218, 223, 238–9
  deficient resources of, 55, 225–7, 241
psychiatrists,
  attitudes of to patients, 29–30,
    216–17, 232–4
  attitudes of to psychologists, etc.,
    140–1, 236–7
  plight of, 247
  role of in commitment and care of
    patients, 223–6
  Russian, 222
  status of, 232, 236
  training of, 134–5, 231–2, 234–6
psychoanalysis,
  aims of, 110
  author's experiences of, 16–25
  cost of, 17, 23, 126, 136–7
  drop out rates from, 106, 137
  efficacy of, 106–8, 169
  length of, 22, 137–8
  popularity of, 109–19, 133
  practice of, 101–2, 111–12, 133–9,
    146
  research on, 96, 105–8
  theory of, 95–101, 103–6, 113–14,
    131–2, 134
  See also Adler, Jung, Reich, etc
psychoanalysts,
  arrogance of, 109–10, 112, 117–19,
    121
  characteristics of, 117, 136–9
  number of, 138
  selection of patients by, 101, 106,
    110, 133
  training of, 111, 134–8
psychodrama, 151
psychology, 96, 140–2, 181, 219–20
  See also clinical psychologists,
    humanistic psychology
psychopathy, 83
psychoses,
  causes of, 88–94
  chemotherapy for, 197, 201–3, 209

functional, 78, 90, 212
organic, 78–82, 212
prevalence of, 89, 90
psychosurgery, 189–94
psychotherapists,
    desirable qualities in, 109, 131, 138,
        144–5, 146–7, 149, 235
    influence of on patients, 114–15,
        133, 227–30
    sexual relations of with patients,
        149, 158, 161, 164, 165
psychotherapy, non-analytic, 140–55
    aims of, 94, 143
    author's experiences of, 44–55
    by laymen, 143, 162–5
    efficacy of, 170
    evaluation of, 106–8, 142, 145–6,
        152–5, 181
    See also marital therapy, psycho-
        analysis, sex therapy
punishment, 172, 175, 177, 178, 182,
    226–7

'randomised control trial', 205
'rationalization', 102
reinforcement, 166, 172, 174–7, 182
relaxation, progressive, 48, 168, 179
religion, 121–3, 133–4
*Report on the Royal Commission on
    Medical Education*, 231, 235
repression, 98, 100, 102, 105, 122, 125
research, *see under* behaviour therapy,
    mental illness, psychoanalysis, etc
resistance, 112, 115, 126, 128
reward, 166, 172, 174–7, 182
Ritalin, 199
Royal College of Psychiatrists, 134,
    232, 235–6

schizophrenia, 81, 82, 121, 145–6, 188,
    197, 201, 209, 213–14, 216–17,
    221–2, 226, 240
    causes of, 88–9, 91
    symptoms of, 79–80
'secondary gain', 172
self-actualization, 122–3, 126, 131,
    144–5, 150, 156, 162
self-esteem,
    lack of in patients, 51, 125, 144
    of analysts, 112
senile dementia, 78
sex therapy, 227–9
sexual desire, *see* libido

sexual deviation, 85–6, 113, 153, 175,
    229
    See also homosexuality
'shaping', 46
sleep, patterns of in depression, 81
slips of the tongue, 95–6, 115
smoking, treatment for, 56–8, 173, 174
social class, 90–1, 233
social workers, 143, 223, 236, 239
society and mental illness, 89–91,
    125–6, 217, 218–19
sociopaths, 85
stigma, *see* mental illness
stress, 92–3, 180, 219
'stress inoculation', 179–80, 183
sublimation, 92, 98, 114
suicide, 42, 85, 158, 186, 195, 214,
    220, 221, 242
superego, 98, 104, 113
Supershrink, 146
symbolism in psychoanalytic theory,
    98, 102, 104
symptom substitution, 169–70, 171,
    172, 182

'T-groups', 153, 155–6
thalidomide, 208–9
Thantos, 103, 104–5, 114
Thomas, R., case of, 192–3
'thrownness', 130–1
toilet training, 99, 105, 127
'token economies', 176–7
tonsillectomy, 187
tranquillizers,
    major, 33, 50, 82, 197, 240
    minor, 33, 50, 168–9, 196, 205, 208
transactional analysis, 151
transference, 100–2, 114, 126, 182
tri-cyclic antidepressants, *see* anti-
    depressants
trusting, exercises in, 38, 73
twin studies, 88–9

unconscious, the, 96–9, 100–2, 104,
    111–13, 115–16, 122–3
unipolar affective illness, 80–1
    See also affective psychoses
U.S. Food & Drug Administration,
    128, 207

Valium, 196
volition, 211, 215–16

will, the, 211, 215–16
witches, 79, 161
womb, physical traumata in, 89
  See also birth trauma
Women's Liberation movement, 127,
  133, 134

See also feminism
word association, 121
World Health Organization, 78, 85
Wyatt v. *Alderholt,* 226
Wyatt v. *Stickney,* 225–6